EXTRA- AND NON-DOCUMENTARY WRITING IN THE CANON OF FORMATIVE JUDAISM

VOLUME ONE

THE POINTLESS PARALLEL

HANS-JÜRGEN BECKER AND THE MYTH OF THE AUTONOMOUS TRADITION IN RABBINIC DOCUMENTS

EXTRA- AND NON-DOCUMENTARY WRITING IN THE CANON OF FORMATIVE JUDAISM

VOLUME ONE

THE POINTLESS PARALLEL

HANS-JÜRGEN BECKER AND THE MYTH OF THE AUTONOMOUS TRADITION IN RABBINIC DOCUMENTS

JACOB NEUSNER

Academic Studies in the History of Judaism
Global Publications, Binghamton University
2001

Library of Congress Cataloging-in-Publication Data:

Jacob Neusner, *Extra- and Non-Documentary Writing in the Canon of Formative Judaism.* Volume One. *The Pointless Parallel: Hans-Jürgen Becker and the Myth of the Autonomous Tradition in Rabbinic Documents.*

1. Judaism   2. Rabbinic Judaism

ISBN 1-586841-06-8

Published and Distributed by:
Academic Studies in the History of Judaism
Global Publications, Binghamton University
LNG 99, Binghamton University
State University of New York at Binghamton
Binghamton, New York, USA 13902-6000
Phone: (607) 777-4495 or 777-6104; Fax: (607) 777-6132
E-mail: pmorewed@binghamton.edu
http://ssips.binghamton.edu

THE SERIES

ACADEMIC STUDIES IN THE HISTORY OF JUDAISM

TABLE OF CONTENTS

PART THREE

SHOWING THAT SHARED TRADITIONS, PRIOR TO AND AUTONOMOUS OF THE TWO TALMUDS DO NOT LINK THE BAVLI TO THE YERUSHALMI

PART FOUR

TOWARD A GENERAL THEORY OF
THE FORMATION OF THE RABBINIC TRADITION

APPENDICES

EXTRA- AND NON-DOCUMENTARY WRITING IN THE CANON OF FORMATIVE JUDAISM

VOLUME TWO

PALTRY PARALLELS

THE NEGLIGIBLE PROPORTION AND PERIPHERAL ROLE OF FREE-STANDING COMPOSITIONS IN RABBINIC DOCUMENTS

TABLE OF CONTENTS

PART TWO

EXTRA- AND NON-DOCUMENTARY WRITING IN PROPORTION AND POSITION

QUANTITATIVE SHOWING THAT A MINISCULE PROPORTION OF RABBINIC DOCUMENTS IS COMPRISED BY FREE-STANDING STORIES AND QUALITATIVE SHOWING THAT THESE FEW FREE-STANDING STORIES ARE TANGENTIAL IN THE COMPOSITIONS WHERE THEY DO OCCUR

2. PROPORTION AND POSITION: EVIDENCE OF SHARED, AUTONOMOUS TRADITIONS IN A SAMPLE OF THE MISHNAH AND THE TOSEFTA

EXTRA- AND
NON-DOCUMENTARY WRITING
IN THE CANON OF FORMATIVE JUDAISM

VOLUME THREE

PERIPATETIC PARALLELS

Table of Contents

II
THE THRICE-TOLD TALE IN RABBINIC STORIES ABOUT PHARISEES BEFORE 70

III
Three Theories of the Peripatetic Saying

IV
Toward a General Theory of the Rabbinical Literature: The Documentary Picture of the Formative Age

Appendices

2. THE BAVLI AT THE END: THE JUDGMENT OOF MEN-
    ACHEM FISH

BIBLIOGRAPHY

PREFACE

I

At issue here is the character of the Rabbinic canonical documents of late antiquity. These are the Mishnah, Abot, the Tosefta, Sifra, Sifré to Numbers, Sifré to Deuteronomy, Mekhilta Attributed to R. Ishmael, the Talmud of the Land of Israel, the Talmud of Babylonia, the four Rabbah-Midrash-compilations of late antiquity, Genesis, Leviticus, Lamentations, Song of Songs, Abot deR. Natan, as well as some minor compilations. Under debate are the following alternative propositions:

Are these writings, respectively, subject to characterization as a whole, or do they lack traits of coherence, whether formal or substantive?

Do they in the aggregate exhibit purpose and plan, or are they mere random collections of free-standing ("autonomous") compositions and composites?

In a long sequence of monographs, devoted to each of the compilations of the Rabbinic canon of the formative age,[1] I have invoked the indicative criteria of rhetoric (form), topic (propositional program), and logic of coherent discourse. On the strength of those criteria I have argued that we may define each of the named documents in comparison and contrast with all the others. The documents are shown to relate in three ways: autonomy, connection, and continuity. Each is distinct from all the others in its particular traits of rhetoric, topic, and logic. None may be characterized as a mere scrapbooks, collected we know not how or why. All exhibit traits that show them to be purposive and pointed. The Rabbinic documents, severally and jointly, constitute components of a coherent canon of ideas, not merely random collec-

---

[1] Listed in the bibliography of my writings, given at the end of the book.

tions of writings about this and that. I have defined in detail
the indicative traits of each of the principal documents, with
the result just now summarized.

The contrary position is represented here by the writings of Goldberg-Schaefer-Becker, which we may call, a
German academic school of Rabbinic studies. The school
takes a position vis-à-vis Rabbinic Judaism that I have characterized elsewhere as nihilistic. The school has produced no
systematic account of the documents, one by one or all at
once. So it has stated a theory of matters in the abstract, but
has not realized that theory in a systematic reading of the
documents in the manner it advocates. But the position of the
Goldberg-Schaefer-Becker school is clear. It is that for antiquity there is nothing we may call "Judaism," a religious system
realized in its canonical writings. Indeed, there are no timely
documents, only diverse MSS of indeterminate location in
time and space. If we were to judge from the publications of
that school, indeed, when it comes to Judaism there is neither
a structure of ideas, nor a system for generating and solving
fresh problems. There is only a vast corpus of variant readings, which add up to nothing in particular, a hodgepodge
and a mess of gibberish. That school, accordingly, has produced little work on the religion, Judaism in late antiquity, to
which the Rabbinic documents attest. Why they find worth in
studying the inchoate texts (by their characterization) I cannot
say, and I can only point to the failure of that school to produce academic scholarship on the religion, Judaism, in the period which they claim to study.

At stake in the debate between the Goldberg-
Schaefer-Becker school and me is the possibility of the definition of Rabbinic Judaism as a coherent religious structure and
system. With determinate documents, each with its proposition and program, we may discern a structure that is embodied in cogent statements, a system that addresses determinate

questions and solves them. So to summarize: those who deny the documentary character of the canonical writings also neglect the study of Rabbinic Judaism, and those who claim to discern in the writings a structure and a system also undertake the description, analysis, and interpretation in context of that Judaism.

I hasten to add, this academic school does not speak for all of German and Austrian scholarship on Judaism in antiquity, as many distinguished names can testify, among them, Johann Maier, emeritus at Cologne University and Günter Stemberger, Professor of Judaic Studies at Vienna University. Important scholarship on Midrash-compilations, scholarship of profound erudition and precision on difficult texts, comes, for instance, from Professor Dagmar Börner-Klein, Duisberg University, and she is not alone among German scholars of the history of Judaism in antiquity.

The documentary hypothesis requires the reading of the writings start to finish and the systematic categorization, by reference to rhetoric, topic, and logic of coherent discourse, of each of the components of each of the writings. That work has been done and has produced sustained results. The rejectionists call attention to the indeterminacy of the manuscript evidence, rich as it is in variant readings, as an argument that the entire documentary enterprise is hopeless to begin with: there are no documents susceptible of characterization, only diverse manuscript testimonies to we know not what. They further point to compositions and composites, as well as singleton-sayings, that are shared among two or more documents. These by definition testify against the documentary hypothesis of the Rabbinic canon.

The principal task, then, for those who hold the parallels to be pointless and the autonomous tradition to be subordinate to its documentary setting(s) is in two parts, affirmative and negative. The former requires exercises in documentary characterization, encompassing both form-analysis and propositional characterization (rhetoric, topic). The latter demands the testing of a null-hypothesis. Chapters One and Two and Three present the form-analytical argument for the documentary hypothesis, using the cases of Genesis Rabbah and Leviticus Rabbah in the former, Leviticus Rabbah, Pesiqta deRab Kahana, and Pesiqta Rabbati, in the second. The latter, in Part Three (Chapter Four) sets forth a null-hypothesis and tests it, with solid results. Then, at Chapter Five, I offer my general theory of the formation of the literary evidence of the Rabbinic tradition. I await the counterpart theory of the rejectionists.

II

What about the myth of the autonomous tradition? Everyone knows that the same composition and even sizable composite may occur in more than one document of the canon of Rabbinic Judaism in its formative age, the first six centuries C.E. A given saying or story may find its way into two or three documents, exhibiting variations as it moves along. The implications of these parallels, which constitute traditions autonomous of any distinctive, determinate documentary setting, bear examination. From the perspective of the documentary reading of the canonical compilations, these parallels make no point at all.

I make that judgment in the context of the contrary claim that the parallels bear implications for the character of the canon itself. The fact that sayings circulate hither and yon leads some to dismiss as null the documentary lines that differentiate one document from another, e.g., the Mishnah or the Talmud of Babylonia from Sifra or Genesis Rabbah. Compilations that can so blatantly overlap — so it is argued — cannot claim the status of autonomous, purposeful documents. The compilations of Rabbinic law, exegesis, and theology therefore should be treated as the result of happenstance, as mere collections of assorted traditions. They should not be read as determinate, defined and deliberate statements in their own terms and framework.

I have argued, on the contrary, that documentary lines signify purpose and viewpoint. Compilers of compositions and composites — I call them "authorships" — impose on their compilations distinctive traits of rhetoric, topic, and logic of coherent discourse. In so doing, they form a purposeful statement, imparting to the parts that they have compiled a cogency and integrity that, on their own, one by one, they do not exhibit. Here I address the challenge that parallels present to that documentary hypothesis of the Rabbinic canon. In Chapter Five I set forth a theory of how the writing down of the Rabbinic tradition took place.

III

How did the debate get underway? It began before I had even enunciated the documentary reading of the Rabbinic canon. The documentary hypothesis of the Rabbinic canon came to merely implicit expression in my work on the Mishnah (together with the Tosefta), *Judaism: The Evidence of the Mishnah.*[2] I did not at that time think through and articulate the implications of a work that read the Mishnah in its own terms and framework, in dialogue with the Tosefta. That is because it struck me as a self-evidently necessary first step: this text by itself, then that text by itself, then both, each in its consequent context established in a canon of documents continuous with one another. Why not read the Mishnah in its

---

[2] *Judaism. The Evidence of the Mishnah.* Chicago, 1981: University of Chicago Press. *Choice,* "Outstanding academic book list" 1982-3. Paperback edition: 1984. Second printing, 1985. Third printing, 1986. Second edition, augmented: Atlanta, 1987: Scholars Press for Brown Judaic Studies. The work appeared also in Italian and in Hebrew.

own terms, since it was, after all, the first document of Rabbinic Judaism beyond Scripture? Beyond Scripture, the Mishnah had no past. It marked the starting point. It therefore seemed to me self-evidently the right way to commence work on the documentary history of the ideas of Rabbinic Judaism. And that is what I contemplated, starting with the first writing. So I read the Mishnah (with the Tosefta) as an autonomous document. I understood that canonical documents also are connected one to another, and, further, that being formed into the canon of Judaism, they form a continuity from each to all.

But reviewers, some of them memorably brutal, immediately challenged the unacknowledged premise of my work, which was, a given Rabbinic document could be defined as autonomous of all other documents, with distinctive traits of topic, rhetoric, and logic of coherent discourse. I took for granted that one could speak of "the Judaism of the Mishnah," that is, the religious structure and system that the Mishnah (and the Tosefta) set forth. I thought it self-evident that the Mishnah (and the Tosefta) provide their own first, best commentary: the very signals embodied in the rhetoric, topic, and logic of coherent discourse that characterize those compilations. That is what I expounded in *Judaism: The Evidence of the Mishnah*.

To be sure, in subsequent work, in a systematic way, I examined further documents, the Yerushalmi and Bavli in the line of the Mishnah, Sifra, the two Sifrés and Mekhilta, and the Rabbah-Midrash-compilations of antiquity, in the line of Scripture, as well as Abot and Abot deRabbi Natan. So I did not neglect the other components of the ancient canon. I further pursued the other two of the three dimensions of canonical context, connection and continuity. That is, I saw each document in succession as autonomous of all others, connected with some others, and continuous, by reason of canonical standing, with every other Rabbinic writing (inclusive of the liturgical documents, so far as these originate in late antiquity). I compared and contrasted two or more documents, e.g., two kindred Midrash-compilations, the two Talmuds, and the like. Nonetheless, the possibility of describing a document as a systematic statement of a cogent system, not only as a component of a larger construction, was challenged. The challenge to what was implicit, in a variety of studies precipitated by my *Judaism: The Evidence of the Mishnah*, then, imposed on me the task of proceeding from the Mishnah to the other documents of the Rabbinic canon, the Yerushalmi and Bavli, the several Midrash-compilations, and the like. That work of documentary description, analysis, and interpretation for the main part of the Rabbinic canon of late antiquity has required twenty years and is now complete, so far as I can accomplish it. Another generation will improve upon and refine the results. But I know of no clearly-pre-Islamic Rabbinic documents of any weight and consequence that await documentary description.

Now, as a matter of fact, the direction of criticism I scarcely anticipated proved the most engaging. It held that the very conception of a document with a set of determinate traits, a document that is to be described, analyzed, and interpreted, in the Rabbinic canon cannot stand. Rabbinic writings are random, scrapbooks not documents of purpose. That is for three reasons:

[1] the indeterminacy of the readings of documents by reason of textual variants;

[2] the porous character of documentary boundaries by reason of the presence of a given composition or composite in two or more documents, thus the composition or composite autonomous of any single document; and

[3] the matter of intertextuality, the flow of thought from document to document, even when a particular passage is not explicitly cited by one document from another.

Now let us take up each of these foci of criticism of the documentary hypothesis of the Rabbinic canon.

IV

Variant Readings: First, critics, represented here by Becker, have maintained that the variations in manuscript testimony are so vast as to deny the cogency and coherence of any compilation. I was accused of ignoring the matter of variant readings, even though my Mishnah- and Tosefta-work systematically attended to them.

My initial encounter with textual variants came with the Mishnah and the Tosefta, and while cognizant of the findings of Y. N. Epstein in his *Mevo lenussah hammishnah* (1954) and lesser works, I saw no variation so fundamental as to deny to the Mishnah all cogency. It is one thing to recognize variations in wording of particular passages. It is another to deny that the Mishnah has no distinctive and definitive traits that characterize the whole: no rhetorical patterns, no topical program, no logic of coherent discourse everywhere took charge of matters. In Saul Lieberman's Tosefta edition, where the variants are carefully collated, variations in detail likewise left ample space for the recognition of something we may regard as a stable and coherent whole: *the* Tosefta, not merely this manuscript's version of the Tosefta and that manuscript's version of the same. Nothing in Lieberman's discussion suggested otherwise. And that is so, even though there are significant MSS variations, as everyone knows.

True, the relatively stable text-tradition of the Mishnah represents a particularly felicitous situation. Some of the Rabbinic compilations, as well as Judaic but not necessarily Rabbinic compilations, are represented in text-traditions of considerable diversity. Among them are compilations with simply chaotic text-traditions. These are problems to be taken into account. Much depends on whether the definition of a given document — its rhetorical, topical, and logical program — can accommodate diverse textual representations of said document.

V

Compositions Autonomous of Documents: Second, the matter of parallels — the "pointless parallels" of the title of this book — came to the fore. Critics argued that the occurrence of the same story or saying in two or more documents calls into question the conception that the compilers of documents exercised taste and judgment in selecting for their distinctive purpose the materials they present to us. The ubiquity of parallels shared by two or more documents bears a compelling implication, some have held. It is that compilers in no way carried out a systematic labor of composition, collection, and arrangement, a labor aimed at making a cogent statement of a systemic order. People made up compositions and even composites, and editors used these ready-made writings when they compiled their collections.

The most systematic statement of the first and the second critiques came from Peter Schaefer and his student, Hans-Jürgen Becker, respectively. The former, in "Research into Rabbinic literature," *Journal of Jewish Studies* 1986, 37:139-152, made much of the diversity of manuscript representations of compilations. The latter, in his *Die grossen rabbinischen Sammelwerke Palaestinas. Zur literarischen Genese von Talmud Yerushalmi und Midrash Bereshit Rabba*,[3] builds on the peripa-

---

[3] Hans-Juergen Becker, *Die grossen rabbinischen Sammelwerke Palaestinas. Zur literarischen Genese von Talmud Yerushalmi und Midrash Bereshit Rabba.* Tuebingen, 1999: J. C. B. Mohr (Paul Siebeck).

tetic saying or story his case against the documentary hypothesis of Rabbinic writings.

To the opposed, anti-documentary reading of the Rabbinic canon, I replied in a variety of books and articles, for example, *Midrash as Literature: The Primacy of Documentary Discourse*. Lanham, 1987: University Press of America *Studies in Judaism* series, *Sifra in Perspective: The Documentary Comparison of the Midrashim of Ancient Judaism* Atlanta, 1988: Scholars Press for Brown Judaic Studies. To Schaefer in particular, I replied in a paper that occurred, most notably, in *The Documentary Foundation of Rabbinic Culture. Mopping Up after Debates with Gerald L. Bruns, S. J. D. Cohen, Arnold Maria Goldberg, Susan Handelman, Christine Hayes, James Kugel, Peter Schaefer, Eliezer Segal, E. P. Sanders, and Lawrence H. Schiffman.* Atlanta, 1995: Scholars Press for South Florida Studies in the History of Judaism. (I reprint the unit on Schaefer in the Second Appendix to this volume.)

The occasion for raising the issue once more, so many years later, is the appearance of Becker's *Habilitationsschrift*, briefly treated in the First Appendix. He takes the position that every manuscript-version of a Rabbinic compilation represents a free-standing statement, so that we have not a single Genesis Rabbah or Yerushalmi but many of them. A student of Schaefer in Berlin and now Professor of Judaic Studies in the Theology Faculty at the University of Göttingen, Becker explicitly positions, as a critique of my documentary hypothesis, his study of four particular points of comparison between the Yerushalmi and Genesis Rabbah. These are those parallel traditions that are supposed to show documentary lines register not at all.

Becker thinks his data call into question the viability of that hypothesis, and he so states at the fore and aft of his exposition of the textual and manuscript variants of his four cases. That he exhibits an imperfect knowledge of that hypothesis does not render null the shank of his book, which presents data that that hypothesis (like any other that pertains) must address. Becker's work of comparing versions of the same story or saying as these occur in two kindred documents is absolutely necessary. But how his results bear upon the documentary hypothesis of the Rabbinic canon requires a clearer understanding of that hypothesis, its claims and implications, than Becker exhibits. He does not include in his bibliography or footnotes the bulk of the discussion of the documentary hypothesis that is in print, much of it for ten or even fifteen years. He just has failed to do his homework.

In fact comparing versions of a story autonomous of any one document presents nothing new. Taking my place in a long tradition of such work, I pursued precisely that kind of comparison in work published more than three decades ago, which Becker does not cite and may even not know. In framing the documentary hypothesis of the Rabbinic canon, I took full cognizance of shared stories and sayings among documents. How do I deal with them? I show in this book that these form a small and inconsequential proportion of the documents that share them. They in no way constitute a formidable obstacle to the characterization of those documents in determinate terms.

Variant readings, free-standing compositions, and the documentary hypothesis: It suffices to say, I concur entirely that variant readings are to be noted, especially where they represent a distinction that makes a difference; and that stories and sayings autonomous of particular documents require study in their own terms. Both approaches are necessary. But they are not sufficient. The full characterization of the canon requires the recognition of the simple fact that the Mishnah is different from Genesis Rabbah, which is different from the Yerushalmi, which is different from the Siddur and Mahzor;

and that all the canonical documents participate in a single system in common.

Before proceeding, we follow the third source of criticism of the documentary reading of the canonical writings, even though it represents a dead-end and has produced no important scholarship since the position was initially proclaimed and episodically instantiated: intertextuality.

VI

Intertextuality: Yet a third group, a circle of literary critics mostly of Jewish origin but not deeply engaged in scholarship on Judaism and its texts but rather on English and American literature, took the view that documentary lines are null. Working on Midrash, they took as the starting point not the largest unit of discourse, the document, but the smallest, the individual unit of thought represented by the simplest complete statement of a thought or a proposition. Intertextuality in this context bore a simple meaning. Texts flow into one another not only formally (through shared compositions, "autonomous traditions") but in more subtle ways, by allusion without explicit citation. I clearly maintained that the Rabbinic documents are intratextual, that is, distinct from one another. The Rabbinic sages explicitly cite received documents and their traditions. I found no place in the projects of that circle, which, as a matter of fact, did not wish to engage with my findings at all. That does not defy understanding: if I was right, they were wrong. Now, a decade later, intertextuality in Rabbinic canonical writings has faded, little came of it, no large exegetical projects of a systematic character results. But it does no harm to dwell on the matter for a moment.

I held — by the late 1980s articulately, not only implicitly — that since the several Rabbinic documents stand distinct from one another, each with its own rhetorical, logical, and topical program, they relate not "intertextually" but "intratextually." That is to say, when the framers of a composition wish to allude to another document, e.g., Scripture, they say so in so many words. They ordinarily give a clear signal that that other document is cited, ordinarily using such citation-language as "as it is said," or "as it is written." The accepted definitions of intertextuality, which emphasize the implicit bonds that form an invisible web holding together all writings, therefore do not apply. Rabbinic literature forms a library, in which a common collection unites discrete items, rather than an undifferentiated body of writing.

The debate on intertextuality proved one-sided. My systematic challenge took the form of two accounts, *Canon and Connection: Intertextuality in Judaism.* Lanham, 1986: University Press of America. *Studies in Judaism* Series. *Midrash as Literature: The Primacy of Documentary Discourse.* Lanham, 1987: University Press of America *Studies in Judaism* series, in addition *to The Documentary Foundation,* cited above. These works rested on a systematic study of documents and their traits. The intertextualists in the Rabbinic canon did not show how they read those same documents, and their arguments from example, not from comprehensive work, proved not compelling in the end. Little has been heard from them in recent times. But they raised important issues and stimulated rigorous thought, for which all must be thankful.

VII

A Community of Texts: The upshot is, the Rabbinic canon is comprised by a community of texts, related in three dimensions: autonomy, connection, and continuity. Documents stand on their own. They intersect at specific points with other documents. And they form a continuity with all other documents, constituting a canon.

To clarify this perspective, consider the analogy of a library. Books brought together form a library. Each title addresses its own program and makes its own points. But books produced by a cogent community constitute not merely a library but a canon: a set of compositions each of which contributes to a statement that transcends its own pages. The books exhibit intrinsic traits that make of them all *a community of texts*. We should know on the basis of those characteristics that the texts form a community even if we knew nothing more than the texts themselves. In the Judaic writings, moreover, the documents at hand are held by Judaism to form a canon.

Seeing the whole as continuous, which is quite natural, later theology maintains that all of the documents of Rabbinic literature find a place in the Torah. But that is an imputed, and theological, not an inductive and intrinsic fact. It is something we know only on the basis of information — theological convictions about the one whole Torah God gave to Moses in two media — deriving from sources other than the texts at hand, which, on their own, do not link each to all and all to every line of each. Extrinsic traits, that is imputed ones, make of the discrete writings a single and continuous, uniform statement: one whole Torah in the mythic language of Judaism. The community of Judaism imputes those traits, sees commonalities, uniformities, deep harmonies: one Torah of one God. In secular language, that community expresses its system — its world view, its way of life, its sense of itself as a society — by these choices, and finds its definition in them. Hence, in the nature of things, the community of Judaism forms a *textual community*. That cogent community that forms a canon out of a selection of books therefore participates in the process of authorship, just as the books exist in at least two dimensions.

Let us turn to the problem of the community of texts, utilizing the dimensions just now defined in our description of the canon. We take the measure of two of the three dimensions now introduced, *autonomy*, on the one side, and *connection*, on the second. Continuity among all documents introduces theological, not literary problems for analysis. That is to say, a book enjoys its own autonomous standing, but it also situates itself in relationship to other books of the same classification. Each book bears its own statement and purpose, and each relates to others of the same classification. The community of texts therefore encompasses individuals who (singly or collectively) comprise (for the authorships: compose) books. But there is a set of facts that indicates how a book does not stand in isolation. These facts fall into several categories. Books may go over the same ground or make use in some measure of the same materials. The linkages between and among them therefore connect them. Traits of rhetoric, logic, and topic may place into a single classification a number of diverse writings. Then there is the larger consensus of members who see relationships between one book and another and so join them together on a list of authoritative writings. So, as is clear, a book exists in the dimensions formed of its own contents and covers, but it also takes its place in the second and third dimensions of relationship to other books.

Then the relationships in which a given document stands may be expressed in the prepositions *between* and *among*. That is to say, in its intellectual traits a document bears relationship, to begin with, to some other, hence we describe relationships between two documents. These constitute formal and intrinsic matters: traits of grammar, arrangements of words and resonances as to their local meaning, structures of syntax of expression and thought. But in its social setting a document finds bonds among three or more documents, with all of which it is joined in the imagination and mind of a community. These range widely and freely, bound by limits not of form and language, but of public policy in behavior and belief. Documents because of their traits of rhetoric, logic, and topic form a community of texts. Documents because of their audience and authority express the intellect of a textual community.

The principal issue worked out in establishing a community of texts is hermeneutical, the chief outcome of defining a textual community, social and cultural. The former teaches us how to read the texts on their own. The latter tells us how to interpret texts in context. When we define and classify the relationships between texts, we learn how to read the components — words, cogent thoughts formed of phrases, sentences, paragraphs — of those texts in the broader context defined by shared conventions of intellect: rhetoric, logic, topic. More concretely, hermeneutical principles tell how, in light of like documents we have seen many times, to approach a document we have never before seen. Hermeneutics teaches the grammar and syntax of thought. Memorizing a passage of a complex text will teach the rhythms of expression and thought that make of the sounds of some other document an intelligible music. Not only so, but documents joined into a common classification may share specific contents, not only definitive traits of expression — meaning and not solely method. That, in the context of the debate on intertextuality, represents the results of my inquiry into the status of the Rabbinic canonical writings, a status captured in the single word, "document," with its explicit definition now set forth.

VIII

The Two Main Points of Debate: The critics thus have pursued two lines of attack on the documentary reading of the Rabbinic canon:

[1] textual variants vitiate the conception of a determinate document to begin with, and

[2] peripatetic sayings and stories demonstrate the irrelevance of documentary boundaries.

Both emphasize the diversity of documentary representations, both in the manuscript traditions and in the inclusion of the same story in more than one document. Each body of evidence is seen to invalidate the claim that the various compilations respond to distinctive programs and purposes, respectively. One approach is to compare and contrast versions of the same story as these occur in two or more Rabbinic documents. The other is to focus upon manuscript variations, some of them of a considerable order, that pertain to a single document. One manuscript represents the document in one way, another in quite a different way, the one including, the other omitting, sizable stretches of writing.

These two matters present no surprises to anybody. They are commonplaces of learning. Differences arise only from diverse assessments of the matters' importance. From the early 1970s forward, I have addressed both matters, textual variations and multiple citations of a single story or saying.

Diverse manuscript testimonies to a given document: As to the former, I addressed the question — important to me as much as to those who regard the canon as essentially chaotic — in two ways. First, in my commentary to the Mishnah (*A History of the Mishnaic Law* [Leiden, 1974-1986: E. J. Brill, in forty three volumes]) I collated variant readings of the Mishnah-text for some of the divisions; I found they yielded distinctions that rarely made much of a difference. And from the perspective of the description, analysis, and interpretation of free-standing documents, the variant readings made no difference at all. That is because, more important, I defined the documentary reading of the canonical documents in such a way as to take account of variations in manuscript representation of documents. The definition of a document

— its description, analysis, and interpretation — never rests
on one reading as against another, but on the indicative traits
that everywhere characterize the whole and establish the
paradigm that governs the parts. Within that definition, the
inclusion or exclusion of one detail or another makes little
difference.

Not only so, but second, as to variant readings of a
given document, I furthermore dealt with the matter explicitly
in my debate with Schaefer. Since to my knowledge he has
not replied in print, in systematic book, to my systematic response to his critique of 1986, I cannot guess at what he may
be thinking. But there is evidence that suggests he lays heavy
stress on variant MSS evidence of a given document. The
evidence takes the form of a series of "books" comprised by
computer printouts of collated variants. Alas, what difference
the distinctions in readings make is difficult to assess. Schaefer's printouts do not encompass systematic reading and interpretation of what is collated. Specifically, Schaefer and his
co-workers mechanically collate variant readings of the various Yerushalmi-tractates. But to my knowledge they have yet
to interpret these variants. I have not seen their Yerushalmi-
commentaries, based on their collation of variant readings,
and I do not know how they interpret these variants in the
context of the Halakhic issues to which, in general, they pertain.

The Goldberg-Schaefer-Becker school in Berlin treats
variant readings as though they contained no implications for
the exegesis of the document and for its contents. Implicitly,
then, Schaefer's presentation of manuscript variants concedes
the limited importance of those variants, and, as I say, explicitly he has said little to establish their cultural consequence.
The Rabbinic tradition in the classical contexts of learning
knows full well the meaning of diverse wordings and readings
of Halakhic rulings, e.g., is able to discern the Halakhic theory

that has generated one reading in preference to another. The freshest beginners in the study of these texts is introduced to the problem of implications of variant wordings and readings, e.g., by Rashi and the Tosafists, among many. Schaefer and his co-workers have thus far declined to pursue the implications of their computer-collations. Thus far, then, they have given us distinctions that make no difference to learning.

But they owe themselves the effort. For the documentary reading of the Rabbinic canon concerns itself with precisely the matter of Rabbinic culture. Not only so, but the classical exegetical tradition of the Halakhic documents takes full account of not only the presence, but also the meaning, of variant readings of Halakhic rulings — the legal theory behind this version as against that — and of this fact, Schaefer and his co-workers exhibit remarkably slight appreciation. So the entire enterprise stands for little more than a formality of arid academicism: collecting and arranging information of no consequence to speak of.

What, second, about peripatetic sayings? As to the circulation of a given story or saying, complete with variations, over two or more compilations, I dealt with that phenomenon systematically between 1969 and 1974. Specifically, I undertook such systematic studies in the comparison and contrast of the same saying or story in circulation in a number of compilations, e.g., *Development of a Legend. Studies on the Traditions about Yohanan ben Zakkai; Rabbinic Traditions about the Pharisees before 70;* and *Eliezer ben Hyrcanus: The Tradition and the Man.*[4] In a long sequence of charts of comparisons of stories

[4] *Development of a Legend. Studies on the Traditions Concerning Yohanan ben Zakkai.* Leiden, 1970: Brill; *The Rabbinic Traditions about the Pharisees before 70.* Leiden, 1971: Brill. I-III; I. *The Rabbinic Traditions about the Pharisees before 70. The Masters;* II. *The Rabbinic Traditions about the Pharisees before 70. The Houses'* III. *The Rabbinic Traditions about the Pharisees before 70. Conclusions'* *Eliezer ben Hyrcanus. The Tradition and the Man.* Leiden, 1973: Brill. I. *Eliezer*

common to two or more documents, I laid out the differences in detailed charts and proposed theories to explain them. Struck by the heavy emphasis on these stories autonomous of particular documents, I restated the main results of those studies as well as others in *The Peripatetic Saying: The Problem of the Thrice-Told Tale in Talmudic Literature*.[5] But I have never addressed the implications of the peripatetic saying or story for the documentary reading of Rabbinic literature. And that brings us to the present exercise. Specifically, just how important, proportionately, are these peripatetic sayings and stories in the setting of the documents that preserve them?

IX

By "the pointless parallel," then, I mean, the existence of parallels in two or more documents, stories that occur here and there but make a documentary difference no where. A documentary difference would impose variables upon the definitive traits of the document. Stated simply: traditions autonomous of particular documents are parachuted down into particular documents, ordinarily for purposes we can readily discern. Their presence never requires the redefinition of the documentary traits of rhetoric, topic, and logic of coherent discourse that prevail throughout the document. Their presence signifies the intent to draw upon extra-documentary data to amplify or illustrate a documentary point.

What I have left until now is the claim that the Rabbinic tradition circulated in autonomous traditions, unaffected by documentary considerations. Those autonomous traditions in stories and sayings that occur in two or more documents, it is held, vitiate the documentary reading of the Rabbinic ca-

---

ben Hyrcanus. The Tradition and the Man. The Tradition; II. *Eliezer ben Hyrcanus. The Tradition and the Man. The Man.*
[5] Chico, 1985: Scholars Press for Brown Judaic Studies.

nonical books. Rabbinic Judaism circulated in free-circulating "traditions" or "texts," and localizing these "traditions" here rather than there forms a happenstance. If texts can fit anywhere, they belong. no where in particular. It is argued that the presence of peripatetic sayings renders null the claim that data in a given compilation has been selected and arranged purposefully. I have maintained that the compilers of a given document impart to their compilation distinctive traits of rhetoric, topic, and logic of coherent discourse.

Others take the view that utilization of a saying or story in a variety of documents calls into question the allegation that documentary lines signal the imposition of a distinctive program, whether of law or theology, upon what lies within those boundaries. The Rabbinic literature, others maintain, is comprised by a formless mass of free-standing traditions, unaffected by the intent and purpose of documentary authorships let alone the authors of the compositions and composites collected by those authorships.

X

How to proceed? The starting point of the documentary reading of the Rabbinic compilations defines the answer. Since I maintain that sayings and stories autonomous of a particular document make little difference in the definition of the documents that contain them, my argument rests on the matter of proportion. Let me state the argument in the form of a question:

Do the various documents mostly collect and arrange this and that, or are they comprised of compositions and composites that conform to the documents' definitive characteristics of rhetoric, topic, and logic of coherent discourse?

Answering that question with some precision requires detailed readings of particular documents, with the question of proportion imposed on samples of each. Those who argue against the documentary reading of the Rabbinic canon argue from example. Becker, for instance, takes four points at which comparable compositions occur in the two kindred documents, the Yerushalmi and Genesis Rabbah. These are as follows: [1] narratives of Creation at Y. Hag. 2:1 and Gen. R. 1-12; [2] Halakhic texts in Genesis Rabbah with parallels in Yerushalmi, [3] Genesis Rabbah parallels in the Babot-tractates of Yerushalmi, and [4] the narratives of the death of R. Samuel bar R. Isaac. On the strength of these four examples, in his beginning and end of a book that fails to expound the contrary position in a competent manner, he mounts his critique of the documentary hypothesis. In these pages I reply by systematically spelling out, in the context of representative documents, precisely what I mean by a documentary reading of a Rabbinic texts, indicating the sorts of data that register. At no point does a particular reading of a MS by itself sustain my argument. In no way do I depend upon one MS version of a document over another. When Becker grasps that fact, he will have to reconsider the critique he has mounted and its relevance.

XI

We come at the end to the issue at hand: the documentary reading of the Rabbinic canon of late antiquity. I alluded at the outset to the issue and what is at stake in the debate. Let me expand on that matter.

The reason one might suppose that, in the case of the formative age of Judaism, a document does not exhibit integrity and is not autonomous is simple. The several writings of the Rabbinic canon of late antiquity, formed from the Mishnah, ca. A.D. 200, through the Talmud of Babylonia, ca. A.D. 600, with numerous items in between, share materials — sayings, tales, protracted discussions. Some of these shared materials derive from explicitly-cited documents. For instance, passages of Scripture or of the Mishnah or of the Tosefta, cited verbatim, will find their way into the two Talmuds. But sayings, stories, and sizable compositions not identified with a given, earlier text and exhibiting that text's distinctive traits will float from one document to the next. How , then, do we know that a given book in the canon of Judaism is something other than a scrapbook?

The choices are clear. One theory is that a document serves solely as a convenient repository of ready-made sayings and stories, available materials that will have served equally well (or poorly) wherever they took up their final location. In accord with that theory it is quite proper in ignorance of all questions of circumstance and documentary or canonical context to compare the exegesis of a verse of Scripture in one document with the exegesis of that verse of Scripture found in some other document. The other theory is that a composition exhibits a viewpoint, a purpose of authorship distinctive to its framers or collectors and arrangers. Such a characteristic, literary purpose — by this other theory — is so powerfully particular to one authorship that nearly everything at hand can be shown to have been (re)shaped for the ultimate purpose of the authorship at hand, that is, collectors and arrangers who demand the title of authors. In accord with this other theory context and circumstance form the prior condition of inquiry, the result, in exegetical terms, the contingent one.

To resort to a less than felicitous neologism, I thus ask what signifies or defines the "document-ness" of a document and what makes a book a book. I therefore wonder whether there are specific texts in the canonical context of Judaism or whether all texts are merely contextual. In framing the question as I have, I of course lay forth the mode of answering it. . We have to confront a single Rabbinic composition, and ask about its definitive traits and viewpoint. When we investigate the textuality of a document, we therefore raise these questions: is it a composition or a scrap book, a cogent proposition made up of coherent parts, or a collage?

The answers help us to determine the appropriate foundations for comparison, the correct classifications for comparative study. Once we know what is unique to a document, we can investigate the traits that characterize all the document's unique and so definitive materials. We ask about whether the materials unique to a document also cohere, or whether they prove merely miscellaneous. If they do cohere, we may conclude that the framers of the document have followed a single plan and a program. That would in my view justify the claim that the framers carried out a labor not only of conglomeration, arrangement and selection, but also of genuine authorship or composition in the narrow and strict sense of the word. If so, the document emerges from authors, not merely arrangers and compositors. For the same purpose, therefore, we also take up and analyze the items shared between that document and some other or among several documents. We ask about the traits of those items, one by one and all in the aggregate. In these stages we may solve for the case at hand the problem of the Rabbinic document: do we deal with a scrapbook or a collage or a cogent composition? A text or merely a literary expression, random and essentially promiscuous, of a larger theological context? That is the choice at hand.

My project here is to find out whether the documentary lines made a difference, that is to say, whether a given composition exhibited distinctive and definitive traits of its own. The alternative was to take the view that pretty much everything in every holy book circulated on its own, without reference to the particular piece of writing in which it made its appearance. In my initial project, the study of Leviticus

Rabbah and Genesis Rabbah[6] summarized here, I proposed
to demonstrate in the case of that compilation of exegeses of
Scripture that a Rabbinic document constitutes a text, not
merely a scrapbook or a random compilation of episodic materials. A text — in the present context — is a document with
a purpose, one that exhibits the traits of the integrity of the
parts to the whole and the fundamental autonomy of the
whole from other texts. I showed that — for those cases —
the document at hand therefore falls into the classification of
a cogent composition, put together with purpose and intended as a whole and in the aggregate to bear a meaning and
state a message.

I have therefore disproved the claim, for those compilations, that a Rabbinic document serves merely as an an-
thology or miscellany or is to be compared only to a scrapbook, made up of this and that. In that exemplary instance I
pointed to the improbability that a document has been
brought together merely to join discrete and ready-made bits
and pieces of episodic discourse. A document in the canon of
Judaism thus does not merely define a context for the aggregation of such already completed and mutually distinct materials. Rather, I proved, that document constitutes a text. So at
issue in the study of any Rabbinic document is what makes a
text a text, that is, the textuality of a document. But it is clear
with Becker's book that the bulk of the research has yet to
find its readers — hence, in the present context, the necessity
to recapitulate part of it and to add to the project where required.

---

[6] *Comparative Midrash: The Plan and Program of Genesis Rabbah and Leviticus
Rabbah.* Atlanta, 1986: Scholars Press for Brown Judaic Studies.

XII

The question then opens: how to account for the corpus of sayings and stories that do circulate hither and yon? I do not know the answer to that question. But I can contribute three exercises aimed at helping to find it, two of them realized, one simply proposed.

Chapter One: I begin with the simplest task, the characterization of documents as a step in the differentiation of one from another. I deal with Genesis Rabbah and Leviticus Rabbah, which have some common traits and go over a single theological program.

Chapters Two and Three: we proceed to a more difficult problem, the relationship between two intersecting documents, which share materials in common. We address Leviticus Rabbah and Pesiqta deRab Kahana, which intersect in substantial ways. Then, in Chapter Three, we turn to Pesiqta deRab Kahana and Pesiqta Rabbati, with further points of intersection. Here, then, we deal with the most difficult problem in documentary differentiation. What I show is simple. We can account for some shared composites by showing that said composites belong to one document and not another, meaning, they conform to the traits definitive of one of the two documents in which they occur and do not conform to the different definitive traits of the other. I can show that, where a given composite occurs in two documents, we are able through ordinary form-analysis to determine to which document the shared ("autonomous") composite is primary, and to which, secondary. We are able to discern which of the two documents has imposed its formal preferences upon the shared composite, and which has simply received it whole — to which it is primary, to which, secondary.

Chapter Four: I can show that, where a given saying generates a sustained analytical discussion in both Talmuds, we have no grounds for forming a hypothesis of a shared tradition on which the two Talmuds systematically draw. That is to say, we cannot reconstruct a common source that stands beyond a composition or composite of the Yerushalmi and the Bavli, respectively. What we do have are singleton sayings, treated this way in one document, that in another — powerful evidence in favor of the distinctive documentary characteristics of each of the Talmuds. So the treatment, distinctive to the respective Talmuds, of what the Talmuds share argues in favor of the purposive, documentary program.

How is this relevant to the issue at hand? Becker, like many others who have argued to the contrary in examining peripatetic sayings and stories, rarely try to explain the variations in a given document's presentation of a story common to several documents. And when they do, it is still more exceptional for them to invoke documentary considerations, e.g., cultural or theological preferences characteristic of one document and not another, in explaining the variations in the versions of the common story. These are ordinarily left uninterpreted — evidence of difference between documents reduced to proof of the irrelevance of documentary lines. But where the two Talmuds invoke a common saying, each does so in its own context and for its own purpose, and where there is a common composition or composite, the variations in wording respond — so I shall show for the case at hand — for a distinctive program characteristic of one document and not the other: this, not that, where the documents intersect on a common saying or story. In other words, distinct wordings of a common story can make a difference, and should be taken as evidence for a distinctive documentary purpose in citing a free-circulating story or saying.

Chapter Five: The outlines of a theory of the formative history of the Rabbinic tradition — not the documents but the tradition that is given concrete expression in those documents — are set forth. I here offer a theory of how the

Rabbinic traditions were written down and collected into documents. I pay close attention to the criteria for the designation of documentary, as distinct from non-documentary, writing. I offer a tentative theory on the sequence taken by types of writing, that is, for circulation outside of documents, for circulation in documents such as we now possess, for circulation in documents that we can imagine but do not possess.

The Unwritten Chapter: that carries us to an exercise, proposed but not realized here. If documentary lines signify nothing, then what are the traits of the Rabbinic writings that float hither and yon? It is a task that I think imposes itself upon the opponents of the documentary reading of the Rabbinic canon. If documentary lines mark no significant barriers between parallels, so that an autonomous tradition supposedly not only circulates but vitiates documentary boundaries, then a task awaits. It is to describe the definitive traits of that autonomous tradition: its topical program, its distinctive rhetorical preferences (or preferences as to genre), its manner of holding together its distinctive components into conglomerates of one kind or another. In other words, can those who make much of traditions autonomous of particular documents anything at all about the shape and structure of those free-circulating traditions? Or do they view them as a mass of distinct singletons, forming no coherent literary corpus at all?

I do not ask for a theory of the literary history of that corpus or of its singleton-components, only some statement that explains about what they are talking to begin with. If these parallel versions make a point, tell us what it is. If the compositions and composites that serve two or more documents and therefore by definition deny documentary lines comprise a tradition, enlighten us on the traits of that "tradition." How has it circulated, in bits and pieces or as a whole, and to what purpose were the parts composed, and if formed into a whole, on what basis were they sewn together? I have answered those questions for the autonomous documents and that proportion of their contents that is particular to them, respectively. This third exercise challenges those who assign weight to the stories that produce parallels in two or more documents. If they register a point on the traits of the Rabbinic canon and its formation, transmission, and utilization, what point is that?

XII

To summarize: I have now noted four distinct exercises in exposition of the documentary hypothesis. Of those exercises that fill the shank of this book, I have chosen to order them in this way, moving from the familiar to the unfamiliar.

The first asks about the comparison and contrast of complete documents, with attention to the topical programs of each.

The second raises the possibility of showing that a shared composition or composite is primary to one document in which it occurs, secondary to (borrowed by) another document that utilizes it. The upshot is, documentary lines to govern, and each document is characterized by determinate, distinctive traits.

The third requires the consideration of a tradition common to the two Talmuds, the comparison and contrast of the two Talmuds' treatment of a given saying or story. In comparing the Yerushalmi's and the Bavli's treatment of a single problem in common, I am able to show that each exhibits its own particular traits. We may readily differentiate one Talmud's treatment of a given saying from the other Talmud's treatment of that same saying.

The fourth asks for a general theory of the literary history of the Rabbinic canon: who wrote what and why?

Obviously, such a general theory at this stage in learning can only lay out lines for further inquiry, nothing more.

A separate exercise, not undertaken here, requires an assessment of the proportion of a given document shared with some other document, from the Mishnah through the Bavli, from the earlier to the later Midrash-compilations. That requires choosing a sample-passage and identifying precisely the points of intersection.

The four exercises form reprises of completed research. It is necessary to restate some matters in this context in particular, because those that argue against the documentary hypothesis of Rabbinic Judaism have some difficulty in following the progress of research. They simply do not grasp, and apparently do not even know, important components of the documentary hypothesis of the Rabbinic canon. If Schaefer has reflected on the critique of his position and responded to it, I do not know where, in a systematic book, he has published his reply. His student, Becker, for example, does not even cite, and also does not seem even to know, the work reviewed here. A comparison of his bibliography of my pertinent writings with the bibliography given at the end of this book suffices to show how much he has neglected. Nor, in his eagerness, does he take account of the view contrary to his own, except superficially to summarize, and facilely to dismiss it. Hence he stands for those participants in the debate who need help in following the debate, specifically, in grasping the evidence and implications thereof that contradict his approach.

XIII

This reprise of scattered results comes about because of the appearance of Becker's book. From the huge holes in his bibliography, I realized that he has an imperfect grasp of the very problem that he imagines he is addressing. He has not understood the documentary hypothesis that he proposes to criticize. I am thankful to Dr. Sarah Pearce, the book editor of *the Journal of Jewish Studies,* who called my attention to Becker's book and asked me to review it briefly.

But I work from the outside inward. Struggling to characterize the Becker-problem, I turned to Professor William Scott Green, University of Rochester. The project began with a discussion of the title — hence, the thesis of the whole — with him.

Jacob Neusner
Research Professor of Religion and Theology
Senior Fellow, Institute of Advanced Theology
Bard College
Annandale-on-Hudson, New York 12504
neusner@webjogger.net

PART ONE

SHOWING THAT, IN INDICATIVE TRAITS, ONE DOCUMENT IS DIFFERENT FROM ANOTHER DOCUMENT

1.

DIFFERENTIATING DOCUMENTS: GENESIS RABBAH AND LEVITICUS RABBAH

I. THE DOCUMENTARY READING OF THE RABBINIC CANON IN THE FORMATIVE AGE

The only way to establish that one document fundamentally differs from some other is to compare documents. To do so I have taken two large and complex ones, Genesis Rabbah and Leviticus Rabbah. The purpose of the exercise requires iteration at the outset of the particular task of this part of the project and its natural continuator in part two. To begin with, for reasons set forth in the Preface, we turn to the characterization of Genesis Rabbah in comparison and contrast with Leviticus Rabbah: does each compilation focus on its own problem, or do they go over the same ideas in random fashion? In Part ii I show how we may characterize the topical program of Genesis Rabbah, and in Part iii, in a different way, I do the same for Leviticus Rabbah. Part iv conducts the comparison of the results. Then in Part v I expand the range of comparison and contrast to encompass other-than-Rabbinic compilations. In this way we see the distinctive and indicative characteristics of each compilation of Midrash-exegeses. That establishes the prima facie case that one compilation differs from another, the foundation of the documentary hypothesis of the Rabbinic canon.

II.   THE PROGRAM OF GENESIS RABBAH

In Genesis Rabbah the entire narrative of Genesis is so formed as to point toward the sacred history of Israel, the Jewish people: its slavery and redemption; its coming Temple in Jerusalem; its exile and salvation at the end of time. The outcome imposes sense and meaning on the interval from creation to redemption. The method of the Midrash is to read the whole into the exposition of the parts. The purpose is to explain the present and to establish clear guidelines on the shape of the future.

The powerful message of Genesis in Genesis Rabbah proclaims that the world's creation commenced a single, straight line of events, leading in the end to the salvation of Israel and through Israel all humanity, which will accept God's dominion as Israel does now in the Torah. Israel's history constitutes the counterpart of creation, and the laws of Israel's salvation affirm the foundation of creation. Therefore a given story out of Genesis, about creation, events from Adam to Noah and Noah to Abraham, the domestic affairs of the patriarchs, or Joseph, will bear a deeper message about what it means to be Israel, on the one side, and what in the end of days will happen to Israel, on the other.

So the persistent theological program requires sages' to search in Scripture for meaning for their own circumstance and for the condition of their people. If, therefore, I had to point to the single most important proposition of Genesis Rabbah, it is that, in the story of the beginnings of creation, humanity, and Israel, we find the message of the meaning and end of the life of the Jewish people. The deeds of the founders supply signals for the children about what is going to come in the future. So the biography of Abraham, Isaac, and Jacob also constitutes a protracted account of the history of Israel later on. If the sages could announce a single syllogism and argue it systematically, that is the proposition upon which they would insist.

Before proceeding, let me give a single example of the tendency of the document as a whole. It derives from the single critical moment, in sages' view, in the narrative of Genesis. The binding of Isaac, critical in sages' reading of lessons taught by Abraham's deeds for the direction of their descendants, formed the centerpiece of their quest for the laws of history as well. At each point, in each detail, they discovered not only what we going to happen but also why. The single most important paradigm for history therefore emerged from the deed at Moriah.

> LVI:I.1.A. "On the third day Abraham lifted up his eyes and saw the place afar off" (Gen. 22:4):
>
> B. "After two days he will revive us, on the third day he will raise us up, that we may live in his presence" (Hos.16:2).
>
> C. On the third day of the tribes: "And Joseph said to them on the third day, 'This do and live'" (Gen. 42:18).
>
> D. On the third day of the giving of the Torah: "And it came to pass on the third day when it was morning" (Ex. 19:16).
>
> E. On the third day of the spies: "And hide yourselves there for three days" (Josh 2:16).
>
> F. On the third day of Jonah: "And Jonah was in the belly of the fish three days and three nights" (Jonah 2:1).
>
> G. On the third day of the return from the Exile: "And we abode there three days" (Ezra 8:32).
>
> H. On the third day of the resurrection of the dead: "After two days he will revive us, on the third day he will raise us up, that we may live in his presence" (Hos. 16:2).
>
> I. On the third day of Esther: "Now it came to pass on the third day that Esther put on her royal apparel" (Est. 5:1).

J. She put on the monarchy of the house of her fathers.

K. On account of what sort of merit?

L. Rabbis say, "On account of the third day of the giving of the Torah."

M. R. Levi said, "It is on account of the merit of the third day of Abraham: 'On the third day Abraham lifted up his eyes and saw the place afar off' (Gen. 22:4)."

2.   A. "...lifted up his eyes and saw the place afar off" (Gen. 22:4):

B. What did he see? He saw a cloud attached to the mountain. He said, "It would appear that that is the place concerning which the Holy One, blessed be he, told me to offer up my son."

The third day marks the fulfillment of the promise, at the end of time of the resurrection of the dead, and, at appropriate moments, of Israel's redemption. The reference to the third day at Gen. 22:2 then invokes the entire panoply of Israel's history. The relevance of the composition emerges at the end. Prior to the concluding segment, the passage forms a kind of litany and falls into the category of a liturgy. Still, the recurrent hermeneutic which teaches that the stories of the patriarchs prefigure the history of Israel certainly makes its appearance. The sages understood that stories about the progenitors, presented in the book of Genesis, define the human condition and proper conduct for their children, Israel in time to come. Accordingly, they systematically asked Scripture to tell them how they were supposed to conduct themselves at the critical turnings of life.

The first thing to notice is how a variety of events is made to prove a syllogism. The stories of Genesis therefore join stories of other times and persons in Israel's history. All of them equally, and timelessly, point to prevailing rules. Syllogistic argument, resting on lists of facts of the same classification, wrests the narrative out of its one-time and time-bound setting and turns it into a statement of rules that prevail everywhere and all the time for Israel. Here is a good example of the mode of argument of the document:

> XCVI:III.1.A. "And when the time drew near that Israel must die, [he called his son Joseph and said to him, 'If now I have found favor in your sight, put your hand under my thigh and promise to deal loyally and truly with me. Do not bury me in Egypt, but let me lie with my fathers; carry me out of Egypt and bury me in their burying place.' He answered, I will do as you have said.' And he said, 'Swear to me.' And he swore to him. Then Israel bowed himself upon the head of his bed]" (Gen. 47:29-31):
>
> B. "There is no man that has power of the spirit...neither is there dominion in the day of death" (Qoh. 8:8).
>
> C. Said R. Joshua of Sikhnin in the name of R. Levi, "As to the trumpets that Moses made in the wilderness, when Moses lay on the point of death, the Holy One, blessed be he, hid them away, so that he would not blow on them and summon the people to him.
>
> D. "This was meant to fulfill this verse: '...neither is there dominion in the day of death' (Qoh. 8:8).
>
> E. "When Zimri did his deed, what is written? 'And Phineas went after the man of Israel into the chamber' (Num. 25:8). So where was Moses, that Phineas should speak before he did?
>
> F. "'...neither is there dominion in the day of death' (Qoh. 8:8).
>
> G. "But the formulation expresses humiliation. Salvation was handed over to Phineas, [and Moses] abased himself.
>
> H. "So too with David: 'How king David was old' (1 Kgs. 1:1). What is stated about him when he lay dying? 'Now the days of David drew near, that he should die' (1 Kgs. 21:1).
>
> I. "What is said is not 'king David,' but merely 'David.'

J. "The same applies to Jacob, when he was on the point of death, he humbled himself to Joseph, saying to him, 'If now I have found favor in your sight.' [So he abased himself, since there is no dominion on the day of death.]

K. "When did this take place? As he drew near the end: 'And when the time drew near that Israel must die.'"

What strikes the exegete is the unprepossessing language used by Jacob in speaking to Joseph. The intersecting verse makes clear that, on the day of one's death, one no longer rules. Several examples of that fact are given, Moses, David, finally Jacob. So the syllogism about the loss of power on the occasion of death derives proof from a number of sources, and the passage has not been worked out to provide the exegesis of our base verse in particular. The exposition is all the more moving because the exegete focuses upon his proposition, rather than on the great personalities at hand. His message obviously is that even the greatest lose all dominion when they are going to die. In this way the deeds of the founders define the rule for the descendants.

As a corollary to the view that the biography of the fathers prefigures the history of the descendants, sages maintained that the deeds of the children — the holy way of life of Israel — follow the model established by the founders long ago. So they looked in Genesis for the basis for the things they held to be God's will for Israel. And they found ample proof. Sages invariably searched the stories of Genesis for evidence of the origins not only of creation and of Israel, but also of Israel's cosmic way of life, its understanding of how, in the passage of nature and the seasons, humanity worked out its relationship with God. The holy way of life that Israel lived through the seasons of nature therefore would make its mark upon the stories of the creation of the world and the beginning of Israel

Part of the reason sages pursued the interest at hand derived from polemic. From the first Christian century theologians of Christianity maintained that salvation did not depend upon keeping the laws of the Torah. Abraham, after all, had been justified and he did not keep the Torah, which, in his day, had not yet been given. So sages time and again would maintain that Abraham indeed kept the entire Torah even before it had been revealed. They further attributed to Abraham, Isaac, and Jacob rules of the Torah enunciated only later on, for example, the institution of prayer three times a day. But the passage before us bears a different charge. It is to Israel to see how deeply embedded in the rules of reality were the patterns governing God's relationship to Israel. That relationship, one of human sin and atonement, divine punishment and forgiveness, expresses the most fundamental laws of human existence. Here is yet another rule that tells sages what to find in Scripture.

> XCVIII:I.1.A. "Then Jacob called his sons [and said, 'Gather yourselves together, that I may tell you what shall befall you in days to come. Assemble and hear, O sons of Jacob, and hearken to Israel, your father. Reuben, you are my first-born, my might and the first fruits of my strength, pre-eminent in pride and pre-eminent in power. Unstable as water, you shall not have pre-eminence, because you went up to your father's bed, then you defiled it, you went up to my couch!']" (Gen. 49:1-4):
>
> B. "I will cry to God Most High, [unto God who completes it for me]" (Ps. 57:3):
>
> C. "I will cry to God Most High:" on the New Year.
>
> D. "...unto God who completes it for me:" on the Day of Atonement.
>
> E. To find out which [goat] is for the Lord and which one is for an evil decree.
>
> 2.   A. Another matter: "I will cry to God Most High, [unto God who completes it for me]" (Ps. 57:3):

B "I will cry to God Most High:" refers to our father, Jacob.

C. "...unto God who completes it for me:" for the
Holy One, blessed be he, concurred with him to give
each of the sons a blessing in accord with his character.

D. "Then Jacob called his sons [and said, 'Gather
yourselves together, that I may tell you what shall befall
you in days to come]."

The intersecting verse invites the comparison of the
judgment of the Days of Awe to the blessing of Jacob, and
that presents a dimension of meaning that the narrative
would not otherwise reveal. Just as God decides which goat
serves what purpose, so God concurs in Jacob's judgment of
which son/tribe deserves what sort of blessing. So Jacob
stands in the stead of God in this stunning comparison of Jacob's blessing to the day of judgment. The link between Jacob's biography and the holy life of Israel is fresh.

What, then, tells sages how to identify the important
and avoid the trivial? The answer derives from the fundamental theological conviction that gives life to their search of
Scripture. It is that the task of Israel is to hope, and the message of Genesis — there for the sages to uncover and make
explicit — is always to hope. For a Jew it is a sin to despair.
This I think defines the iron law of meaning, telling sages
what matters and what does not, guiding their hands to take
up those verses that permit expression of hope — that above
all. Given the definitive event of their day — the conversion
of the great empire of Rome to Christianity — the task of
hope proved not an easy assignment.

XCVIII:XIV.4.A. "I hope for your salvation, O Lord"
(Gen. 49:18):

B. Said R. Isaac, "All things depend on hope, suffering depends on hope, the sanctification of God's
name depends on hope, the merit attained by the fa-

thers depends on hope, the lust for the age to come depends on hope.

C. "That is in line with this verse: 'Yes, in the way of your judgments, O Lord, we have hoped for you, to your name, and to your memorial, is the desire of our soul' (Is. 26:8). 'The way of your judgments refers to suffering.

D. "'...to your name:' this refers to the sanctification of the divine name.

E. "'...and to your memorial:' this refers to the merit of the fathers.

F. "'...is the desire of our soul:' this refers to the lust for the age to come.

G. "Grace depends on hope: 'O Lord, be gracious to us, we have hoped for you' (Is. 33:2).

H. "Forgiveness depends on hope: 'For with you is forgiveness' (Ps. 133:4), then: 'I hope for the Lord' (Ps. 130:5).'"

The interesting unit is No. 4, which is explicit on the critical importance of hope in the salvific process, and which further links the exclamation to the setting in which it occurs. This seems to me to typify the strength of the exegesis at hand, with its twin-powers to link all details to a tight narrative and to link the narrative to the history of Israel.

Sages read the narrative of creation and the fall of Adam to testify to the redemption and the salvation of Israel. Let me begin with a single example of the syllogism at hand and then offer a more general statement of it. The following passage provides a stunning example of the basic theory of sages on how the stories of creation are to be read:

XXIX:III.1.A. "And Noah found grace" (Gen. 6:8):

B. Said R. Simon, "There were three acts of finding on the part of the Holy One, blessed be he:

C. "'And you found [Abraham's] heart faithful before you' (Neh. 9:8).

D. "'I have found David my servant' (Ps. 89:21).

> E. "'I found Israel like grapes in the wilderness' (Hos. 9:10)."
>
> F. His fellows said to R. Simon, "And is it not written, 'Noah found grace in the eyes of the Lord' (Gen. 6:8)?"
>
> G. He said them, "He found it, but the Holy One, blessed be he, did not find it."
>
> H. Said R. Simon, "'He found grace in the wilderness' (Jer. 31:1) on account of the merit of the generation of the Wilderness."

The proposition draws on the verse at hand, but makes its own point. It is that the grace shown to Noah derived from Israel. Noah on his own — that is, humanity — enjoyed salvation only because of Israel's merit. The proposition is striking and daring. God "found," that is, made an accidental discovery, of a treasure, consisting only of three: Abraham, David, and Israel. These stand for the beginning, the end, and the holy people that started with Abraham and found redemption through David. As if to underline this point, we refer, H, to the generation of the Wilderness and its faith, which merited gaining the Land.

A cogent and uniform world-view accompanied the sages at hand when they approached the text of Genesis. This world-view they systematically joined to that text, fusing the tale at hand with that larger context of imagination in which the tale was received and read. Accordingly, when we follow the sages' mode of interpreting the text, we find our way deep into their imaginative life. Scripture becomes the set of facts that demonstrate the truth of the syllogisms that encompassed and described the world, as sages saw it. The next stage in my demonstration of the systematic and deeply polemical reading at hand will take the simple form of successive illustration of the basic thesis. That thesis is that Israel's salvific history informs and infuses the creation of the world. That story takes on its true meaning from what happened to

Israel, and it follows that Israel's future history accounts for the creation of the world.

> XX:I.1.A. "Then the Lord God said to the serpent, 'Because you have done this, cursed are you above all cattle and above all wild animals'" (Gen. 3:14):
>
> B. "A slanderer shall not be established in the earth; the violent and wicked man shall be hunted with thrust upon thrust" (Ps. 140:12).
>
> C. Said R. Levi, "In the world to come the Holy One, blessed be he, will take the nations of the world and bring them down to Gehenna. He will say to them, 'Why did you impose fines upon my children.' They will say to him, 'Some of them slandered others among them. The Holy One, blessed be he, will then take these [Israelite slanderers] and those and bring them down to Gehenna."
>
> 2. A. Another interpretation: "A slanderer" refers to the snake, who slandered his creator.
>
> B. "Will not be established [standing upright] on earth:" "Upon your belly you shall go" (Gen. 3:14).
>
> C. "The violent and wicked man shall be hunted:" What is written is not "with a thrust" but "with thrust after thrust," [since not only the serpent was cursed]. What is written is "thrust after thrust," for man was cursed, woman was cursed, and the snake was cursed.
>
> D. "And the Lord God said to the serpent...."

We have an exegesis of a base verse and intersecting verse, that is in that "classic" form in which the intersecting verse is fully worked out and only then drawn to meet the base verse. No. 1 treats the intersecting verse as a statement on its own, and then No. 2 reads the verse in line with Gen. 3:14. But the intersecting verse is hardly chosen at random, since it speaks of slander in general, and then at No. 2 the act of slander of the snake is explicitly read into the intersecting verse. So the intersection is not only thematic, not by any means. The upshot of the exercise links Israel's history to the history of humanity in the garden of Eden. No. 1 focuses upon the sacred history of Israel, making the point that slanderers in Israel cause the nation's downfall, just as the snake caused the downfall of humanity, the point

> XIX:VII.1.A. "And they heard the sound of the Lord God walking in the garden in the cool of the day" (Gen. 3:8):
> 2.   A. Said R. Abba bar Kahana, "The word is not written, 'move,' but rather, 'walk,' bearing the sense that [the Presence of God] leapt about and jumped upward.
>
> B. "[The point is that God's presence leapt upward from the earth on account of the events in the garden, as will now be explained:] The principal location of the Presence of God was [meant to be] among the creatures down here. When the first man sinned, the Presence of God moved up to the first firmament. When Cain sinned, it went up to the second firmament. When the generation of Enosh sinned, it went up to the third firmament. When the generation of the Flood sinned, it went up to the fourth firmament. When the generation of the dispersion [at the tower of Babel] sinned, it went up to the fifth. On account of the Sodomites it went up to the sixth, and on account of the Egyptians in the time of Abraham it went up to the seventh.
>
> C. "But, as a counterpart, there were seven righteous men who rose up: Abraham, Isaac, Jacob , Levi, Kohath, Amram, and Moses. They brought the Presence of God [by stages] down to earth.
>
> D. "Abraham brought it from the seventh to the sixth, Isaac brought it from the sixth to the fifth, Jacob brought it from the fifth to the fourth, Levi brought it down from the forth to the third, Kohath brought it down from the third to the second, Amram brought it down from the second to the first. Moses brought it down to earth."
>
> E. Said R. Isaac, "It is written, 'The righteous will inherit the land and dwell therein forever' (Ps. 37:29). Now what will the wicked do? Are they going to fly in the air? But that the wicked did not make it possible for

the Presence of God to take up residence on earth [is
what the verse wishes to say]."

What is striking is the claim that while the wicked
(gentiles) drove God out of the world, the righteous (Israelites) brought God back into the world. This theme, linking
the story of the fall of man to the history of Israel, with Israel
serving as the counterpart and fulfillment of the fall at creation. The next composition still more strikingly shows that
the creation and fall of man finds its counterpart in the formation and sanctification of Israel. So Israel serves, as did the
first man, as the embodiment of humanity. But while Adam
sinned and was driven from paradise, Israel through atonement will bring humanity salvation. In this way the book of
Genesis serves a purpose quite pertinent to the theological
program of the compilers of Genesis Rabbah.

> XIX:IX.1.A. "And the Lord God called to the man and
> said to him, 'Where are you?'" (Gen. 3:9):
> B. [The word for "where are you" yields conso-
> nants that bear the meaning,] "How has this happened
> to you?"
> C. [God speaks:] "Yesterday it was in accord with
> my plan, and now it is in accord with the plan of the
> snake. Yesterday it was from one end of the world to
> the other [that you filled the earth], and now: 'Among
> the trees of the garden' (Gen. 3:8) [you hide out]."
> 2. A. R. Abbahu in the name of R. Yosé bar Haninah:
> "It is written, 'But they are like a man [Adam], they
> have transgressed the covenant' (Hos. 6:7).
> B. "'They are like a man,' specifically, like the first
> man. [We shall now compare the story of the first man
> in Eden with the story of Israel in its land.]
> C. "'In the case of the first man, I brought him
> into the garden of Eden, I commanded him, he violated
> my commandment, I judged him to be sent away and
> driven out, but I mourned for him, saying
> "How..."'[which begins the book of Lamentations,

hence stands for a lament, but which, as we just saw, also is written with the consonants that also yield, 'Where are you'].

D. "'I brought him into the garden of Eden,' as it is written, 'And the Lord God took the man and put him into the garden of Eden' (Gen. 2:15).

E. "'I commanded him,' as it is written, 'And the Lord God commanded...' (Gen. 2:16).

F. "'And he violated my commandment,' as it is written, 'Did you eat from the tree concerning which I commanded you' (Gen. 3:11).

G. "'I judged him to be sent away,' as it is written, "And the Lord God sent him from the garden of Eden' (Gen. 3:23).

H. "'And I judged him to be driven out.' 'And he drove out the man' (Gen. 3:24).

I. "'But I mourned for him, saying, "How..."'.' 'And he said to him, "Where are you"' (Gen. 3:9), and the word for 'where are you' is written, 'How....'

J. "'So too in the case of his descendants, [God continues to speak,] I brought them into the Land of Israel, I commanded them, they violated my commandment, I judged them to be sent out and driven away but I mourned for them, saying, "How...."'"

K. "'I brought them into the Land of Israel.' 'And I brought you into the land of Carmel' (Jer. 2:7).

L. "'I commanded them.' 'And you, command the children of Israel' (Ex. 27:20). 'Command the children of Israel' (Lev. 24:2).

M. "'They violated my commandment.' 'And all Israel have violated your Torah' (Dan. 9:11).

N. "'I judged them to be sent out.' 'Send them away, out of my sight and let them go forth' (Jer 15:1).

O. "'....and driven away.' 'From my house I shall drive them' (Hos. 9:15).

P. "'But I mourned for them, saying, "How...."'" 'How has the city sat solitary, that was full of people' (Lam. 1:1)."

No. 1 simply contrasts one day with the next, a stunning and stark statement, lacking all decoration. No. 1 certainly sets the stage for No. 2 and the whole must be regarded as a cogent, thoughtful composition. The other, No. 2, equally simply compares the story of man in the Garden of Eden with the tale of Israel in its Land. Every detail is in place, the articulation is perfect, and the result, completely convincing as an essay in interpretation. All of this rests on the simple fact that the word for "where are you" may be expressed as "How...," which, as is clear, invokes the opening words of the book of Lamentations. So Israel's history serves as a paradigm for human history, and vice versa. What then is the point? It is obedience, as the following indicates:

XIX:XI.1.A. "The man said, 'The woman whom you gave to be with me gave me fruit of the tree, and I ate'" (Gen. 3:12):

B. There are four on whose pots the Holy One, blessed be he, knocked, only to find them filled with piss, and these are they: Adam, Cain, the wicked Balaam, and Hezekiah.

C. Adam: "The man said, 'The woman whom you gave to be with me gave me fruit of the tree and I ate" (Gen. 3:12).

D. Cain: "And the Lord said to Cain, 'Where is Abel, your brother?'" (Gen. 4:9).

E. The wicked Balaam: "And God came to Balaam and said, 'What men are these with you?'" (Num. 22:9)

F. Hezekiah: "Then came Isaiah the prophet to king Hezekiah and said to him, 'What did these men say?'" (2 Kgs. 20:14).

G. But Ezekiel turned out to be far more adept than any of these: "'Son of man, can these bones live?' And I said, 'O Lord God, you know'" (Ez. 37:3).

H. Said R., Hinena bar Pappa, "The matter may be compared to the case of a bird that was caught by a hunter. The hunter met someone who asked him, 'Is this bird alive or dead?'

I. "He said to him, 'If you want, it is alive, but if you prefer, it is dead.' So: "'Will these bones live?" And he said, "Lord God, you know.""

The colloquy once more serves to find in Israel's history a counterpart to the incident at hand. Only Ezekiel knew how to deal with a question that bore with it the answer: God will do as he likes, God knows the answer. That is, the sole appropriate response is one of humility and acceptance of God's will. With what result? With the result of the salvation of humanity through Israel. History through Israel becomes the story of the salvation of humanity:

> XXI:I.1.A. "Then the Lord God said, 'Behold, the man has become like one of us, [knowing good and evil, and now, lest he put forth his hand and take also of the tree of life and eat and live forever]'" (Gen. 3:22):
>
> B. "It is written, 'Then I heard a holy one speaking, and another holy one said to that certain one who spoke'" (Dan. 8:13).
>
> C. "The one" refers to the Holy One, blessed be he: "The Lord, our God, the Lord is One" (Deut. 6:4).
>
> D. "Holy," for everyone says before him, "Holy...."
>
> E. "Speaking" means "issuing harsh decrees against his creatures."
>
> F. [For example,] "Thorns and thistles it shall bring forth to you" (Gen. 3:18).
>
> G. "And another holy one said to that certain one who spoke:"
>
> H. R. Huna said, "It was to Mr. So-and-so."
>
> I. Aqilas translated the passage, "It was to one who was within that he spoke, meaning the first man, whose presence lay within [and closer to God than] that of the serving angels [since he stood closer to God than they did]." [The remainder of the exegesis flows from Aqilas's view of the locus of discourse.]
>
> J. "How long shall be the vision concerning the continual burnt offering?" (Dan. 8:13);
>
> K. "Will the decree that has been issued against the first man go on forever?"

L. "And the transgression that causes desolation" (Deut. 8:13):

M. "So too will his transgression desolate him even in the grave?"

N. "To give both the sanctuary and the host to be trampled underfoot" (Dan. 8:13):

O. "Will he and his descendants be made into chaff before the angel of death?"

P. "And he said to me, 'Until evening, morning two thousand and three hundred, then shall the sanctuary be victorious'" (Dan. 8:14):

Q. R. Azariah, R. Jonathan b. Haggai in the name of R. Isaac: "In any case in which it is evening, it is not morning, and in any case in which it is morning, it surely is not evening. [So what is the sense of this passage?] But when it is morning for the nations of the world, it is evening for Israel, and as to 'morning,' at that time [at which it is morning for Israel],' then 'shall the sanctuary be victorious,' for at that time I shall declare him justified of that decree: 'Behold, let the man become like one of us' (Gen. 3:22)."

The fully exploited intersection of the intersecting and base verses turns the statement of Gen. 3:22 into a powerful promise. Man will indeed become like the One, at the time that the gentiles reach their evening, and Israel, morning. So once more the condition of Israel serves as a paradigm for the human situation, but this in a most concrete and specific way. The nations of the world embody the curse of God to man, and Israel, the promised future blessing. The framer of the passage carefully avoids speculation on the meaning of the numbers used in Daniel's passage, so the apocalyptic power of Daniel's vision serves the rather generalized messianic expectations of sages, without provoking dangerous speculation on the here and now.

XXI:VII.3.A. Judah b. Padaiah interpreted, "Who will remove the dust from between your eyes, O first Man! For you could not abide in the commandment that ap-

plied to you for even a single hour, and lo, your children can wait for three years to observe the prohibition
of the use of the fruit of a tree for the first three years
after it is planted: 'Three years shall it be as forbidden
to you, it shall not be eaten' (Lev. 19:23)."

B. Said R. Huna, "When Bar Qappara heard this,
he said, 'Well have you expounded matters, Judah, son
of my sister!'"

No. 3 then compares the character of Israel to the
character of the first man, calling Israel "descendants of the
first man" and pointing out that they can observe a commandment for a long time. The example is apt, since Israel
observes the prohibition involving the fruit of a newly
planted tree, and does so for three years, while the first man
could not keep his hands off a fruit tree for even an hour.
This of course restates with enormous power the fact that Israel's history forms the counterpart to the history of humanity. But while the first man could not do what God demanded, Israel can and does do God's will. We come at the
end to a simple and clear statement of the main point of it all:

LXXXIII:V.1.A. Wheat, straw, and stubble had a fight.

B. Wheat said, "It was on my account that the field
was sown."

C. Stubble said, "It was on my account that the
field was sown."

D. Wheat said, "The day will come and you will
see."

E. When the harvest time came, the householder
began to take the stubble and burn it, and the straw and
spread it, but the wheat he made into heaps.

F. Everyone began to kiss the wheat. [I assume this
is a reference to the messianic passage, "Kiss the son"
which is also to be translated, "Kiss the wheat" (Ps.
2:12).]

G. So too Israel and the nations of the world have
a fight.

H. These say, "It was on our account that the world was created," and those say, "It was on our account that the world was created."

I. Israel says, "The day will come and you will see."

J. In the age to come: "You shall fan them and the wind will carry them away" (Is. 41:16).

K. As to Israel: "And you shall rejoice in the Lord, you shall glory in the Holy One of Israel" (Is. 41:16).

Here at the end sages make explicit their basic view. The world was created for Israel, and not for the nations of the world. At the end of days everyone will see what only Israel now knows. Since sages read Genesis as the history of the world with emphasis on Israel, the lives portrayed, the domestic quarrels and petty conflicts with the neighbors, as much as the story of creation itself, all serve to yield insight into what was to be. We now turn to a detailed examination of how sages spelled out the historical law at hand. The lives of the patriarchs signaled the history of Israel. Every detail of the narrative therefore served to prefigure what was to be, and Israel found itself, time and again, in the revealed facts of the history of the creation of the world, the decline of humanity down to the time of Noah, and, finally, its ascent to Abraham, Isaac, and Israel. In order to illustrate the single approach to diverse stories, whether concerning Creation, Adam, and Noah, or concerning Abraham, Isaac, and Jacob, we focus on two matters, Abraham, on the one side, and Rome, on the other. In the former we see that Abraham serves as well as Adam to prove the point of it all. In the latter we observe how, in reading Genesis, the sages who compiled Genesis Rabbah discovered the meaning of the events of their own day.

Let us begin with an exemplary case of how sages discovered social laws of history in the facts of Scripture. What Abraham did corresponds to what Balaam did, and the same law of social history derives proof from each of the two contrasting figures.

> LV:VIII.1.A. "And Abraham rose early in the morning,
> [saddled his ass, and took two of his young men with
> him, and his son Isaac, and he cut the wood for the
> burnt offering and arose and went to the place which
> God had told him]" (Gen. 22:3):
>
> B. Said R. Simeon b. Yohai, "Love disrupts the
> natural order of things, and hatred disrupts the natural
> order of things.
>
> C. "Love disrupts the natural order of things we
> learn from the case of Abraham: '...he saddled his ass.'
> But did he not have any number of servants? But that
> proves love disrupts the natural order of things.
>
> D. "Hatred disrupts the natural order of things we
> learn from the case of Balaam: 'And Balaam rose up
> early in the morning and saddled his ass' (Num. 22:21).
> But did he not have any number of servants? But that
> proves hatred disrupts the natural order of things.
>
> E. "Love disrupts the natural order of things we
> learn from the case of Joseph: 'And Joseph made his
> chariot ready' (Gen. 46:29). But did he not have any
> number of servants? But that proves love disrupts the
> natural order of things.
>
> F. "Hatred disrupts the natural order of things we
> learn from the case of Pharaoh: 'And he made his char-
> iot ready' (Ex. 14:6). But did he not have any number
> of servants? But that proves hatred disrupts the natural
> order of things."
>
> 2.   A. Said R. Simeon b. Yohai, "Let one act of sad-
> dling an ass come and counteract another act of sad-
> dling the ass. May the act of saddling the ass done by
> our father Abraham, so as to go and carry out the will
> of him who speak and brought the world into being
> counteract the act of saddling that was carried out by
> Balaam when he went to curse Israel.
>
> B. "Let one act of preparing counteract another act
> of preparing. Let Joseph's act of preparing his chariot
> so as to meet his father serve to counteract Pharaoh's
> act of preparing to go and pursue Israel."

C. R. Ishmael taught on Tannaite authority, "Let the sword held in the hand serve to counteract the sword held in the hand.

D. "Let the sword held in the hand of Abraham, as it is said, 'Then Abraham put forth his hand and took the knife to slay his son' (Gen. 22:10) serve to counteract the sword taken by Pharaoh in hand: 'I will draw my sword, my hand shall destroy them' (Ex. 15:9)."

We see that the narrative is carefully culled for probative facts, yielding laws. One fact is that there are laws of history. The other is that laws may be set aside, by either love or hatred. Yet another law of history applies in particular to Israel, as distinct from the foregoing, deriving from the life of both Israel and the nations, Abraham and Balaam. What follows presents the law that Israel never is orphaned of holy and heroic leaders.

LVIII:II.1.A. "The sun rises and the sun goes down" (Qoh. 1:5):

B. Said R. Abba, "Now do we not know that the sun rises and the sun sets? But the sense is this: before the Holy One, blessed be he, makes the sun of one righteous man set, he brings up into the sky the sun of another righteous man.

C. "On the day that R. Aqiba died, Our Rabbi [Judah the Patriarch] was born. In his regard, they recited the following verse: 'The sun rises and the sun goes down' (Qoh. 1:5).

D. "On the day on which Our Rabbi died, R. Adda bar Ahbah was born. In his regard, they recited the following verse: 'The sun rises and the sun goes down' (Qoh. 1:5).

E. "On the day on which R. Ada died, R. Abin was born. In his regard, they recited the following verse: 'The sun rises and the sun goes down' (Qoh. 1:5).

F. "On the day on which R. Abin died, R. Abin his son was born. In his regard, they recited the following verse: 'The sun rises and the sun goes down' (Qoh. 1:5).

G. "On the day on which R. Abin died, Abba Hoshaiah of Taraya was born. In his regard, they recited the following verse: 'The sun rises and the sun goes down' (Qoh. 1:5).

H. "On the day on which Abba Hoshaiah of Taraya died, R. Hoshaiah was born. In his regard, they recited the following verse: 'The sun rises and the sun goes down' (Qoh. 1:5).

I. "Before the Holy One, blessed be he, made the sun of Moses set, he brought up into the sky the sun of Joshua: 'And the Lord said to Moses, Take you Joshua, the son of Nun' (Num. 27:18).

J. "Before the Holy One, blessed be he, made the sun of Joshua set, he brought up into the sky the sun of Othniel, son of Kenaz: 'And Othniel the son of Kenaz took it' (Joshua 15:17).

K. "Before the Holy One, blessed be he, made the sun of Eli set, he brought up into the sky the sun of Samuel: 'And the lamp of God was not yet gone out, and Samuel was laid down to sleep in the Temple of the Lord' (1 Sam. 3:3)."

L. Said R. Yohanan, "He was like an unblemished calf."

M. [Reverting to K:] "Before the Holy One, blessed be he, made the sun of Sarah set, he brought up into the sky the sun of Rebecca: 'Behold Milcah also has borne children' (Gen. 22:20). 'Sarah lived a hundred and twenty-seven years. These were the years of the life of Sarah' (Gen. 23:1)."

One rule of Israel's history is yielded by the facts at hand. Israel is never left without an appropriate hero or heroine. The relevance the long discourse becomes clear at the end. Each story in Genesis may forecast the stages in Israel's history later on, beginning to end. A matter of deep concern focused sages' attention on the sequence of world-empires to which, among other nations, Israel was subjugated, Babylonia, Media, Greece, and Rome — Rome above all. What will follow? Sages maintained that beyond the rule of Rome lay the salvation of Israel:

> XLII:IV.1.A. "And it came to pass in the days of Amraphel" (Gen. 14:1):
>
> 4.   A. Another matter: "And it came to pass in the days of Amraphael, king of Shinar" (Gen. 14:1) refers to Babylonia.
>
>   B. "Arioch, king of Ellasar" (Gen. 14:1) refers to Greece.
>
>   C. "Chedorlaomer, king of Elam" (Gen. 14:1) refers to Media.
>
>   D. "And Tidal, king of Goiim [nations]" (Gen. 14:1) refers to the wicked government [Rome], which conscripts troops from all the nations of the world.
>
>   E. Said R. Eleazar bar Abina, "If you see that the nations contend with one another, look for the footsteps of the king-messiah. You may know that that is the case, for lo, in the time of Abraham, because the kings struggled with one another, a position of greatness came to Abraham."

Obviously, No. 4 presents the most important reading of Gen. 14:1, since it links the events of the life of Abraham to the history of Israel and even ties the whole to the messianic expectation. I suppose that any list of four kings will provoke inquiry into the relationship of the entries of that list to the four kingdoms among which history, in Israel's experience, is divided. The process of history flows in both directions. Just as what Abraham did prefigured the future history of Israel, so what the Israelites later on were to do imposed limitations on Abraham. Time and again events in the lives of the patriarchs prefigure the four monarchies, among which, of course, the fourth, last, and most intolerable was Rome. Here is another such exercise in the recurrent proof of a single proposition.

XLIV:XVII.4.A. "[And it came to pass, as the sun was going down,] lo, a deep sleep fell on Abram, and lo, a dread and great darkness fell upon him" (Gen. 15:12):

B. "...lo, a dread" refers to Babylonia, as it is written, "Then was Nebuchadnezzar filled with fury" (Gen. 3:19).

C. "' and darkness" refers to Media, which darkened the eyes of Israel by making it necessary for the Israelites to fast and conduct public mourning.

D. "...great..." refers to Greece.

E. R. Simon said, "The kingdom of Greece set up one hundred and twenty commanders, one hundred and twenty hyparchs, and one hundred and twenty generals."

F. Rabbis said, "It was sixty of each, as it is written, 'Serpents, fiery serpents, and scorpions' (Gen. 8:15). Just as the scorpion produces sixty eggs at a time, so the kingdom of Greece set up sixty at a time."

G. "...fell upon him" refers to Edom, as it is written, "The earth quakes at the noise of their fall" (Jer. 49:21).

H. Some reverse matters:

I. "...fell upon him" refers to Babylonia, since it is written, "Fallen, fallen is Babylonia" (Is. 21:9).

J. "...great..." refers to Media, in line with this verse: "King Ahasuerus did make great" (Est. 3:1).

K. "' and darkness" refers to Greece, which darkened the eyes of Israel by its harsh decrees.

L. "...lo, a dread" refers to Edom, as it is written, "After this I saw...,a fourth beast, dreadful and terrible" (Dan. 7:7).

No. 4 successfully links the cited passage once more to the history of Israel. Israel's history falls under God's dominion. Whatever will happen carries out God's plan. The fourth kingdom is part of that plan, which we can discover by carefully studying Abraham's life and God's word to him. What of Rome in particular? Edom, Ishmael, and Esau all stand for Rome, perceived as a special problem, an enemy who also is a brother. In calling now-Christian Rome brother, sages conceded the Christian claim to share in the patrimony of Israel. For example, Ishmael, standing for Christian Rome, claims God's blessing, but Isaac gets it, as Jacob will take it from Esau.

> XLVII:V.1.A. "God said, 'No, but Sarah your wife [shall bear you a son, and you shall call his name Isaac. I will establish my covenant with him as an everlasting covenant for his descendants after him.] As for Ishmael, I have heard you. Behold, I will bless him and make him fruitful and multiply him exceedingly. He shall be the father of twelve princes, and I will make him a great nation]'" (Gen. 17:19-20).
>
> B. R. Yohanan in the name of R. Joshua b. Hananiah, "In this case the son of the servant-woman might learn from what was said concerning the son of the mistress of the household:
>
> C. "'Behold, I will bless him' refers to Isaac.
>
> D. "'...and make him fruitful' refers to Isaac.
>
> E. "'...and multiply him exceedingly' refers to Isaac.
>
> F. "'...As for Ishmael, I have informed you' through the angel. [The point is, Freedman, p. 401, n. 4, explains, Ishmael could be sure that his blessing too would be fulfilled.]"
>
> G. R. Abba bar Kahana in the name of R. Birai: "Here the son of the mistress of the household might learn from the son of the handmaiden:
>
> H. "'Behold, I will bless him' refers to Ishmael.
>
> I. "'...and make him fruitful' refers to Ishmael.
>
> J. "'...and multiply him exceedingly' refers to Ishmael.
>
> K. "And by an argument a fortiori : 'But I will establish my covenant with Isaac' (Gen. 17:21)."
>
> 2. A. Said R. Isaac, "It is written, 'All these are the twelve tribes of Israel' (Gen. 49:28). These were the descendants of the mistress [Sarah].
>
> B. "But did Ishmael not establish twelve?

C. "The reference to those twelve is to princes, in line with the following verse: 'As princes and wind' (Prov. 25:14). [But the word for prince also stands for the word vapor , and hence the glory of the sons of Ishmael would be transient (Freedman, p. 402, n. 2).]

D. "But as to these tribes [descended from Isaac], they are in line with this verse: 'Sworn are the tribes of the word, selah' (Hab. 3:9). [Freedman, p. 402, n. 3: The word for tribe and for staff or rod, in the cited verse, are synonyms, both meaning tribes, both meaning rods, and so these tribes would endure like rods that are planted.]"

Nos. 1 and 2 take up the problem of the rather fulsome blessing assigned to Ishmael. One authority reads the blessing to refer to Isaac, the other maintains that the blessing refers indeed to Ishmael, and Isaac will gain that much more. No. 2 goes over the same issue, now with the insistence that the glory of Ishmael will pass like vapor, while the tribes of Isaac will endure as well planted rods. The polemic against Edom/Rome, with its transient glory, is familiar.

Reading the book of Genesis as if it portrayed the history of Israel and Rome defines the given of Genesis Rabbah. For that is the single obsession binding sages of the document at hand to common discourse with the text before them. Why Rome in the form it takes in Genesis Rabbah? And how come the obsessive character of sages disposition of the theme of Rome? Were their picture merely of Rome as tyrant and destroyer of the Temple, we should have no reason to link the text to the problems of the age of redaction and closure. But now it is Rome as Israel's brother, counterpart, and nemesis, Rome as the one thing standing in the way of Israel's, and the world's, ultimate salvation. So the stakes are different, and much higher. It is not a political Rome but a Christian and messianic Rome that is at issue: Rome as surrogate for Israel, Rome as obstacle to Israel. Why? It is because Rome now confronts Israel with a crisis, and the program of Genesis Rabbah constitutes a response to that crisis. Rome in the fourth century became Christian. Sages respond by facing that fact quite squarely and saying, "Indeed, it is as you say, a kind of Israel, an heir of Abraham as your texts explicitly claim. But we remain the sole legitimate Israel, the bearer of the birthright — we and not you. So you are our brother: Esau, Ishmael, Edom." And the rest follows.

By rereading the story of the beginnings, sages discovered the answer and the secret of the end. Rome claimed to be Israel, and, indeed, sages conceded, Rome shared the patrimony of Israel. That claim took the form of the Christians' appropriate of the Torah as "the Old Testament," so sages acknowledged a simple fact in acceding to the notion that, in some way, Rome too formed part of Israel. But it was the rejected part, the Ishmael, the Esau, not the Isaac, not the Jacob. The advent of Christian Rome precipitated the sustained, polemical, and, I think, rigorous and well-argued rereading of beginnings in light of the end. Rome then marked the conclusion of human history as Israel had known it. Beyond? The coming of the true Messiah, the redemption of Israel, the salvation of the world, the end of time. So the issues were not inconsiderable, and when the sages spoke of Esau/Rome, as they did so often, they confronted the life-or-death decision of the day.

Let us begin with a simple example of how ubiquitous is the shadow of Ishmael/Esau/Edom/Rome. Whenever sages reflect on future history, their minds turn to their own day. They found the hour difficult, because Rome, now Christian, claimed that very birthright and blessing that they understood to be theirs alone. Christian Rome posed a threat without precedent. Now another dominion, besides Israel's, claimed the rights and blessings that sustained Israel. Wherever in Scripture they turned, sages found comfort in the iteration that the birthright, the blessing, the Torah, and the hope — all belonged to them and to none other. As the several antagonists of Israel stand for Rome in particular, so the traits of Rome, as sages perceived them, characterized the biblical heroes. Esau provided a favorite target. From the womb Israel and Rome contended.

> LXIII:VI.11.A. "And the children struggled together [within her, and she said, 'If it is thus, why do I live?' So she went to inquire of the Lord. And the Lord said to her, 'Two nations are in your womb, and two peoples, born of you, shall be divided; the one shall be stronger than the other, and the elder shall serve the younger']" (Gen. 25:22-23):
>
> B. R. Yohanan and R. Simeon b. Laqish:
>
> C. R. Yohanan said, "[Because the word, 'struggle,' contains the letters for the word, 'run,'] this one was running to kill that one and that one was running to kill this one."
>
> D. R. Simeon b. Laqish: "This one releases the laws given by that one, and that one releases the laws given by this one."
>
> 2.   A. R. Berekhiah in the name of R. Levi said, "It is so that you should not say that it was only after he left his mother's womb that [Esau] contended against [Jacob].
>
> B. "But even while he was yet in his mother's womb, his fist was stretched forth against him: 'The wicked stretch out their fists [so Freedman] from the womb' (Ps. 58:4)."
>
> 3.   A. "And the children struggled together within her:"
>
> B. [Once more referring to the letters of the word "struggled," with special attention to the ones that mean, "run,"] they wanted to run within her.
>
> C. When she went by houses of idolatry, Esau would kick, trying to get out: "The wicked are estranged from the womb" (Ps. 58:4).

D. When she went by synagogues and study-houses, Jacob would kick, trying to get out: "Before I formed you in the womb, I knew you" (Jer. 1:5)."

Nos. 1-3 take for granted that Esau represents Rome, and Jacob, Israel. Consequently the verse underlines the point that there is natural enmity between Israel and Rome. Esau hated Israel even while he was still in the womb. Jacob, for his part, revealed from the womb those virtues that would characterize him later on, eager to serve God as Esau was eager to worship idols

> LXIII:VII.2.A. "Two nations are in your womb, [and two peoples, born of you, shall be divided; the one shall be stronger than the other, and the elder shall serve the younger]" (Gen. 25:23):
> B. There are two proud nations in your womb, this one takes pride in his world, and that one takes pride in his world.
> C. This one takes pride in his monarchy, and that one takes pride in his monarchy.
> D. There are two proud nations in your womb.
> E. Hadrian represents the nations, Solomon, Israel.
> F. There are two who are hated by the nations in your womb. All the nations hate Esau, and all the nations hate Israel.
> G. [Following Freedman's reading:] The one whom your creator hates is in your womb: "And Esau I hated" (Mal. 1:3).

The syllogism invokes the base-verse as part of its repertoire of cases. No. 2 augments the statement at hand, still more closely linking it to the history of Israel. What follows explicitly introduces the issue of the Messiah:

> LXIII:VIII.3.A. "The first came forth red:"
> B. R. Haggai in the name of R. Isaac: "On account of the merit attained by obeying the commandment,

'You will take for yourself on the first day...,' (Lev. 23:40),

C. "I shall reveal myself to you as the First, avenge you on the first, rebuild the first, and bring you the first.

D. "I shall reveal myself to you the First: 'I am the first and I am the last' (Is. 44:6).

E. "...avenge you on the first: 'Esau, 'The first came forth red.'

F. "...rebuild the first: that is the Temple, of which it is written, 'You throne of glory, on high from the first, you place of our sanctuary' (Jer. 17:12).

G. "...and bring you the first: that is, the messiah-king: 'A first unto Zion will I give, behold, behold them, and to Jerusalem' (Is. 41:27)."

LXIII:X.1.A. "[When the boys grew up,] Esau was a skilful hunter, [a man of the field, while Jacob was a quiet man, dwelling in tents]" (Gen. 25:27):

B. He hunted people through snaring them in words [as the Roman prosecutors do:] "Well enough, you did not steal. But who stole with you? You did not kill, but who killed with you?"

2. A. R. Abbahu said, "He was a trapper and a fieldsman, trapping at home and in the field.

B. "He trapped at home: 'How do you tithe salt?' [which does not, in fact, have to be tithed at all!]

C. "He trapped in the field: 'How do people give tithe for straw?' [which does not, in fact, have to be tithed at all!]"

3. A. R. Hiyya bar Abba said, "He treated himself as totally without responsibility for himself, like a field [on which anyone tramples].

B. "Said the Israelites before the Holy One, blessed be he, 'Lord of all ages, is it not enough for us that you have subjugated us to the seventy nations, but even to this one, who is subjected to sexual intercourse just like a woman?'

C. "Said to them the Holy One, blessed be he, 'I too will exact punishment from him with those same words: 'And the heart of the mighty men of Edom at that day shall be as the heart of a woman in her pangs' (Jer. 49:22).

4.   A. "...while Jacob was a quiet man, dwelling in tents" (Gen. 25:27):

B. There is a reference to two tents, that is, the school house of Shem and the school house of Eber.

Nos. 1-3 deal with the description of Esau, explaining why he was warlike and aggressive. Nothing Esau did proved sincere. He was a hypocrite, even when he tried to please his parents.

> LXV:I.1.A. "When Esau was forty years old, he took to wife Judith, the daughter of Beeri, the Hittite, and Basemath the daughter of Elon the Hittite; and they made life bitter for Isaac and Rebecca" (Gen. 26:34-35):
>
> B. "The swine out of the wood ravages it, that which moves in the field feeds on it" (Ps. 80:14).
>
> C. R. Phineas and R. Hilqiah in the name of R. Simon: "Among all of the prophets, only two of them spelled out in public [the true character of Rome, represented by the swine], Asaf and Moses.
>
> D. "Asaf: 'The swine out of the wood ravages it.'
>
> E. "Moses: 'And the swine, because he parts the hoof' (Deut. 14:8).
>
> F. "Why does Moses compare Rome to the swine? Just as the swine, when it crouches, puts forth its hoofs as if to say, 'I am clean,' so the wicked kingdom steals and grabs, while pretending to be setting up courts of justice.
>
> G. "So Esau, for all forty years, hunted married women, ravished them, and when he reached the age of forty, he presented himself to his father, saying, 'Just as father got married at the age of forty, so I shall marry a wife at the age of forty.'
>
> H. "'When Esau was forty years old, he took to wife Judith, the daughter of Beeri, the Hittite, and Basemath the daughter of Elon the Hittite.'"

The exegesis of course once more identifies Esau with Rome. The round-about route linking the fact at hand,

Esau's taking a wife, passes through the territory of Roman duplicity. Whatever the government does, it claims to do in the general interest. But it really has no public interest at all. Esau for his part spent forty years pillaging women and then, at the age of forty, pretended, to his father, to be upright. That, at any rate, is the parallel clearly intended by this obviously unitary composition. The issue of the selection of the intersecting verse does not present an obvious solution to me; it seems to me only the identification of Rome with the swine accounts for the choice. The contrast between Israel and Esau produced the following anguished observation. But here the Rome is not yet Christian, so far as the clear reference is concerned. The union of the two principal motifs of exegesis, the paradigmatic character of the lives of the patriarchs and matriarchs, the messianic message derived from those lives, is effected in the following:

> LXXXIII:I.1.A. "These are the kings who reigned in the land of Edom before any king reigned over the Israelites: Bela the son of Beor reigned in Edom, the name of his city being Dinhabah" (Gen. 36:31-32):
>
> B. R. Isaac commenced discourse by citing this verse: "Of the oaks of Bashan they have made your oars" (Ez. 27:6).
>
> C. Said R. Isaac, "The nations of the world are to be compared to a ship. Just as a ship has its mast made in one place and its anchor somewhere else, so their kings: 'Samlah of Masrekah' (Gen. 36:36), 'Shaul of Rehobot by the river' (Gen. 36:27), and: 'These are the kings who reigned in the land of Edom before any king reigned over the Israelites.'"
>
> 2.   A. ["An estate may be gotten hastily at the beginning, but the end thereof shall not be blessed" (Prov. 20:21)]: "An estate may be gotten hastily at the beginning:" "These are the kings who reigned in the land of Edom before any king reigned over the Israelites."

B. "...but the end thereof shall not be blessed:"
"And saviors shall come up on mount Zion to judge
the mount of Esau" (Ob. 1:21).

No. 1 contrasts the diverse origin of Roman rulers
with the uniform origin of Israel's king in the house of David.
No. 2 makes the same point still more forcefully. How so?
Though Esau was the first to have kings, his land will eventu-
ally be overthrown (Freedman, p. 766, n. 3). So the point is
that Israel will have kings after Esau no longer does, and the
verse at hand is made to point to the end of Rome, a striking
revision to express the importance in Israel's history to events
in the lives of the patriarchs.

The final passage once more stresses the correspondence between Israel's and Edom's governments, respectively. The reciprocal character of their histories is then stated
in a powerful way, with the further implication that, when the
one rules, the other waits. So now Israel waits, but it will rule.
The same point is made in what follows, but the expectation
proves acute and immediate.

> LXXXIII:IV.3.A. "Magdiel and Iram: these are the
> chiefs of Edom, that is Esau, the father of Edom, ac-
> cording to their dwelling places in the land of their pos-
> session" (Gen. 36:42):
> B. On the day on which Litrinus came to the
> throne, there appeared to R. Ammi in a dream this
> message: "Today Magdiel has come to the throne."
> C. He said, "One more king is required for Edom
> [and then Israel's turn will come]."
> 4. A. Said R. Hanina of Sepphoris, "Why was he
> called Iram? For he is destined to amass [a word using
> the same letters] riches for the king-messiah."
> B. Said R. Levi, "There was the case of a ruler in
> Rome who wasted the treasuries of his father. Elijah of
> blessed memory appeared to him in a dream. He said to
> him, 'Your fathers collected treasures and you waste
> them.'

C. "He did not budge until he filled the treasuries again."

Nos. 3 presents once more the theme that Rome's rule will extend only for a foreordained and limited time, at which point the Messiah will come. No. 4 explains the meaning of the name Iram. The concluding statement also alleges that Israel's saints even now make possible whatever wise decisions Rome's rulers make. That forms an appropriate conclusion to the matter. How the compilers of Leviticus Rabbah deal with the situation we shall now see.

III.   THE PROGRAM OF LEVITICUS RABBAH

It is simple on formal-analytical grounds to distinguish a passage primary to Genesis Rabbah from one that is primary to Leviticus Rabbah. Propositions in Genesis Rabbah are ordinarily framed as exegeses of verses of Scripture. By contrast Leviticus Rabbah is not an exegetical document. They frame their ideas as large-scale composites that demonstrate propositions, to which exegesis of verses of Scripture contributes.

The framers of Leviticus Rabbah treat topics, not particular verses. They make generalizations that are freestanding. They express cogent propositions through extended compositions, not episodic ideas. Earlier, in Genesis Rabbah, as we have seen, things people wished to say were attached to predefined statements based on an existing text, constructed in accord with an organizing logic independent of the systematic expression of a single, well-framed idea. That is to say, the sequence of verses of Genesis and their contents played a massive role in the larger-scale organization of Genesis Rabbah and expression of its propositions. Now the authors of Leviticus Rabbah so collected and arranged their materials that an abstract proposition emerges. That proposition is not expressed only or mainly through episodic restatements, assigned, as I said, to an order established by a base text (whether Genesis or Leviticus, or a Mishnah-tractate, for that matter). Rather it emerges through a logic of its own. What is new is the move from an essentially exegetical mode of logical discourse to a fundamentally philosophical one. It is the shift from discourse framed around an established (hence old) text to syllogistic argument organized around a proposed (hence new) theorem or proposition. What changes, therefore, is the way in which cogent thought takes place, as people moved from discourse contingent on some prior principle of organization to discourse autonomous of a ready-made program inherited from an earlier paradigm.

What happens in Leviticus Rabbah (and, self-evidently, in other documents of the same sort, e.g., Pesiqta deRab Kahana)? Reading one thing in terms of something else, the builders of the document systematically adopted for themselves the reality of the Scripture, its history and doctrines. They transformed that history from a sequence of one-time events, leading from one place to some other, into an ever-present mythic world. No longer was there one Moses, one David, one set of happenings of a distinctive and never-to-be-repeated character. Now whatever happens, of which the thinkers propose to take account, must enter and be absorbed into that established and ubiquitous pattern and structure founded in Scripture. It is not that biblical history repeats itself. Rather, biblical history no longer constitutes history as a story of things that happened once, long ago, and pointed to some one moment in the future. Rather it becomes an account of things that happen every day — hence, an ever-present mythic world, as I said.

That is why, in Leviticus Rabbah, Scripture as a whole does not dictate the order of discourse, let alone its character.

In this document they chose in Leviticus itself a verse here, a phrase there. These then presented the pretext for propositional discourse commonly quite out of phase with the cited passage. The verses that are quoted ordinarily shift from the meanings they convey to the implications they contain, speaking about something, anything, other than what they seem to be saying. So the as-if frame of mind brought to Scripture brings renewal to Scripture, seeing everything with fresh eyes. And the result of the new vision was a reimagining of the social world envisioned by the document at hand, I mean, the everyday world of Israel in its Land in that difficult time. For what the sages now proposed was a reconstruction of existence along the lines of the ancient design of Scripture as they read it. What that meant was that, from a sequence of one-time and linear events, everything that happened was turned into a repetition of known and already experienced paradigms, hence, once more, a mythic being. The source and core of the myth, of course, derive from Scripture — Scripture reread, renewed, reconstructed along with the society that revered Scripture.

So the mode of thought that dictated the issues and the logic of the document, telling the thinkers to see one thing in terms of something else, addressed Scripture in particular and collectively. And thinking as they did, the framers of the document saw Scripture in a new way, just as they saw their own circumstance afresh, rejecting their world in favor of Scripture's, reliving Scripture's world in their own terms. That, incidentally, is why they did not write history, an account of what was happening and what it meant. It was not that they did not recognize or appreciate important changes and trends reshaping their nation's life. They could not deny that reality. In their apocalyptic reading of the dietary and leprosy laws, they made explicit their close encounter with the history of the world as they knew it. But they had another mode of responding to history. It was to treat history as if it were already known and readily understood. Whatever happened had already happened. Scripture dictated the contents of history, laying forth the structures of time, the rules that prevailed and were made known in events. Self-evidently, these same thinkers projected into Scripture's day the realities of their own, turning Moses and David into rabbis, for example. But that is how people think in that mythic, enchanted world in which, to begin with, reality blends with dream, and hope projects onto future and past alike how people want things to be.

Let us turn, now, from these somewhat abstract observations to a concrete account of what happened, in particular, when the thinkers at hand undertook to reimagine reality — both their own and Scripture's. Exactly how did they think about one thing in terms of another, and what did they choose, in particular, to recognize in this rather complex process of juggling unpalatable present and unattainable myth? We turn to the specifics by reverting to the tried and true method of listing all the data and classifying them. Exactly what did the framers of Leviticus Rabbah learn when they opened the book of Leviticus? To state the answer in advance, when they read the rules of sanctification of the priesthood, they heard the message of the salvation of all Israel. Leviticus became the story of how Israel, purified from social sin and sanctified, would be saved.

We take up the classifications of rules that sages located in the social laws of Leviticus. The first, and single paramount, category takes shape within the themes associated with the national life of Israel. The principal lines of structure flow along the fringes: Israel's relationships with others. These are (so to speak) horizontal, with the nations, and vertical, with God. But, from the viewpoint of the framers of the document, the relationships form a single, seamless web, for

Israel's vertical relationships dictate the horizontals as well; when God wishes to punish Israel, the nations come to do the work. The relationships that define Israel, moreover, prove dynamic, not static, in that they respond to the movement of the Torah through Israel's history. When the Torah governs, then the vertical relationship is stable and felicitous, the horizontal one secure, and, when not, God obeys the rules and the nations obey God. So the first and paramount, category takes shape within the themes associated with the national life of Israel. The principal lines of structure flow along the fringe, Israel's relationships with others. The relationships form a single, seamless web, for Israel's vertical relationships dictate the horizontals as well; when God wishes to punish Israel, the nations come to do the work. The relationships that define Israel, moreover, prove dynamic, not static, in that they respond to the movement of the Torah through Israel's history. When the Torah governs, then the vertical relationship is stable and felicitous, the horizontal one secure, and, when not, God obeys the rules and the nations obey God.

I now catalogue and classify all of the propositions emerging from the paragraphs of thought of Leviticus Rabbah. My effort is to state, as simply and accurately as I can, what the framer of a given paragraph wished to express, either directly or through rich illustrative materials.

THE NATIONAL LIFE OF ISRAEL: ISRAEL, GOD, AND THE NATIONS

> I:XI. Torah is life to Israel, poison to nations.
> I:XII. Gentiles have no prophets.
> I:XIII. Gentile prophets are inferior.
> II:I. Israel is precious to God.
> II:IV-V. God gave Israel many laws so as to express his love and ongoing concern. This was because they enthroned God at the Red Sea.

II:VI. Scripture is so worded as to treat Israel with respect.

V:II. God punishes Israel's sins by placing gentile rulers over them, e.g., Sennacherib.

V:VII. Virtues of Israel are vices for nations [see I:XI, XIII].

VI:I. Israel are God's witnesses.

VI:V. Israel violated its oath at Sinai, but God forgave Israel. [Also: VII:I.]

VII:IV. God is concerned not to waste Israel's resources.

X:I-III. God favors prophets and priests who justify Israel.

XII:II. God meets Israel in the tent of meeting.

XIII:II. Israel alone was worthy to receive the Torah. By observing food taboos, Israel shows its special position. [Also: XIII:III.]

XIII:IV-V. Food taboos symbolize Israel's fate among the nations. The four kingdoms as exemplary of food laws.

XV:IX. Skin ailments symbolize Israel's fate among the nations. The four kingdoms.

[XVI:I. Leprosy as punishment for social sins, e.g., gossip.]

XVII:I. Israel is singled out to be punished for specific sins. Others suffer at last judgment.

XVII:V. If Israel sins in the Land, it will be punished as Canaan was.

XVII:VI. Canaanites hid their treasures, and by afflicting the houses, God revealed the hiding place.

XVII:VII. The Temple's affliction is symbolized by the leprosy disease affecting houses.

XVIII:II. Individuals and nations cause their own punishment. [Also: XVIII:III.]

XVIII:IV. Israel was unafflicted at Sinai. After they sinned, various afflictions appeared.

XVIII:V. God governs Israel the same way kings govern kingdoms. But God heals with that with which he punishes.

XIX:IV. Israel's sins provoke punishment.

XX:VIII-IX. Sins in the cult caused death of Nadab and Abihu.

XX:X. Social sins and the death of Nadab and Abihu. Snootiness, pride.

XXI:XI. Israel is sustained by merits of the patriarchs.

XXII:VIII. God permitted sacrifice as an antidote to sin.

XXIII:I-III. Israel is the rose, the nations, the thorns. Various circumstances in Israel's history at which that fact was shown.

XXIII:V. Israel among the nations is steadfast in loyalty to God and will be redeemed.

XXIII:VI. Israel was created only to do religious duties and good deeds.

XXIII:VII. Israel must be different from gentiles, particularly in sexual practices. [Also XXIII:IX, XXIII:XIII.]

XXIV:I-II. When God exalts a people, it is done justly and so his act endures.

XXV:I. The Torah is what protects Israel.

XXV:IV. God kept his promises to the patriarchs to favor their descendants.

XXVII:V. God favors the victim.

XXVII:VI. God shows Israel special favor, which disappoints the nations. He does not demand much from Israel. [Also: XXVII:VIII.]

XXVII:IX. The animals used in the cult stand for the meritorious ancestors.

XXVII:XI. God will ultimately save Israel even from its cruelest enemies.

XXVIII:III. God asks very little of Israel.

XXVIII:IV. Merely with prayer Israel is saved, not with weapons.

XXVIII:VI. The merit of the religious duty of the sheaf of first fruits causes Israel to inherit the land, peace is made, Israel is saved.

XXIX:II. Israel's suffering among the nations is due to Jacob's lack of faith.

XXIX:V. Israel is redeemed because of keeping commandments. [Also: XXIX:VIIIB.]

XXIX:VII. Israel is saved through the merit of the patriarchs. [Also: XXIX:VIII, XXIX:X.]

XXX:I. Israel serves Esau [Rome] because of insufficient devotion to Torah study.

XXX:II. Israel's victory is signified by palm branches.

XXX:IX-XII. The symbols of Sukkot stand for God, the patriarchs, Israel's leaders, Israel. [Also: XXX:XIV.]

XXXI:III. God wants from Israel something he surely does not need, e.g., lamp, and that is the mark of God's love. [Also: XXXI:IV, XXXII:VIII.]

XXXII:I. Israel is reviled among the nations but exalted by God.

XXXII:VIII. God goes into exile with Israel.

XXXIII:VI. Israel, sold to the nations, joins their Creator with them.

XXXIV:VI. God forgives Israel's sin and repeatedly redeems them.

XXXIV:XIII. If Israel is not liberal to the poor, their wealth will go to Esau [Rome].

XXXV:I. If Israel attains merit, curses are turned into blessings.

XXXVI:II. Israel compared to a vine.

XXXVI:III. Patriarchs left their merit to Israel.

XXXVI:IV. World was created through the merit of Jacob.

XXXVI:V. Israel saved through the merits of the patriarchs.

XXXVI:VI. That merit yet endures.

The recurrent messages may be stated in a single paragraph. God loves Israel, so gave them the Torah, which defines their life and governs their welfare. Israel is alone in its category (sui generis), so what is a virtue to Israel is a vice to the nation, life-giving to Israel, poison to the gentiles. True, Israel sins, but God forgives that sin, having punished the nation on account of it. Such a process has yet to come to an end, but it will culminate in Israel's complete regeneration.

Meanwhile, Israel's assurance of God's love lies in the many expressions of special concern, for even the humblest and most ordinary aspects of the national life: the food the nation eats, the sexual practices by which it procreates.

These life-sustaining, life-transmitting activities draw God's special interest, as a mark of his general love for Israel. Israel then is supposed to achieve its life in conformity with the marks of God's love. These indications moreover signify also the character of Israel's difficulty, namely, subordination to the nations in general, but to the fourth kingdom, Rome, in particular. Both food laws and skin diseases stand for the nations. There is yet another category of sin, also collective and generative of collective punishment, and that is social. The moral character of Israel's life, the treatment of people by one another, the practice of gossip and small-scale thuggery — these too draw down the divine penalty. The nation's fate therefore corresponds to its moral condition. The moral condition, however, emerges not only from the current generation. Israel's richest hope lies in the merit of the ancestors, thus in the Scriptural record of the merits attained by the founders of the nation, those who originally brought it into being and gave it life.

The world to come is so portrayed as to restate these same propositions. Merit overcomes sin, and doing religious duties or supererogatory acts of kindness will win merit for the nation that does them. Israel will be saved at the end of time, and the age, or world, to follow will be exactly the opposite of this one. Much that we find in the account of Israel's national life, worked out through the definition of the liminal relationships, recurs in slightly altered form in the picture of the world to come.

ISRAEL AND THE WORLD TO COME
SALVIFIC DOCTRINES AND SYMBOLS

II:II. In this world and in the world to come, Israel, Levites, priesthood, heave offerings, firstlings, Land, Jerusalem, etc., will endure.

III:I. Israel will be redeemed on the Sabbath.

VII:III. Israel will be redeemed through the merit of Torah study.

IX:I. The thanksgiving offering will continue in the world to come. [Also: IX:VIII.]

X:IX. Jerusalem in the world to come.

XI:II. Rebuilding of Jerusalem in the world to come.

XVII:VII. Temple will be rebuilt.

XXI:I-IV. Israel is saved because of the merit of the people at various turnings in their history, e.g., at the Red Sea. Also through merit of atonement.

XXI:V-VI. Religious duties counteract sin.

XXIII:V. Israel will be saved through its steadfast faith.

XXIII:VI. Israel will be redeemed when Esau no longer rules.

XXX:XVI. Through merit of lulab, Temple will be rebuilt.

XXXI:XI. Merit of eternal light brings messiah.

The world to come will right all presently unbalanced relationships. What is good will go forward, what is bad will come to an end. The simple message is that the things people revere, the cult and its majestic course through the year, will go on; Jerusalem will come back, so too the Temple, in all their glory. Israel will be saved through the merit of the ancestors, atonement, study of Torah, practice of religious duties. The prevalence of the eschatological dimension at the formal structures, with its messianic and other expressions, here finds its counterpart in the repetition of the same few symbols in the expression of doctrine. The theme of the moral life of Israel produces propositions concerning not only the individual but, more important, the social virtues that the community as a whole must exhibit.

THE LAWS OF SOCIETY FOR ISRAEL'S HOLY COMMUNITY

I:X. Israel became punishable for violating divine law only after the Torah was taught to them a second time in the tent of meeting.

II:VII. Offerings should not derive from stolen property. [Also: III:IV.]

III:I. Not expiating sin through an inexpensive offering is better than doing so through an expensive one. Better not sin at all. [Also: IX:I, IX:V, IX:VIII.]

III:II-III. God will not despise a meager offering of a poor person. [Also: III:V, VIII:IV.]

IV:I. God punishes with good reason and not blindly.

IV:II. The soul wants to do ever more religious duties.

IV:III. Unwitting sin is caused by haste.

IV:IV-V. Soul and body are jointly at fault for sin.

IV:VI. Israelites are responsible for one another.

IV:VIII. Soul compared to God.

V:IV. Philanthropy makes a place for the donor.

V:VIII. Israel knows how to please God.

VI:III. False oath brings terrible punishment.

VII:II. If one repents sin, it is as if he made an offering in the rebuilt Temple.

VII:II. God favors the contrite and penitent. [Also: VII:VI, VIII:I, IX:I, IV, VI, God favors the thanksgiving offering.]

IX:III. God favors those who bring peace even more than those who study Torah.

IX:IX. Peace is the highest value.

X:V. Repentance and prayer effect atonement for sin.

X:VI. Priests' acts effect atonement.

XI:V. God responds to human virtue by acting in the same way.

XII:I, IV. Wine leads to poverty, estrangement.

XIV:V. Even the most pious person has a sinful side to his nature.

XV:IV. Gossip causes a specific ailment. God punishes Israel because he cares about Israel's moral condition.

XV:V. Sin of mother effects embryo.

XV:VI. Correspondence of sin and punishment. People get what they deserve.

XVI:I. Leprosy punishes gossip, other sins. [Also: XVI:II, XVII:III, XVIII:IV.]

XVI:V. Sinning through speech — general principle and particular examples.

XVI:VI. Skin disease and gossip. [Also: XVI:VII.]

XVI:VIII. People cause their own ailments through sin.

XVII:II. Diseases afflicting a house and the sin of the owner.

XVII:IV. God penalizes first property, then the person.

XXII:VI. Thievery is tantamount to murder.

XXII:X. For each prohibition there is a release.

XXIII:X-XI. God rewards those who avoid sin.

XXIII:XII. Adultery may be in one's mind.

XXIV:VI. Sanctification is through avoiding sexual misdeed.

XXIV:VII. Israel must remain holy if God is to be in its midst. [Also: XXIV:VIII.]

XXV:III. People are like God when they plant trees.

XXVI:II. God's pure speech versus humanity's gossip.

XXVII:I. God seeks justice, but it may be fully worked out only in the world to come. [Also: XXVII:II.]

XXX:V. One cannot serve God with stolen property. [Also: XXX:VI.]

XXXII:V. Israel keeps itself sexually pure.

XXXIII:I. What people say has the power of life and death.

XXXIV:II. God repays generosity.

XXXIV:V. People should not envy one another.

XXXIV:VIII. God rewards generosity. [Also: XXXIV:IX, XXXIV:X, XXXIV:XI.]

XXXV:VII. If Israel keeps the commandments, it is as if they made them.

XXXVII:I. It is unwise to vow.

First of all, the message to the individual constitutes a revision, for this context, of the address to the nation: humility as against arrogance, obedience as against sin, constant concern not to follow one's natural inclination to do evil or to overcome the natural limitations of the human condition. Israel must accept its fate, obey and rely on the merits accrued through the ages and God's special love. The individual must conform, in ordinary affairs, to this same paradigm of patience and submission.

Great men and women, that is, individual heroes within the established paradigm, conform to that same pattern, exemplifying the national virtues. Among these, of course, Moses stands out; he has no equal. The special position of the humble Moses is complemented by the patriarchs and by David, all of whom knew how to please God and left as an inheritance to Israel the merit they had thereby attained.

ISRAEL'S LEADERS: PRIESTS, RABBIS, PROPHETS

I:I. Prophets are messengers to mortals, and Moses was the greatest of them.

I:III. Moses had several names.

I:IV. Abraham, Jacob, David, Moses were recognized by God.

I:V. Moses was humble.

I:VI. Moses' teaching was precious in God's view.

I:VII. God recognized how much honor was paid to him by Moses.

I:VIII. God showed special favor to Moses.

I:IX. As above.

I:XII. After tent of meeting was built, prophecy ceased among gentiles.

I:XIV. Moses was superior to all other Israelite prophets.

[III:VI. Priests have every right to the residue of the meal offering.]

V:VII. The elders sustain Israel through their merits, which they pass on.

V:VIII. David knows how to please God.

X:I. God favored Abraham because he sought mercy.

X:II. The great prophets all loved to justify Israel.

XI:VIII. Israel can do nothing without its leaders.

While we find numerous stories about rabbis in the modern (fourth-century) mold, Yohanan, Simeon b. Laqish, Yudan, not to mention Hillel, they usually exemplify established social policies or virtues. They scarcely exhibit distinctive traits of personality. They do not stand comparison with the scriptural figures and only rarely appear in the same supernatural framework. Such stories do not belong in the present classification at all. When we do find them, we observe that they exemplify such common virtues as are catalogues in the earlier lists.

If we now ask about further recurring themes or topics, there is one so commonplace that we should have to list the majority of paragraphs of discourse of Leviticus Rabbah in order to provide a complete list. It is the list of events in Israel's history, meaning, in this context, Israel's history solely in scriptural times, down through the return to Zion. The one-time events of the generation of the flood, Sodom and Gomorrah, the patriarchs and the sojourn in Egypt, the exodus, the revelation of the Torah at Sinai, the golden calf, the Davidic monarchy and the building of the Temple, Sennacherib, Hezekiah, and the destruction of northern Israel, Nebuchadnezzar and the destruction of the Temple in 586, the life of Israel in Babylonian captivity, Daniel and his associates, Mordecai and Haman — these events occur over and over again. They turn out to serve as paradigms of sin and atonement, steadfastness and divine intervention, and equivalent lessons. We find, in fact, a fairly standard repertoire of scriptural heroes or villains, on the one side, and conventional lists of Israel's enemies and their actions and downfall, on the other. The boastful, for instance, include (VII:VI) the generation of the flood, Sodom and Gomorrah, Pharaoh, Sisera, Sennacherib, Nebuchadnezzar, the wicked empire (Rome) — contrasted to Israel, "despised and humble in this world." The four kingdoms recur again and again, always ending, of course, with Rome, with the repeated message that after Rome will come Israel. But Israel has to make this happen through its faith and submission to God's will. Lists of enemies ring the changes on Cain, the Sodomites, Pharaoh, Sennacherib, Nebuchadnezzar, Haman.

Accordingly, the mode of thought brought to bear upon the theme of history remains exactly the same as before: list making, with data exhibiting similar taxonomic traits drawn together into lists based on common monothetic traits or definitions. These lists then through the power of repetition make a single enormous point. They prove a social law of history. The catalogues of exemplary heroes and historical events serve a further purpose. They provide a model of how contemporary events are to be absorbed into the biblical paradigm. Since biblical events exemplify recurrent happenings, sin and redemption, forgiveness and atonement, they lose their one-time character. At the same time and in the same way, current events find a place within the ancient, but eternally present, paradigmatic scheme. So no new historical events, other than exemplary episodes in lives of heroes, demand narration because, through what is said about the past, what was happening in the times of the framers of Leviticus Rabbah would also come under consideration. This mode of dealing with biblical history and contemporary events produces two reciprocal effects. The first is the mythicization of biblical stories, their removal from the framework of ongoing, unique patterns of history and sequences of events and their transformation into accounts of things that happen all the time. The second is that contemporary events too lose all of their specificity and enter the paradigmatic framework of established mythic existence. So (1) the Scripture's myth happens every day, and (2) every day produces reenactment of the Scripture's myth.

In seeking the substance of the mythic being invoked by the exegetes at hand, who read the text as if it spoke about something else and the world as if it lived out the text, we uncover a simple fact. At the center of the pretense, that is, the as-if mentality of Leviticus Rabbah and its framers, we find a simple proposition. Israel is God's special love. That love is shown in a simple way. Israel's present condition of subordination derives from its own deeds. It follows that God cares, so Israel may look forward to redemption on God's part in response to Israel's own regeneration through repentance. When the exegetes proceeded to open the scroll of Leviticus, they found numerous occasions to state that proposition in concrete terms and specific contexts. The sinner brings on his own sickness. But God heals through that very ailment. The nations of the world govern in heavy succession, but Israel's lack of faith guaranteed their rule and its moment of renewal will end it. Israel's leaders — priests, prophets, kings — fall into an entirely different category from those of the nations, as much as does Israel. In these and other concrete allegations, the same classical message comes forth.

Accordingly, at the foundations of the pretense lies the long-standing biblical-Jewish insistence that Israel's sorry condition in no way testifies to Israel's true worth — the grandest pretense of all. All of the little evasions of the primary sense in favor of some other testify to this, the great denial that what is, is what counts. Leviticus Rabbah makes that statement with art and imagination. But it is never subtle about saying so.

Salvation and sanctification join together in Leviticus Rabbah. The laws of the book of Leviticus, focused as they are on the sanctification of the nation through its cult, in Leviticus Rabbah indicate the rules of salvation as well. The message of Leviticus Rabbah attaches itself to the book of Leviticus, as if that book had come from prophecy and addressed the issue of the meaning of history and Israel's salvation. But the book of Leviticus came from the priesthood and spoke of sanctification. The paradoxical syllogism — the as-if reading, the opposite of how things seem — of the composers of Leviticus Rabbah therefore reaches simple formulation. In the very setting of sanctification we find the promise of salvation. In the topics of the cult and the priesthood we uncover the national and social issues of the moral life and redemptive hope of Israel. The repeated comparison and contrast of priesthood and prophecy, sanctification and salvation, turn out to produce a complement, which comes to most perfect union in the text at hand.

The focus of Leviticus Rabbah and its laws of history is upon the society of Israel, its national fate and moral condition. Indeed, nearly all of the parashiyyot of Leviticus Rabbah turn out to deal with the national, social condition of Israel, and this in three contexts: (1) Israel's setting in the history of the nations, (2) the sanctified character of the inner life of Israel itself, (3) the future, salvific history of Israel. So the biblical book that deals with the holy Temple now is shown to address the holy people. Leviticus really discusses not the consecration of the cult but the sanctification of the nation — its conformity to God's will laid forth in the Torah, and God's rules. So when we review the document as a whole and ask what is that something else that the base text is supposed to address, it turns out that the sanctification of the cult stands for the salvation of the nation. So the nation now is like the cult then, the ordinary Israelite now like the priest then. The holy way of life lived now, through acts to which merit accrues, corresponds to the holy rites then. The process of metamorphosis is full, rich, complete. When everything stands for something else, the something else repeatedly turns out to be the nation. This is what our document spells out in exquisite detail, yet never missing the main point.

IV.   COMPARING THE PROGRAMS OF GENE-SIS RABBAH AND LEVITICUS RABBAH

A single program of theological conviction unites the two Rabbah-compilations. But we may distinguish the program of the one document from that of the other. Let us speak first of continuities, then of the propositional autonomy of each.

If we summarize the principal doctrines of each of them, the paramount corpus of shared ideas comes to the fore. It is the story that Scripture tells, now continued to encompass contemporary Israel. Let us begin with the earlier of the two documents, commonly held to have reached closure about fifty years before the other. Genesis Rabbah, ca 350-400, in the aggregate proposes to demonstrate that the very creation of the world testifies to the salvation of Israel. The facts of creation, recorded in the book of Genesis, point toward the coming age. What Adam cast in shadow, Israel illuminates. Where humankind went wrong, Israel will go right. The future now stands revealed through the lives of Israel's founders; even now Israel's holy way of life demonstrates the matter. Just as humanity's sins drove God upward from the world, so Israel's saints, Abraham, Isaac, Jacob, and on to

Moses, brought God back down. Israel needs to keep the faith and to hope. Humanity's hope indeed is Israel. God's plan governs, and Israel in its Land compares to Adam in the Garden of Eden. So reality is formed of two components: humanity, Israel, dark, light, sin, redemption. What changes the rules of history? Love on the one side, hatred on the other. As to the present, that too contains no secrets. The story of Edom, Ishmael, Esau precurses Rome, and the salvation of Jacob, Israel in the present age. What Rome now does Esau long ago did. But Jacob held the birthright then, and Israel does today. Time and again a single message makes its appearance, a message of courage in the face of despair, renewal in spite of the signs of the times. The same mode of thought — turning the one-time narrative of a biblical story into a paradigm of the rules underlying existence — characterizes Leviticus Rabbah, ca. 400-450, as well. The message goes over familiar ground,

But Leviticus Rabbah addresses not event but social laws. Israel is unique, the counterpart of the nation. God loves Israel so as to care about how life is transmitted, in food and in procreation. True, the four kingdoms have troubled Israel's life, but beyond the fourth, Rome, is the rule of Israel. Indeed the food laws and the skin diseases of Leviticus serve as metaphors for the nations, and the holy way of life of Israel therefore constitutes an acting out of the paradigm of universal human history. What must Israel do? It must so constitute its social life as to form a holy community. What this means is that Israel must form its moral condition to correspond to God's demands. The Torah supplies the rules that Israel must keep, it therefore serves as source of the laws of Israel's history and salvation. Among the immoral acts to be avoided, one stands out, gossip, the opposite of pure speech. And what people say to, and about, one another surely remains under Israel's control. Sifting and resifting the para-

digmatic events of Israel's history, we find the patterns of sin
and atonement, warrant for Israel's loyalty to and trust in
God. God cares, Israel therefore hopes. Genesis, with its
myths about creation and stories about the founders of Israel,
Abraham, Isaac, Jacob, and Joseph and his brothers, tells the
story of Israel's salvation. Leviticus, with its cultic rules about
sacrifice and uncleanness, tells the rules governing Israel's
salvation.

The difference between Genesis Rabbah and Leviticus Rabbah derives from the character of Genesis and Leviticus, respectively. The profound correspondence between the
one and the other rests upon the simple fact that the framers
of the two documents, living within the same century and in
the same crisis of confidence, propose to say the same thing.
They affirm that God still loves Israel, so confirming Israel's
sanctification here and now and salvation in time to come.
But each document focuses on its assigned biblical book, and
there is no confusing the topical program of the one with that
of the other.

What, then, of continuities between them — and beyond their limits? Let me then state the program of both
compilations: Genesis Rabbah and Leviticus Rabbah take up
Israel's position in creation, hence also among the nations
and as part of history, stating that, in the here and now, Israel's life is holy, and, in time to come, Israel will be saved.
How do we know it? Because in the very facts of Scripture, as
they deal with humanity and creation, in Genesis, and the distinctive way of life of Israel, in Leviticus, prove it — when
rightly interpreted. In the context of the system of Judaism
presented by the canon of late antiquity, summarized so
handsomely by the Talmuds of the Land of Israel and of
Babylonia, for example, none of these messages presents surprises. Indeed, all of them will strike the contemporary histo-
rian of Judaism as commonplaces, as indeed in later times

they became. Yet if we set side by side the points of interest and emphasis, the modes of thought and the specific statements, of the compilers of prior composites and compositions in the canon at hand, the picture would change. Specifically, the powerful interest in history and salvation, the recurring emphasis on the correspondence between Israel's holy way of life and the salvation of Israel in history, the reading of Scripture as an account of the present and future — these will have struck the compositors of other documents as fresh.

The authors of the Mishnah, with its close companion in the Tosefta, the compilers of tractate Abot, the author-compilers of Sifra to Leviticus — none of these circles of authorship took so keen an interest in the issue of salvation or in the correspondence between the biblical narrative and contemporary history. That fact is particularly striking when we compare the exegesis of Leviticus composed by the authors of the Sifra to the treatment of the same book in Leviticus Rabbah. To state matters simply, there is nothing in common, nothing whatsoever, except the biblical text itself. The points of emphasis, the decisions as to form and style, composition, order, and proportion, characteristic of the Mishnah and its fellows contrast starkly with their equivalents in the two Rabbah-Midrashim. So, as we survey the established context for compiling sayings to be preserved, we find it difficult to identify a prior circle of compositors with the same plan and program as those of Genesis Rabbah and Leviticus Rabbah.

That simple fact makes all the more striking the agreement of the two groups upon a single theological program, imparting to the simple observations we have just made a significance otherwise lacking. It is when we compare what these compositors wish to emphasize, their points of stress, with the plan and program of their counterpart, earlier documents, that the true character of the Rabbah-compositors' theological and literary concurrence, their agreement on a single program and plan, fully reveals itself.

V.   THE CENTRALITY OF REDACTION IN THE FORMULATION AND SELECTION OF EXEGESES OF SCRIPTURE

We come now to the implications, for other documents, of the autonomy, connection, and continuity of Genesis Rabbah and Leviticus Rabbah. Bases for analysis, comparison, and contrast derive from points of differentiation, not sameness. Comparing what unrelated groups said about the same matter tells us only facts, not their meaning. Comparison defines the foundations of the documentary hypothesis, e.g., comparison of Midrash-exegeses of one document with those found in another.

But the purpose of comparison, including comparative Midrash, is interpretation. We might as well attempt to differentiate within diverse ages and formulations of Israelite culture on the basis of so commonplace an activity as writing books or eating bread. True enough, diverse groups wrote diverse books, e.g., some long, some short, and, we might imagine, also baked their bread in diverse ways, e.g., with or without yeast, with wheat, spelt, or barley. But so what? What else do we learn if we know that some people wrote long books and ate rye bread, other people wrote short books and ate barley or whole wheat bread? Only if we can show that people did these things in a way or for a purpose that differentiated one group from another, for example, as a mode of expressing ideas particular to themselves, their condition and context, can we answer the question, so what? That is why comparing merely what people said about the same thing, whether the weather or the meaning of Genesis 49:10, without regard to the circumstance in which they said it, meaning, in our case, to begin with the particular book and canon in which what they said is now preserved — that sort of comparison produces knowledge of a merely formal character.

Let me now spell this out, since we cannot understand how comparative Midrash has been carried on to this time without a clear picture of the prevailing, and false, fundamental premise as to category-formation and classification. Midrash, meaning exegesis of Scripture, by itself presents nothing new in Israelite culture. Explaining the verses of holy books, even before the formation of the Holy Book, went on routinely. The activity of scriptural exegesis constituted a prevailing convention of thought, and therefore by itself cannot yield points of differentiation. Why what diverse groups said about the same verse would form a consequential area of comparative study therefore demands explanation, for the answer is not self-evident. Any program of comparing the exegeses of a verse without reference to documentary (therefore social and historical) context will have to sort out the results of millennia of responses to Scripture. But the work of sorting things out in the end may prove unable to conduct other than a merely formal analysis of the diverse results: comparing apples to Australians because both begin with an A.

Let us dwell on the simple fact that exegesis of Scripture was routine and ubiquitous even in the times in which various books of the Hebrew Bible were coming into being. A simple instance of the so-called "internal-biblical" exegetical mode, for example, is given by a contrast of Ps. 106:32-33 and Num. 20:2-13. The former of the two passages supplies a motive for the action described in the latter. We begin with the story, as narrated at Num. 20:10-13.

> And Moses and Aaron gathered the assembly together before the rock, and he said to them, "Hear now, you rebels; shall we bring forth water for you out of this rock?" And Moses lifted up his hand and struck

the rock with his rod twice; and water came forth
abundantly, and the congregation drank, and their cattle. And the Lord said to Moses and Aaron, "Because
you did not believe in me, to sanctify me in the eyes of
the people of Israel, therefore you shall not bring this
assembly into the land which I have given them." These
are the waters of Meribah, where the people of Israel
contended with the Lord, and he showed himself holy
among them.

Why then did Moses strike the rock? The foregoing
account at best suggests an implicit motive for his action. The
author of Ps. 106:32-33 makes it explicit: "They angered him
at the waters of Meribah, and it went ill with Moses on their
account; for they made his spirit bitter, and he spoke words
that were rash." Now what is important in this instance is
simply the evidence of how, within the pages of the Hebrew
Scriptures, a program of exegesis people now call Midrash
reaches full exposure.

Furthermore, we need not hunt at length for evidence
of the work of collecting such exercises in exegesis — of rewriting an old text in light of new considerations or values.
Such a vast enterprise is handsomely exemplified by the book
of Chronicles which, instead of merely commenting on
verses, actually rewrites the stories of Samuel and Kings.
Anyone who without attention to the larger documentary
context — the respective programs of the compilations as a
whole — compares what the compilers of Samuel and Kings
say about a given incident with what the compilers of
Chronicles say about the same incident then misses the point
of the difference between the reading of the one and that of
the other. For, as everyone now knows, the difference derives
from the documentary context — there alone. So without
asking first of all about the plan and program of the documents, the formal comparison of contents produces facts, but

no insight into their meaning. That, in my view, is the present situation of comparative Midrash.

Obviously, neither of these two biblical cases — the one of exegesis, the other of composition or compilation of exegeses — by itself can prove the point. Both serve merely to provide instances of the antiquity of both making up and also purposefully compiling exegeses of Scripture. They call into question any notion that a distinctive historical circumstance — that of late antiquity, for example — frames the context in which we are to read all works of exegesis of Scripture. They further show the futility of comparing bits of information that have not been interpreted as part of their original context, meaning, in the case of Samuel-Kings as against Chronicles, the larger theological program of the later compilation. For when people wished to deliver a powerful argument for a basic proposition, they did so by collecting and arranging exegeses of Scripture — and, it goes without saying, also by producing appropriate exegeses of Scripture for these compilations. That is to say, compilers also participated in the framing or rewriting of what they compiled, so that all we have is what they chose to give us in the language and form they selected. That is why I maintain study of comparative Midrash must begin with the outermost point of contact, namely, the character of the compilation of exegeses. Comparing one compilation with another then defines the first stage of the comparison of exegeses: compilations, contents, principles of hermeneutics alike.

To gain perspective on this proposition, we now turn to two fairly systematic efforts at compiling exegeses of Scripture specifically in order to make some polemical point. These present us with parallels to what is at hand in the work of the earliest composers of exegeses within the Rabbinic movement. We have now seen how the compilers of Genesis Rabbah and Leviticus Rabbah made their collections of exegeses in order to demonstrate propositions critical to their theological program. We detected little that was wholly random in either proposition or proportion, selection and arrangement of exegeses or propositions on the meaning of specific verses of Scripture. All aspects — mode of exegesis, result of exegesis, purpose of compilation alike — addressed the point of the document as a whole, carried out the established purpose. The two compilations form harmonious and unified statements. That is the centerpiece of my argument as to both their form and their substance, plan and meaning alike.

Let us now broaden the range of inquiry, if only briefly, and ask whether the same fact characterizes other documents. That is to say, on our own, let us conduct a brief exercise in comparative Midrash . The instincts follow will demonstrate in settings far removed in time and theological context from the world that produced Genesis Rabbah and Leviticus Rabbah how exegetes and compilers carried out their work. They once more demonstrate the unity of form and meaning, of purpose and proposition. The selection of exegeses, the creation of exegeses, the arrangement and compilation of exegeses, the use of a particular formal technique, and the larger polemic or theological proposition that motivated the compilers and exegetes alike — all of these together join in producing the document as we know it. Therefore we compare document to document, not uninterpreted detail ripped from one document to an equivalent detail seized from some other.

Recalling the exercises already completed, we ask two questions.

First, what is the formal character of the unit of discourse?

Second, how are the units of discourse put together by redactors into a large-scale composition?

We turn first to two passages of exegesis, one of Hosea, the other of Nahum, found in the Essene Library of Qumran. As presented by Geza Vermes, the exegeses do form something we might call a collection, or at least a chapter, that is, a systematic treatment of a number of verses in sequence. Vermes's presentation is a follows:

Commentary on Hosea
In this interpretation, the unfaithful wife is the Jewish people, and her lovers are the Gentiles who have led the nation astray.

"[She knew not that] it was I who gave her [the new wine and oil], who lavished [upon her silver] and gold which they [used for Baal]" (2:8).

Interpreted, this means that [they ate and] were filled, but they forgot God who.... They cast His commandments behind them which He had sent [by the hand of] His servants the Prophets, and they listened to those who led them astray. They revered them, and in their blindness they feared them as though they were gods.

"Therefore I will take back my corn in its time and my wine [in its season]. I will take away my wool and my flax lest they cover [her nakedness]. I will uncover her shame before the eyes of [her] lovers [and] no man shall deliver her from out of my hand" (2:9-10).

Interpreted, this means that He smote them with hunger and nakedness that they might be shamed and disgraced in the sight of the nations on which they relied. They will not deliver them from their miseries.

"I will put an end to her rejoicing, [her feasts], her [new] moons, her Sabbaths, and all her festivals" (2:11).

Interpreted, this means that [they have rejected the ruling of the law, and have] followed the festivals of the nations. But [their rejoicing shall come to an end and] shall be changed into mourning.

I will ravage [her vines and her fig trees], of which she said, 'They are my wage [which my lovers have given me]'. I will make of them a thicket and the [wild beasts] shall eat them...." (2:12).

On the Commentary on Nahum, Vermes comments: "For a correct understanding of the interpretation of Nahum 2:12, the reader should bear in mind the biblical order that only the corpses of executed criminals should be hanged (Deut. 21:21). Hanging men alive, i.e., crucifixion, was a sacrilegious novelty. Some translators consider the mutilated final sentence unfinished, and render it: 'For a man hanged alive on a tree shall be called...' The version given here seems more reasonable. The passage is as follows:

> "[Where is the lions' den and the cave of the young lions?]" (2:11).
>
> [Interpreted, this concerns]...a dwelling-place for the ungodly of the nations.
>
> "Whither the lion goes, there is the lion's cub, [with none to disturb it]" (2:11b).
>
> [Interpreted, this concerns Demetrius king of Greece who sought, on the counsel of those who seek smooth things, to enter Jerusalem. [But God did not permit the city to be delivered] into the hands of the kings of Greece, from the time of Antiochus until the coming of the rulers of the Kittim. But then she shall be trampled under their feet....
>
> "The lion tears enough for its cubs and it chokes prey for its lionesses" (2:12a).
>
> [Interpreted, this] concerns the furious young lion who strikes by means of his great men, and by means of the men of his council.
>
> "[And chokes prey for its lionesses; and it fills] its caves [with prey] and its dens with victims" (2:12a-b).
>
> Interpreted, this concerns the furious young lion [who executes revenge] on those who seek smooth things and hangs men alive, [a thing never done] formerly in Israel. Because of a man hanged alive on [the]

tree, He proclaims, "Behold I am against [you, says the Lord of Hosts]."

"[I will burn up your multitude in smoke], and the sword shall devour your young lions. I will [cut off] your prey [from the earth]" (2:13):

[Interpreted]..."your multitude" is the bands of his army...and his "young lions" are...his "prey" is the wealth which [the priests] of Jerusalem have [amassed], which...Israel shall be delivered....

"[And the voice of your messengers shall no more be heard]" (2:13b).

[Interpreted]...his "messengers" are his envoys whose voice shall no more he heard among the nations.

Treating the materials presented by Vermes as a document, we simply cannot categorize these several "units of discourse" within the established framework of taxonomy suitable for the Genesis Rabbah and Leviticus Rabbah. For we do not have (1) a word-for-word or point-by-point reading, in light of other verses of Scripture, of the verses that are cited, let alone (2) an expansion on the topics of the verses. The forms serving the two Rabbah-compilations obviously do not apply. What we have is an entirely different sort of exegesis, given in an entirely different form, namely, a reading of the verses of Scripture in light of an available scheme of concrete events. The exegete wises to place into relationship to Scripture things that have happened in his own day. His form serves that goal.

If the generative principle of exegesis seems alien, the criterion of composition as a whole is entirely familiar. The compiler wished to present amplifications of the meaning of a verse of Scripture, not word-for-word or phrase-for-phrase interpretations. He also has not constructed a wide-ranging discussion of the theme of the verse. Let me with appropriate emphasis state the main point.

The framer of the passage selected a mode of constructing his unit of discourse wholly congruent with the purpose for which, to begin with, he undertook the exegesis of the passage.

He wished to read the verses of Scripture in light of events. So he organized his unit of discourse around the sequence of verses of Scripture under analysis. Had he wanted, he might have provided a sequential narrative of what happened, then inserting the verse he found pertinent, thus: "X happened, and that is the meaning of (biblical verse) Y." (Such a mode of organizing exegeses served the school of Matthew, but not the framer of the text at hand. I do not know why). In any event the construction at hand is rather simple. The far more complex modes of constructing units of discourse in Genesis Rabbah and Leviticus Rabbah served a different purpose. They are made up, moreover, of different approaches to the exegesis of Scripture. So we see that the purpose of exegesis makes a deep impact upon not only the substance of the exegesis, but also, and especially, upon the formal and redactional characteristics of the document, the mode of organizing the consequent collection of exegeses.

Obviously, there were diverse ways both of undertaking scriptural exegesis and of organizing the collections of such exegeses. In the setting of examples of these other ways in which earlier Jews had responded to verses of Scripture and then collected and organized their responses, we see that there was more than a single compelling way in which to do the work. It follows that the way in which the framers of Genesis Rabbah and Leviticus Rabbah did the work was not predictable. Their mode of formulation, organization, and composition therefore is not to be taken for granted. It represented a distinctive choice among possibilities others in Israelite culture had explored.

It may now be fairly argued that the rather episodic sets of exegeses presented to us by the Essene library of

Qumran cannot be called documents and compared to the sustained and purposeful labor of both exegesis and composition revealed in the earliest Rabbinic collections. Accordingly, let us turn, for a second exercise of comparison, to an exegetical passage exhibiting clear-cut and fixed forms of rhetoric, both of the exegetical passage itself, and of the composition of several exegetical passages into a large-scale discourse — hence, units of discourse to be compared with units of discourse of Genesis Rabbah. We find in the literary composition of the school that produced the Gospel of Matthew a powerful effort to provide an interpretation of verses of Scripture in line with a distinct program of interpretation. Furthermore, the selection and arrangement of these scriptural exegeses turn out to be governed by the large-scale purpose of the framers of the document as a whole.

To illustrate these two facts, I present four parallel passages, in which we find a narrative, culminating in the citation of a verse of Scripture, hence a convention of formal presentation of ideas, style and composition alike. In each case, the purpose of the narrative is not only fulfilled in itself, but also in a subscription linking the narrative to the cited verse and stating explicitly that the antecedent narrative serves to fulfill the prediction contained in the cited verse, hence a convention of theological substance. We deal with Matthew 1:18-23, 2:1-6, 2:16-18, and 3:1-3.

> Mt. 1:18-23
>
> Now the birth of Jesus Christ took place in this way. When his mother Mary had been betrothed to Joseph, before they came together she was found to be with child of the Holy Spirit; and her husband Joseph, being a just man and unwilling to put her to shame, resolved to divorce her quietly. But as he considered this, behold, an angel of the Lord appeared to him in a dream, saying, "Joseph, son of David, do not fear to take Mary your wife, for that which is conceived in her

is of the Holy Spirit; she will bear a son, and you shall call his name Jesus, for he will save his people from their sins." All this took place to fulfill what the Lord had spoken by the prophet: "Behold, a virgin shall conceive and bear a son, and his name shall be called Emmanuel" (which means, God with us).

MT. 2:1-6

Now when Jesus was born in Bethlehem of Judea in the days of Herod the king, behold, wise men from the East came to Jerusalem, saying, "Where is he who has been born king of the Jews? For we have seen his star in the East, and have come to worship him." When Herod the king heard this, he was troubled, and all Jerusalem with him; and assembling all the chief priests and scribes of the people, he inquired of them where the Christ was to be born. They told him, "In Bethlehem of Judea; for so it is written by the prophet: "And you, O Bethlehem, in the land of Judah, are by no means least among the rulers of Judah; for from you shall come a ruler who will govern my people Israel.""

Mt. 2:16-18

Then Herod, when he saw that he had been tricked by the wise men, was in a furious rage, and he sent and killed all the male children in Bethlehem and in all that region who were two years old or under, according to the time which he had ascertained from the wise men. Then was fulfilled what was spoken by the prophet Jeremiah: "A voice was heard in Ramah, wailing and loud lamentation, Rachel weeping for her children; she refused to be consoled, because they were no more."

MT. 3:1-3

In those days came John the Baptist, preaching in the wilderness of Judea, "Repent, for the kingdom of heaven is at hand." For this is he who was spoken of by the prophet Isaiah when he said, "The voice of one crying in the wilderness: Prepare the way of the Lord, make his paths straight."

The four passages show us a stunningly original mode of linking exegeses. The organizing principle derives from the sequence of events of a particular biography, rather than the sequence of verses in a given book of Scripture or of sentences of the Mishnah. The biography of the person under discussion serves as the architectonic of the composition of exegeses into a single statement of meaning. This mode of linking exegeses — that is, composing them into a large-scale collection, such as we have at hand in the earliest Rabbinic compilations — shows us another way than the way taken at Qumran, on the one side, and among the late fourth and fifth centuries' compilers of Rabbinic collections of exegeses, on the other.

To be sure a few stories about the life of Hillel were linked to a sequential set of verses of Deut. 15:1ff. Perhaps someone may have thought of linking events of Hillel's life to a contiguous group of verses. But no "life" of a sage of antiquity forms the base line for a composition, whether made up of exegeses, or (more likely) of legal opinions. There are a few chapters in the Mishnah, e.g., M. Kelim chapter 24, that systematically express the generative principle of a single authority; there are many pericopes (units of discourse) framed around opinions of a single authority, and a great many around disagreements between two or more fixed names. But these are not comparable.

The passages of Matthew, therefore, indicate a clear-cut, distinctive choice on how to compose a "unit of discourse" and to join several congruent units of discourse into a sustained statement, a document. The choice is dictated by the character and purpose of the composition at hand. Since the life of a particular person — as distinct from events of a particular character — forms the focus of discourse, telling a story connected with that life and following this with a citation of the biblical verse illustrated in the foregoing story constitutes the generative and organizing principle of the several units of discourse, all of them within a single taxon. The taxon is not only one-dimensional. It also is rather simple in both its literary traits and its organizing principle. We discern extremely tight narration of a tale, followed by a citation of a verse of Scripture, interpreted only through the device of the explicit joining language: This (1) is what that (2) means. What we see so clearly in the work of the school of Matthew is a simple fact. The work of making up exegeses of Scripture, selecting the appropriate ones and saying important things about them, and the labor of collecting and compiling these exegeses of Scripture into a larger composite together express a single principle, make a single statement, carry out the purposes of a single polemic. Let me once more give proper emphasis to this simple result:

> *Three things go together:*
>
> *(1) the principles of exegesis,*
>
> *(2) the purposes of exegesis, and*
>
> *(3) the program of collecting and arranging exegeses into compilations.*

That is the fact of Matthew. It is true of Sifra. Here I have tried to demonstrate that it is the fact of Genesis Rabbah and Leviticus Rabbah as well.[1] So we see a simple fact. First, what people wished to say about the meaning of a verse of Scripture and, second, why they then proposed to collect

---

[1] In time to come, detailed analysis of the various compilations of biblical exegeses produced at diverse places and times within Judaism, from the fifth century to the eighteenth, will tell us whether or not it is so later on as well. At this point the differentiation of the medieval Midrash-compilations from those of late antiquity, and the correlation of the medieval Midrash-compilations with traits of the time and place in which they reached closure, has yet to be undertaken in a systematic way.

what they had said into cogent compositions — these two considerations cohere.

So the task of documentary differentiation has now been defined. It requires us to say in connection with compilations of scriptural exegeses what we think generated comments on biblical verses. It demands that we explain how composing these particular comments on these selected verses into compilations or compositions made sense to composers. For the Rabbinic canon we now are well on the way to describing, analyzing, and interpreting the context — the life-situation — of those documents. We know how to carry out the comparison of document to document, one whole compilation of exegeses of Scripture with another whole compilation. The implications of these comparisons for the characterization of the Rabbinic canon as a composite of well-crafted documents, each with its own distinctive rhetoric, topical, and logical traits, are self-evident. So much for documents that differ fundamentally in the form-analytical perspective. What about those that are constructed within the same formal paradigms? To answer that question, we turn to Leviticus Rabbah and Pesiqta deRab Kahana.

PART TWO

SHOWING THAT A SHARED PERICOPE IS PRIMARY TO ONE DOCUMENT, SECONDARY TO ANOTHER

2.

THE SHARED PERICOPE AND THE PRIOR CLAIM OF LEVITICUS RABBAH

THE RELATIONSHIP BETWEEN LEVITICUS RABBAH AND PESIQTA DERAB KAHANA

THE FORM-ANALYTICAL PERSPECTIVE

A principal focus of the critics of the documentary hypothesis identifies materials that occur in two or more documents as evidence of the nullity of documentary boundaries. In this chapter we take up a large-scale example of parallel use of materials in two documents. What we shall see is that, even where the materials are repeated, the documentary traits of one of the two compilations define matters. We may therefore say, the shared materials are primary to the document the formal traits of which predominate, and they are secondary to the document the formal traits of which are in context not definitive. It is, simply put, a case of borrowing by the one document of materials original to the other. Here the presence of parallels supports the documentary reading of the canonical compilations. Now to the case in point.

Of the twenty-eight Pisqa'ot of Pesiqta deRab Kahana, five occur also in Leviticus Rabbah. I shall now show that the shared Pisqa'ot in fact are distinctive to Leviticus Rabbah and violate the rhetorical preferences characteristic of the twenty-three Pisqa'ot that are unique to Pesiqta deRab Kahana. That fact will then close the possibility that materials produced we know not where were chosen at random and promiscuously by the framers of diverse documents and will demonstrate the opposite. The authorships of documents, illustrated here by that of Pesiqta deRab Kahana, followed a clearly-defined rhetorical plan. That plan, moreover, may be shown to be distinctive to the document that the authorship has created by comparison of pericopes of a document that are shared with other documents to those that are unique to the document at hand.

In order to demonstrate these propositions, I have first to establish the traits of the rhetorical plan of Pesiqta deRab Kahana. This I do inductively, by dealing first with a single Pisqa', then with two further Pisqa'ot, so showing that rhetorically distinctive forms paramount in one Pisqa' in fact define the rhetorical plan of two others. Then I compare the rhetorical forms of Pesiqta deRab Kahana with the forms of a parashah of Leviticus Rabbah that occurs also in Pesiqta deRab Kahana. In that comparison I am able to demonstrate that the characteristic forms of the latter do not occur in the shared Pisqa'/parashah at all, and that other forms do. I am further able to explain the rhetorical differences between the two documents. We begin with our initial exercise, the proposal of a hypothesis on the definitive rhetorical program of the document.

I.   LITERARY STRUCTURES OF PE-SIQTA DERAB KAHANA PISQA' 6

I use some analytical language that requires definition at the outset. Specifically, I refer, first, to contrastive verse and base verse, and these prove to be the prime building blocks of rhetorical analysis. The base verse is the recurrent

verse of Scripture that defines the point of recurrent reference for all Pisqa'ot but two or three. I call it base verse simply because it forms the basis of all discourse and imparts
unity to each Pisqa'. The contrastive verse is a verse that will
be introduced to clarify the meaning of the base verse. The
contrast between the one and the other then yields a syllogism, and the purpose of the whole, as I shall show, is that
syllogistic discourse. While in the body of the translation, I
have used the language appropriate in earlier documents,
hence intersecting verse and base verse, here a more exact usage is required, because, as I have noted, the function of the
intersecting verse in Leviticus Rabbah, which is to permit extended discussion of everything but the base verse, here
shifts.

Now the function of the outside verse (here: contrastive verse) is to establish the main point of the syllogism, and
it is in the intersecting of the contrastive verse and the base
verse that that syllogism is brought to clear statement. We
shall see, overall, that Pesiqta deRab Kahana presents its syllogisms in a far more powerful and direct medium of rhetoric
than does Leviticus Rabbah. Second, I refer to an implicit syllogism. By syllogism I mean a proposition that forms the recurrent principle a Pisqa' wishes to express and to prove in
the way its authorship deems plausible and compelling. .It is
implicit because it is never stated in so many words, yet it is
readily recognized and repeatedly imputed to one set of
verses after another. The implicit syllogism, as we shall see,
reaches expression in one of two ways, one through what I
call propositional form, the other through exegetical form.
Let me state with appropriate emphasis the rhetorical program represented by the two forms we shall now discern. *Both
are ways of stating in the idiom our authorship has chosen, in the media
of expression they have preferred, and through the modes of demonstration and evidentiary proof they deem probative, a truth they never spell*

out but always take for granted we shall recognize and adopt.

VI:I

1. A. If I were hungry, I would not tell you, for the world and all that is in it are mine. [Shall I eat the flesh of your bulls or drink the blood of he-goats? Offer to God the sacrifice of thanksgiving and pay your vows to the Most High. If you call upon me in time of trouble, I will come to your rescue and you shall honor me] (Ps. 50:12-15):

B. Said R. Simon, "There are thirteen traits of a merciful character that are stated in writing concerning the Holy One, blessed be he.

C. "That is in line with this verse of Scripture: The Lord passed by before him and proclaimed, The Lord, the Lord, God, merciful and gracious, long-suffering and abundant in goodness and truth; keeping mercy unto the thousandth generation, forgiving iniquity, transgression, and sin, who will be no means clear (Ex. 34:6-7).

D. "Now is there a merciful person who would hand over his food to a cruel person [who would have to slaughter a beast so as to feed him]?

E. "One has to conclude: If I were hungry, I would not tell you."

2. A. Said R. Judah bar Simon, "Said the Holy One, blessed be he, 'There are ten beasts that are clean that I have handed over to you [as valid for eating], three that are subject to your dominion, and seven that are not subject to your dominion.

B. "'Which are the ones that are subject to your dominion? The ox, sheep, and he-goat (Deut. 14:4).

C. "'Which are the ones not subject to your dominion? The hart, gazelle, roebuck, wild goat, ibex, antelope, and mountain sheep (Deut. 14:5).

D. "'Now [in connection with the sacrificial cult] have I imposed on you the trouble of going hunting in hills and mountains to bring before me an offering of one of those that are not in your dominion?

E. "'Have I not said to you only to bring what is

in your dominion and what is nourished at your stall?'

    F.   "Thus: If I were hungry, I would not tell you."

3.   A.   Said R. Isaac, "It is written, [The Lord spoke to Moses and said, Give this command to the Israelites:] See that you present my offerings, the food for the food-offering of soothing odor, to me at the appointed time. [Tell them: This is the food-offering which you shall present to the Lord: the regular daily whole-offering of two yearling rams without blemish. One you shall sacrifice in the morning and the second between dusk and dark] (Num. 28:1-4).

    B.   "Now is there any consideration of eating and drinking before Me?

    C.   "Should you wish to take the position that indeed there is a consideration of eating and drinking before me, derive evidence to the contrary from my angels, derive evidence to the contrary from my ministers: ...who makes the winds your messengers, and flames of fire your servants (Ps. 104:4).

    D.   "Whence then do they draw sustenance? From the splendor of the Presence of God.

    E.   "For it is written, In the light of the presence of the King they live (Prov. 16:15).'"

    F.   R. Haggai in the name of R. Isaac: "You have made heaven, the heaven of heavens...the host...and you keep them alive (Neh. 9:6, meaning, you provide them with livelihood [Leon Nemoy, cited by Braude and Kapstein, p. 125, n. 4]."

4.   A.   Said R. Simeon b. Laqish, "It is written, This was the regular whole-offering made at Mount Sinai, a soothing odor, a food-offering to the Lord (Num. 28:6).

    B.   "[God says,] 'Now is there any consideration of eating and drinking before Me?

    C.   "Should you wish to take the position that indeed there is a consideration of eating and drinking before me, derive evidence to the contrary from Moses, concerning whom it is written, And he was there with the Lord for forty days and forty nights. Bread he did not eat, and water he did not drink (Ex. 34:28).

 D. "'Did he see me eating or drinking?

 E. "'Now that fact yields an argument a fortiori: now if Moses, who went forth as my agent, did not eat bread or drink water for forty days, is there going to be any consideration of eating and drinking before me?

 F. "Thus: If I were hungry, I would not tell you."

5. A. Said R. Hiyya bar Ba, "'Things that I have created do not need [to derive sustenance] from things that I have created, am I going to require sustenance from things that I have created?

 B. "'Have you ever in your life heard someone say, 'Give plenty of wine to this vine, for it produces a great deal of wine'?

 C. "'Have you ever in your life heard someone say, 'Give plenty of oil to this olive tree, for it produces a great deal of oil'?

 D. "'Things that I have created do not need [to derive sustenance] from things that I have created, am I going to require sustenance from things that I have created?'

 E. "Thus: If I were hungry, I would not tell you."

6. A. Said R. Yannai, "Under ordinary circumstances if someone passes though the flood of a river, is it possible for him to drink a mere two or three logs of water? [Surely not. He will have to drink much more to be satisfied.]

 B. "[God speaks:] 'But as for Me, I have written that a mere single log of your wine shall I drink, and from that I shall derive full pleasure and satisfaction.'"

 C. R. Hiyya taught on Tannaite authority, "The wine for the proper drink-offering shall be a quarter of a hin for each ram; you are to pour out this strong drink in the holy place as an offering to the Lord (Num. 28:7).

 D. "This statement bears the sense of drinking to full pleasure, satisfaction, and even inebriation."

7. A. Yosé bar Menassia in the name of R. Simeon

b. Laqish, "When the libation was poured out, the stoppers [of the altar's drains] had to be stopped up [Braude and Kapstein, p. 126: so that the wine over-flowing the altar would make it appear that God could not swallow the wine fast enough]."

B. Said R. Yosé bar Bun, "The rule contained in the statement made by R. Simeon b. Laqish is essential to the proper conduct of the rite [and if the drains are not stopped up, the libation offering is invalid and must be repeated]."

8. A. {God speaks:] "I assigned to you the provi-sion of a single beast, and you could not carry out the order. [How then are you going to find the resources actually to feed me? It is beyond your capacity to do so.]'

B. "And what is that? It is the Behemoth on a thousand hills (Ps. 50:10)."

C. R. Yohanan, R. Simeon b. Laqish, and rabbis:

D. R. Yohanan said, "It is a single beast, which crouches on a thousand hills, and the thousand hills produce fodder, which it eats. What verse of Scripture so indicates? Now behold Behemoth which I made...Surely the mountains bring him forth food (Job 40:15)."

E. R. Simeon b. Laqish said, "It is a single beast, which crouches on a thousand hills, and the thousand hills produce all sorts of food for the meals of the right-eous in the coming age.

F. "What verse of Scripture so indicates? Flocks shall range over Sharon and the Vale of Achor be a pasture for cattle; they shall belong to my people who seek me (Is. 65:10)."

G. Rabbis said, ""It is a single beast, which crouches on a thousand hills, and the thousand hills produce cattle, which it eats.

H. "And what text of Scripture makes that point? And all beasts of the field play there (Job 40:20)."

I. But can cattle eat other cattle?

J. Said R. Tanhuma, "Great are the works of our God (Ps. 111:2), how curious are the works of the Holy

One, blessed be he."

K.   And whence does it drink?

L.   It was taught on Tannaite authority: R. Joshua b. Levi said, "Whatever the Jordan river collects in six months it swallows up in a single gulp.

M.   "What verse of Scripture indicates it? If the river is in spate, he is not scared, he sprawls at his ease as the Jordan flows to his mouth (Job 40:23)."

N.   Rabbis say, "Whatever the Jordan river collects in twelve months it swallows up in a single gulp.

O.   "What verse of Scripture indicates it? he sprawls at his ease as the Jordan flows to his mouth (Job 40:23).

P.   "And that suffices merely to wet his whistle."

Q.   R. Huna in the name of R. Yosé: "It is not even enough to wet his whistle."

R.   Then whence does it drink?

S.   R. Simeon b. Yohai taught on Tannaite authority, "And a river flowed out of Eden (Gen. 2:10), and its name is Yubal, and from there it drinks, as it is said, That spreads out its roots by Yubal (Jer. 17:8).æ

T.   It was taught on Tannaite authority in the name of R. Meir, "But ask now the Behemoth (Job 12:7) — this is the Behemoth of the thousand hills (Ps. 50:10), and the fowl of the heaven will tell you (Job 12:7), that is the ziz-bird (Ps. 50:10), or speak to the earth that it tell you (Job 12:8) — this refers to the Garden of Eden. Or let the fish of the sea tell you (Job 12:8) — this refers to Leviathan.

U.   "Who does not know among all these that the hand of the Lord has done this (Job 12:9)."

9.   A.   "I gave you a single king, and you could not provide for him. [How then are you going to find the resources actually to feed me? It is beyond your capacity to do so.] And who was that? It was Solomon, son of David."

B.   The bread required by Solomon in a single day was thirty kors of fine flower and sixty kors of meal (1 Kgs. 5:2).

C.   Said R. Samuel bar R. Isaac, "These were

kinds of snacks. But as to his regular meal, no person could provide it: Ten fat oxen (1 Kgs 5:3), fattened with fodder, and twenty oxen out of the pasture and a hundred sheep (1 Kgs 5:3), also out of the pasture; and harts, gazelles, roebucks, and fatted fowl (1 Kgs. 5:3)."

D.   What are these fatted fowl?

E.   R. Berekhiah in the name of R. Judah said, "They were fowl raised in a vivarium."

F.   And rabbis say, "It is a very large bird, of high quality, much praised, which would go up and be served on the table of Solomon every day."

G.   Said R. Judah bar Zebida, "Solomon had a thousand wives, and every one of them made a meal of the same dimensions as this meal. Each thought that he might dine with her."

H.   "Thus: If I were hungry, I would not tell you."

10.   A.   "One mere captive I handed over to you, and you could barely sustain him too. [How then are you going to find the resources actually to feed me? It is beyond your capacity to do so.]"

B.   And who was that? It was Nehemiah, the governor:

C.   Now that which was prepared for one day was one ox and six choice sheep, also fowls were prepared for me, and once in ten days store of all sorts of wine; yet for all this I demanded not the usual fare provided for the governor, because the service was heavy upon this people (Neh. 5:18).

D.   What is the usual fare provided for the governor?

E.   Huna bar Yekko said, "[Braude and Kapstein, p. 114:] It means gourmet food carefully cooked in vessels standing upon tripods."

F.   "Thus: If I were hungry, I would not tell you."

11.   A.   It has been taught on Tannaite authority: The incense is brought only after the meal (M. Ber. 6:6).

B.   Now is it not the case that the sole enjoyment that the guests derive from the incense is the scent?

C.   Thus said the Holy One blessed be he, "My

children, among all the offerings that you offer before
me, I derive pleasure from you only because of the
scent: the food for the food-offering of soothing odor,
to me at the appointed time.

The passage commences with what is clearly the contrastive verse, Ps. 50:12, which stands in stark contrast to the
base verse, Num. 28:1ff., because what the latter requires, the
former denigrates. No. 1 is open-ended, in that it does not
draw us back to the base verse at all. It simply underlines one
meaning to be imputed to the contrastive verse. No. 2 pursues the theme of the base verse — the selection of beasts for
the altar — and reverts to the intersecting one. Nos. 3, 4 and
5 then draw us back to the base verse, but in a rather odd
way. They treat it as simply another verse awaiting consideration, not as the climax of the exercise of explication of the
many senses of the contrastive verse. The purpose of the
composition before us is not to explore the meanings of the
contrastive verse, bringing one of them to illuminate, also, the
base verse. The purpose of the composition before us is to
make a single point, to argue a single proposition, through a
single-minded repertoire of relevant materials, each of which
makes the same point as all the others. We may say that if a
principal interest of the components of Leviticus Rabbah is
exegetical, another principal interest, syllogistic, the sole interest of our authorship in the type of form before us is to invoke an contrastive verse to make the point that the base
verse must be shown to establish. Before explaining the implications of that simple fact, let me complete the review of
the whole.

I see No. 5 as the conclusion of the main event, that
is to say, the contrastive verse has laid down its judgment on
the sense of the base verse and established the syllogism. No.
6 then underlines that single point by saying that the natural
world presents cases in which considerable volumes of food

or drink are necessary to meet this-worldly requirements. How then can we hope to meet the supernatural requirements of God? That point, made at No. 6, 8, 9, and 10, is essentially secondary to what has gone before. So we have a composition of two elements, Nos. 1-5, the systematic exposition of the base verse in terms of the single proposition of the interesting verse, then No. 6-10, the secondary point that reinforces the main one. No. 11 resolves the enormous tension created by the contrast between the base verse and the contrastive verse. I do not need the food, but I get pleasure from the smell.

Let me now revert to the main formal point at hand. If, therefore, we were to draw a contrast between the contrastive verse-base verse construction as we know it in Leviticus Rabbah and the counterpart before us, we should have to see them as essentially different modes of organizing and expressing an idea. The difference may be stated very simply. Leviticus Rabbah's compositors draw on materials that systematically expound the intersecting verse in a variety of ways, and only then draw back to the base verse to impute to it a fresh and unusual sense, invited by one of the several possible interpretations laid out by the intersecting verse. The framers of Pesiqta deRab Kahana, by contrast, draw upon an contrastive verse in order to make a point — one point — which then is placed into relationship with the base verse and which imposes its meaning on the base verse.

What this means is that our document aims at making a single point, and at doing so with a minimum of obfuscation through exploration of diverse possibilities. The function of the contrastive verse is not to lay forth a galaxy of hermeneutical possibilities, one of which will be selected. It is, rather, to present a single point, and it is that point that we shall then impose upon our base verse. What that fact means, overall, is that our document aims at a syllogism, expressed singly and forcefully, rather than at a diversity of explanation of a verse that, in the end, will yield a syllogism. The difference between Leviticus Rabbah's intersecting verse and base verse construction and Pesiqta deRab Kahana's contrastive verse and base verse construction is sharp and total. The form — one verse, then another verse — looks the same. But the deeper structure is utterly unrelated.

The foregoing analysis has presented us with our first hypothetical rhetorical pattern, one formed out of the comparison and contrast of two verses of Scripture, with the result that a well-formed syllogism emerges. Let me now offer a clear description of the rhetorical pattern I believe underlies VI:I.

1.   THE PROPOSITIONAL FORM: The implicit syllogism is stated through the intervention of an contrastive verse into the basic proposition established by the base verse.

This form cites the base verse, then a contrastive verse. Sometimes the base verse is not cited at the outset, but it is always used to mark the conclusion of the Pisqa'. The sense of the latter is read into the former, and a syllogism is worked out, and reaches intelligible expression, through the contrast and comparison of the one and the other. There is no pretense at a systematic exegesis of the diverse meanings imputed to the contrastive verse, only the comparison and contrast of two verses, the external or intersecting and the base verses, respectively. The base verse, for its part, also is not subjected to systematic exegesis. This represents, therefore, a strikingly abstract and general syllogistic pattern, even though verses are cited to give the statement the formal character of an exegesis. But it is in no way an exegetical pattern. The purpose of this pattern is to impute to the base verse the sense generated by the intersection of the base verse and the contrastive verse. Since the contrastive verse dictates the sense to be imputed to the base verse, therefore its fundamental proposition, we should further expect that the contrastive verse-base verse form will come first in the unfolding of a Pisqa', as it does here. For any further exposition of a proposition will require a clear statement of what, in fact, is at stake in a given Pisqa', and that, as I said, is the contribution of the contrastive verse-base verse form.

VI:II

1. A. A righteous man eats his fill, [but the wicked go hungry] (Prov. 13:25):

B. This refers to Eliezer, our father Abraham's servant, as it is said, Please let me have a little water to drink from your pitcher (Gen. 24:17) — one sip.

C. ...but the wicked go hungry:

D. This refers to the wicked Esau, who said to our father, Jacob, Let me swallow some of that red pottage, for I am famished (Gen. 28:30).

2. A. [And Esau said to Jacob, Let me swallow some of that red pottage, for I am famished (Gen. 25:30):]

B. Said R. Isaac bar Zeira, "That wicked man opened up his mouth like a camel. He said to him, 'I'll open up my mouth, and you just toss in the food.'

C. "That is in line with what we have learned in the Mishnah: People may not stuff a camel or force food on it, but may toss food into its mouth [M. Shab. 24:3]."

3. A. Another interpretation of the verse, A righteous man eats his fill:

B. This refers to Ruth the Moabite, in regard to whom it is written, She ate, was satisfied, and left food over (Ruth 2:14).

C. Said R. Isaac, "You have two possibilities: either a blessing comes to rest through a righteous man, or a blessing comes to rest through the womb of a righteous woman.

D. "On the basis of the verse of Scripture, She ate, was satisfied, and left food over, one must conclude that a blessing comes to rest through the womb of a righteous woman."

E.   ...but the wicked go hungry:

F.   This refers to the nations of the world.

4.   A.   Said R. Meir, "Dosetai of Kokhba asked me, saying to me, "What is the meaning of the statement, '...but the wicked go hungry?'

B.   "I said to him, 'There was a gentile in our town, who made a banquet for all the elders of the town, and invited me along with them. He set before us everything that the Holy One, blessed be he, had created on the six days of creation, and his table lacked only soft-shelled nuts alone.

C.   "What did he do? He took the tray from before us, which was worth six talents of silver, and broke it.

D.   "I said to him, 'On what account did you do this? [Why are you so angry?]'

E.   "He said to me, 'My lord, you say that we own this world, and you own the world to come. If we don't do the eating now, when are we going to eat [of every good thing that has ever been created]?'

F.   "I recited in his regard, ...but the wicked go hungry."

5.   A.   Another interpretation of the verse, A righteous man eats his fill, [but the wicked go hungry] (Prov. 13:25):

B.   This refers to Hezekiah, King of Judah.

C.   They say concerning Hezekiah, King of Judah, that [a mere] two bunches of vegetables and a litra of meat did they set before him every day.

D.   And the Israelites ridiculed him, saying, "Is this a king? And they rejoiced over Rezin and Remaliah's son (Is. 8:6). But Rezin, son of Remaliah, is really worthy of dominion."

E.   That is in line with this verse of Scripture: Because this people has refused the waters of Shiloah that run slowly and rejoice with Rezin and Remaliah's son (Is. 8:6).

F. What is the sense of slowly?

G. Bar Qappara said, "We have made the circuit of the whole of Scripture and have not found a place that bears the name spelled by the letters translated slowly.

H. "But this refers to Hezekiah, King of Judah, who would purify the Israelites through a purification-bath containing the correct volume of water, forty seahs, the number signified by the letters that spell the word for slowly."

I. Said the Holy One, blessed be he, "You praise eating? Behold the Lord brings up the waters of the River, mighty and many, even the king of Assyria and all his glory, and he shall come up over all his channels and go over all his bands and devour you as would a glutton (Is. 8:7)."

6. A. ...but the wicked go hungry: this refers to Mesha.

B. Mesha, king of Moab, was a noked (2 Kgs. 3:4). What is the sense of noked? It is a shepherd.

C. "He handed over to the king of Israel a hundred thousand fatted lambs and a hundred thousand wool-bearing rams (2 Kgs. 3:4)."

D. What is the meaning of wool-bearing rams?

E. R. Abba bar Kahana said, "Unshorn."

7. A. Another interpretation of the verse, A righteous man eats his fill, [but the wicked go hungry] (Prov. 13:25):

B. This refers to the kings of Israel and the kings of the House of David.

C. ...but the wicked go hungry are the kings of the East:

D. R. Yudan and R. Hunah:

E. R. Yudan said, "A hundred sheep would be served to each one every day."

F. R. Hunah said, "A thousand sheep were served to each one every day."

8. A. Another interpretation of the verse, A right-

eous man eats his fill (Prov. 13:25):

    B.   this refers to the Holy One, blessed be he.

    C.   Thus said the Holy One blessed be he, "My children, among all the offerings that you offer before me, I derive pleasure from you only because of the scent: the food for the food-offering of soothing odor, to me at the appointed time."

Our contrastive verse now makes the point that the righteous one gets what he needs, the wicked go hungry, with a series of contrasts at Nos. 1, 2, 3, 5, 6, 7, leading to No. 8: the Holy One gets pleasure from the scent of the offerings. I do not see exactly how the contrastive verse has enriched the meaning imputed to the base verse. What the compositors have done, rather, is to use the contrastive verse to lead to their, now conventional, conclusion, so 8.C appears tacked on as a routine conclusion, but, as before, turns out to be the critical point of cogency for the whole. Then the main point is that God does not need the food of the offerings; at most he enjoys the scent. The same point is made as before at VI:I.11: what God gets out of the offering is not nourishment but merely the pleasure of the scent of the offerings. God does not eat; but he does smell. The exegesis of Prov. 13:25, however, proceeds along its own line, contrasting Eliezer and Esau, Ruth and the nations of the world, Hezekiah and Mesha, Israel's kings and the kings of the East, and then God — with no contrast at all.

    VI:III

1.   A.   You have commanded your precepts to be kept diligently (Ps. 119:4):

    B.   Where did he give this commandment? In the book of Numbers. [Braude and Kapstein, p. 132: "In Numbers you did again ordain...Where did God again ordain? In the Book of Numbers."]

    C.   What did he command?

    D.   To be kept diligently (Ps. 119:4): The Lord

spoke to Moses and said, Give this command to the Israelites: See that you present my offerings, the food for
the food-offering of soothing odor, to me at the appointed time.

E. That is the same passage that has already occurred [at Ex. 29:38-42] and now recurs, so why has it
been stated a second time?

F. R. Yudan, R. Nehemiah, and rabbis:

G. R. Yudan said, "Since the Israelites thought,
'In the past there was the practice of making journeys,
and there was the practice of offering daily whole offerings. Now that the journeying is over, the daily whole
offerings also are over.'

H. "Said the Holy One, blessed be he, to Moses,
'Go, say to Israel that they should continue the practice
of offering daily whole offerings.'"

I. R. Nehemiah said, "Since the Israelites were
treating the daily whole offering lightly, said the Holy
One, blessed be he, to Moses, 'Go, tell Israel not to
treat the daily whole offerings lightly.'"

J. Rabbis said, "[The reason for the repetition is
that] one statement serves for instruction, the other for
actual practice."

2. A. R. Aha in the name of R. Hanina: "It was so
that the Israelites should not say, 'In the past we offered sacrifices and so were engaged [in studying about]
them, but now that we do not offer them any more, we
also need not study about them any longer.'

B. "Said the Holy One, blessed be he, to them,
'Since you engage in studying about them, it is as if you
have actually carried them out.'"

3. A. R. Huna made two statements.

B. R. Huna said, "All of the exiles will be gathered together only on account of the study of Mishnah-
teachings.

C. "What verse of Scripture makes that point?
Even when they recount [Mishnah-teachings] among
the gentiles, then I shall gather them together (Hos.
8:10)."

D.   R. Huna made a second statement.

E.   R. Huna said, "From the rising of the sun even to the setting of the sun my name is great among the nations, and in every place offerings are presented to my name, even pure offerings (Malachi 1:11). Now is it the case that a pure offering is made in Babylonia?

F.   "Said the Holy One, blessed be he, 'Since you engage in the study of the matter, it is as if you offered it up.'"

4.   A.   Samuel said, "And if they are ashamed of all that they have done, show them the form of the house and the fashion of it, the goings out and the comings in that pertain to it, and all its forms, and write it in their sight, that they may keep the whole form of it (Ez. 43:11).

B.   "Now is there such a thing as the form of the house at this time?

C.   "But said the Holy One, blessed be he, if you are engaged in the study of the matter, it is as if you were building it.'"

5.   A.   Said R. Yosé, "On what account do they begin instruction of children with the Torah of the Priests [the book of Leviticus]?

B.   "Rather let them begin instruction them with the book of Genesis.

C.   "But the Holy One, blessed be he said, 'Just as the offerings [described in the book of Leviticus] are pure, so children are pure. Let the pure come and engage in the study of matters that are pure.'"

6.   A.   R. Abba bar Kahana and R. Hanin, both of them in the name of R. Azariah of Kefar Hitayya: "[The matter may be compared to the case of] a king who had two cooks. The first of the two made a meal for him, and he ate it and liked it. The second made a meal for him, and he ate it and liked it.

B.   "Now we should not know which of the two he liked more, except that, since he ordered the second, telling him to make a meal like the one he had prepared, we know that it was the second meal that he liked more.

C.   "So too Noah made an offering and it pleased God: And the Lord smelled the sweet savor (Gen. 8:21).

D.   "And Israel made an offering to him, and it pleased the Holy One, blessed be he.

E.   "But we do not know which of the two he preferred.

F   "On the basis of his orders to Israel, saying to them, See that you present my offerings, the food for the food-offering of soothing odor, to me at the appointed time, we know that he preferred the offering of Israel [to that of Noah, hence the offering of Israel is preferable to the offering of the nations of the world]."

7.   A.   R. Abin made two statements.

B.   R. Abin said, "The matter may be compared to the case of a king who was reclining at his banquet, and they brought him the first dish, which he ate and found pleasing. They brought him the second, which he ate and found pleasing. He began to wipe the dish.

C.   "I will offer you burnt offerings which are to be wiped off (Ps. 66:15), like offerings that are to be wiped off I shall offer you, like someone who wipes the plate clean."

D.   R. Abin made a second statement:

E.   "The matter may be compared to a king who was making a journey and came to the first stockade and ate and drank there. Then he came to the second stockade and ate and drank there and spent the night there.

F.   "So it is here. Why does the Scripture repeat concerning the burnt offering: This is the Torah of the burnt offering (Lev. 3:5), It is the burnt offering Lev. 6:2)? It is to teach that the whole of the burnt offering is burned up on the fires [yielding no parts to the priests]."

The rhetorical pattern now shifts. We have interest in the contrast between our base verse and another one that goes over the same matter. That contrast, to be sure, is invited by Ps. 119:4. But that contrastive verse does not function in such a way as to lead us to our base verse, but rather, as is clear, to lead us to the complementary verse for our base verse. That is, therefore, a different pattern from the one we have identified. The exegesis moves from text to context. We have two statements of the same matter, in Numbers and in Exodus, as indicated at No. 1. Why is the passage repeated? No. 1 presents a systematic composition on that question, No. 2 on another. No. 3 serves as an appendix to No. 2, on the importance of studying the sacrifices. But No. 3 obviously ignores our setting, since it is interested in the Mishnah-study in general, not the study of the laws of the sacrifices in particular. No. 4 goes on with the same point. No. 5 then provides yet another appendix, this one on the study of the book of Leviticus, with its substantial corpus of laws on sacrifice. No. 6 opens a new inquiry, this time into the larger theme of the comparison of offerings. It has no place here, but is attached to No. 7. That item is particular to Leviticus 6:2, but it concerns the same question we have here, namely, the repetition of statements about sacrifices, this timed Lev. 3:5, 6:2. So Nos. 6, 7 are tacked on because of the congruence of the question, not the pertinence of the proposition. In that case we look to No. 1 for guidance, and there we find at issue is the convergence of two verses on the same matter, and that is what stands behind our composition.

The rhetorical pattern is hardly clear. I see a problem — the convergence of verses — but not a pattern that would precipitate expectation of recurrent examples.

VI:IV

1.   A.   ...the regular daily whole-offering of two yearling rams without blemish:

B.   [Explaining the selection of the lambs,] the House of Shammai and the House of Hillel [offered opinions as follows:]

C.   The House of Shammai say, "Lambs are chosen because the letters that spell the word for lamb can
also be read to mean that 'they cover up the sins of Israel,' as you read in Scripture: He will turn again and
have compassion upon us, he will put our iniquities out
of sight (Micah 7:19)."

D.   And the House of Hillel say, "Lambs are selected because the letters of the word lamb can yield
the sound for the word, clean, for they clean up the sins
of Israel.

E.   "That is in line with this verse of Scripture: If
your sins are like scarlet, they will be washed clean like
wool (Is. 1:18)."

F.   Ben Azzai says, "...the regular daily whole-
offering of two yearling rams without blemish are
specified because they wash away the sins of Israel and
turn them into an infant a year old."

2.   A.   [...the regular daily whole-offering of] two
[yearling rams without blemish. One you shall sacrifice
in the morning and the second between dusk and dark]:

B.   Two a day on account of [the sins of] the day.

C.   Two a day to serve as intercessor for that day:
They shall be mine, says the Lord of hosts, on the day
that I do this, even my own treasure, and I will spare
them, as a man spares his son who serves him (Malachi
3:17).

D.   Two a day meaning that they should be
slaughtered in correspondence to that day in particular.

E.   Two a day meaning that one should know in
advance which has been designated to be slaughtered in
the morning and which at dusk.

3.   A.   ...a daily whole offering:

B.   Said R. Yudan in the name of R. Simon, "No
one ever spent the night in Jerusalem while still bearing
sin. How so? The daily whole offering of then morning
would effect atonement for the sins that had been
committed overnight, and the daily whole offering of
dusk would effect atonement for the transgressions that

had been committed by day.

C.   "In consequence, no one ever spent the night in Jerusalem while still bearing sin.

D.   "And what verse of Scripture makes that point? *Righteousness will spend the night in it* (Is. 1:21)."

4.   A.   R. Judah bar Simon in the name of R. Yohanan: "There were three statements that Moses heard from the mouth of the Almighty, on account of which he was astounded and recoiled.

B.   "When he said to him, *And they shall make me a sanctuary* [and I shall dwell among them] (Ex. 25:8), said Moses before the Holy One, blessed be he, 'Lord of the age, lo, the heavens and the heavens above the heavens cannot hold you, and yet you yourself have said, *And they shall make me a sanctuary* [and I shall dwell among them] .'

C.   "Said to him the Holy One, blessed be he, 'Moses, it is not the way you are thinking. But there will be twenty boards' breadth at the north, twenty at the south, eight at the west, and I shall descend and shrink my Presence among you below.'

D.   "That is in line with this verse of Scripture: *And I shall meet you there* (Ex. 25:20).

E.   "When he said to him, *My food which is presented to me for offerings made by fire* [you shall observe to offer to me] (Num. 28:2), said Moses before the Holy One, blessed be he, 'Lord of the age, if I collect all of the wild beasts in the world, will they produce one offering [that would be adequate as a meal for you]?

F.   "'If I collect all the wood in the world, will it prove sufficient for one offering,' as it is said, *Lebanon is not enough for altar fire, nor the beasts thereof sufficient for burnt offerings* (Is. 40:16).

G.   "Said to him the Holy One, blessed be he, "Moses, it is not the way you are thinking. But: *You shall say to them, This is the offering made by fire* [he lambs of the first year without blemish, two day by day] (Num. 28:3), and not two at a time but one in the

morning and one at dusk, as it is said, One lamb you
will prepare in the morning, and the other you will prepare at dusk (Num. 28:4).'

H.   "And when he said to him, When you give the
contribution to the Lord to make expiation for your
lives (Ex. 30:15), said Moses before the Holy One,
blessed be he, 'Lord of the age, who can give redemp-
tion-money for his soul?

I.   "'One brother cannot redeem another (Ps.
49:8), for too costly is the redemption of men's souls
(Ps. 49:9).'

J.   "Said the Holy One, blessed be he, to Moses,
'It is not the way you are thinking. But: This they shall
give — something like this [namely, the half-shekel
coin] they shall give"

The rhetorical pattern is clear: the base verse is analyzed, clause by clause. The point that is made is that the offerings achieve expiation and serve as intercessors. That is the
same proposition that the contrastive verse wishes to establish. The exegesis of the components of the base verse accounts for the miscellany with which our Pisqa' draws to a
close. But the point is cogent. The daily whole offering effects atonement for sins of the preceding day. No. 1 makes
that point in one way, No. 2 in another. Deriving from elsewhere, No. 3, bearing in its wake No. 4, says the same thing
yet a third time. So the miscellany is a composite but makes a
single point in a strong way.

The form in its purest exemplification would give us
the base verse clause by clause, with each of the clauses subjected to amplification and exposition. The rhetorical pattern
then may be described as follows:

2.   **THE EXEGETICAL FORM:** The implicit
syllogism is stated through a systematic exegesis of the components of the base verse on their own.

That proposition is taken to be the message established by the base verse. So the base verse now serves as the

structural foundation for the pericope. This form cites the base verse alone. A syllogism is worked out, and reaches intelligible expression, through the systematic reading of the individual components of the base verse. The formal traits: [1] citation of a base verse, [2] a generalization or syllogistic proposition worked out through details of the base verse. We should moreover anticipate that the exegetical form will follow in sequence upon the propositional form, since the propositional form through the interplay of contrastive verse and base verse establishes the theorem to be worked out, and only then does the exegetical form undertake the secondary amplification of that same message, now in terms of the base verse alone. If this scheme is a sound one, then we should always find the sequence [1] propositional and [2] exegetical form.

Whether or not the authorship of Pesiqta deRab Kahana required for the accomplishment of its purpose more than the two forms identified here will be seen when we survey the entire document's rhetorical character. First we have to test the hypothesis framed here concerning the identification and definition of the recurrent rhetorical patterns of choice. At issue are two matters. First, we wish to know whether the formulations we have defined in fact dictate the mode of discourse at all, and this in regard to both the pattern of formulating ideas and also the sequence by which the two hypothetical forms or patterns occur, first one, then the other. Second, we want to find out whether these are not only necessary but also sufficient, or whether we shall have to define (not invent) yet other formal patterns to account for the recurrent modes by which intelligible propositions are framed.

II. LITERARY STRUCTURES OF PE-SIQTA DERAB KAHANA PISQA'OT 14 AND 22

So far as I can see, the large units of Pisqa' 6 all fall within the two patterns for formal compositions that we have now identified. Do these suffice or are other formal patterns to be defined? To answer these questions we proceed to two further Pisqa'ot, selected at random. I then conduct a test by examining a Pisqa' that occurs also in another document, that is, Pisqa' 27, which is shared with Leviticus Rabbah. This will allow us a negative test, since, if my claim is correct that Pe-siqta deRab Kahana is the work of a distinctive authorship, which has made its singular choices as to rhetoric, then a Pisqa' not particular to that authorship should exhibit different traits.

Since my principal purpose is to test our hypothetical scheme of the rhetorical patterns of the document, the principal point of exposition addresses the question of whether we deal with propositional form, exegetical form, or some other.

XIV:I

1.   A.   Therefore hear me you men of understanding, far be it from God that he should do wickedness, and from the almighty that he should do wrong. [For according to the work of a man he will requite him, and according to his ways he will make it befall him] (Job 34:10-11):

B.   R. Azariah, R. Jonathan bar Haggai in the name of R. Samuel bar R. Isaac, "[With reference to the verse, Then Jacob became angry and upbraided Laban. Jacob said to Laban, 'What is my offense? What is my sin, that you have hotly pursued me? Although you have felt through all my goods, what have you found of all your household goods? Set it here before my kinsmen and your kinsmen that they may decide between us two' (Gen. 31:36-37),] "Better the captiousness of the fathers than the irenic obsequiousness of the sons.

C.   "[We learn the former from this verse:] Then Jacob became angry and upbraided Laban. Jacob said to Laban, "What is my offense? What is my sin, that you have hotly pursued me? [Gen. R. 74:10 adds: You might imagine that, in consequence, there would be a brawl. But in fact there was nothing but an effort at reconciliation. Jacob made every effort to reconcile his father-in-law: Although you have felt through all my goods, what have you found of all your household goods? Set it here before my kinsmen and your kinsmen that they may decide between us two.]

D.   "[We learn about] the irenic obsequiousness of the sons from the case of David:

E.   "And David fled from Naioth in Ramah and came and said before Jonathan, What have I done? What is my iniquity? and what is my sin before your father, that he seeks my life? (1 Sam. 20:1).

F.   "Even while he is trying to reconcile with the other, he mentions bloodshed.

G.   Said R. Simon, "Under ordinary circumstances, when a son-in-law is living with his father in law and then proceeds to leave the household of his father in law, is it possible that the father-in-law will not find in his possession even the most minor item? But as to this [Jacob], even a shoelace, even a knife, was not found in his possession.

H.   "That is in line with this verse of Scripture: Although you have felt through all my goods, what have you found of all your household goods? Set it here before my kinsmen and your kinsmen that they may decide between us two.

I.   "Said the Holy One, blessed be he, 'By your life! In the very language by which you have rebuked your father-in-law, I shall rebuke your children: What wrong did your fathers find in me that they went far from me and went after worthlessness and became worthless?'"

The issue before us is whether the contrastive verse opens up any aspect of the base verse. Clearly, the first point of interest is the use of the word "hear," shared by Job 34:10 and Jer. 2:4. But what is to be heard? It is that there is good reason for what God does (Job 34:10), and it must follow that God's complaint — there must be good reason for what man does — is justified. That seems to me a solid basis for classifying the composition as the Propositional Form. The implicit syllogism — there is a common bond of rationality that accounts for God's and man's deeds — is stated through the intervention of an contrastive verse into the basic proposition established by the base verse.

XIV:II

1. A. [For the simple are killed by their turning away, and the complacence of fools destroys them;] but he who listens to me will dwell secure, and will be at ease, [without dread of evil] (Prov. 1:33):

B. There are four categories of hearing.

C. There is one who listens and loses, there is one who listens and gains, one who does not listen and loses, one who does not listen and gains.

D. There is one who listens and loses: this is the first Man: And to Man he said, Because you listened to the voice of your wife (Gen. 3:17).

E. What did he lose? For you are dust and to dust you will return (Gen. 3:19).

F. ...who listens and gains: this is our father, Abraham: Whatever Sarah says to you, Listen to her voice (Gen. 21:12).

G. How did he gain? For through Isaac will you have descendents (Gen. 21:12)

H. ...who does not listen and gains: this refers to Joseph: And he did not listen to her, to lie with her (Gen. 39:11).

I. How did he gain? And Joseph will place his hand over your eyes (Gen. 46:4).

J. ...who does not listen and loses: this refers to Israel: They did not listen to me and did not pay attention (Jer. 7:26).

K. What did they lose? Him to death, to death, and him to the sword, to the sword (Jer. 15:2).

2.   A.   Said R. Levi, "The ear is to the body as the kiln to pottery. Just as in the case of a kiln, when it is full of pottery, if you kindle a flame under it, all of the pots feel it,

B.   "so: Incline your ear and go to me and listen and let your souls live (Is. 55:3)."

The choice of the contrastive verse is accounted for by the reference at Prov. 1:33 to "he who listens will dwell secure." The proposition is that listening to God will produce a gain to a faithful people, in the model of Abraham. The category, once more, is the Propositional Form.

XIV:III

1.   A.   If you are willing and listen, you shall eat the good of the land; but if you refuse and rebel, [you shall be devoured by the sword; for the mouth of the Lord has spoken] (Is. 1:19-20):

B.   [...you shall eat the good of the land:] You shall eat carobs.

C.   Said R. Aha, "When an Israelite has to eat carobs, he will carry out repentance.

D.   Said R. Aqiba, "As becoming is poverty for a daughter of Jacob as a red ribbon on the breast of a white horse."

2.   A.   Said R. Samuel bar Nahman, "Even while a palace is falling, it is still called a palace, and even when a dung heap rises, it is still called a dung heap.

B.   "Even while a palace is falling, it is still called a palace: Hear the word of the Lord, O House of Jacob, and all the families of the House of Israel (Jer. 2:4-6). When while they are declining, he still calls them the House of Israel.

C.   "...and even when a dung heap rises, it is still called a dung heap: Behold the land of the Chaldeans

— this is the nation that was nothing (Is. 23:13) — would that they were still nothing!"

3.   A.   Said R. Levi, The matter may be compared to the case of a noble woman who had two family members at hand, one a villager, the other a city-dweller. The one who was a villager, [when he had occasion to correct her,] would speak in words of consolation: 'Are you not the daughter of good folk, are you not the daughter of a distinguished family.'

   B.   "But the one who was a city-dweller, [when he had occasion to correct her,] would speak in words of reprimand: 'Are you not the daughter of the lowest of the poor, are you not the daughter of impoverished folk?'

   C.   "So too in the case of Jeremiah, since he was a villager, from Anathoth, he would go to Jerusalem and speak to Israel in words of consolation [and pleading,] Hear the word of the Lord, O House of Jacob, [and all the families of the House of Israel. Thus says the Lord: "What wrong did your fathers find in me that they went far from me and went after worthlessness and became worthless? They did not say, "Where is the Lord who brought us up from the Land of Egypt, who led us in the wilderness, in a land of deserts and pits, in a land of drought and deep darkness, in a land that none passes through, where no man dwells?"] (Jer. 2:4-6).

   D.   "'These are the improper deeds which your fathers did.'

   E.   "But Isaiah, because he was a city dweller, from Jerusalem, would speak to Israel in terms of reprimand: Hear the word of the Lord, you rulers of Sodom, attend, you people of Gomorrah, to the instruction of our God (Is. 1:10).

   F.   "'Do you not come from the mold of the people of Sodom.'"

4.   A.   Said R. Levi, "Amoz and Amaziah were brothers, and because Isaiah was the son of the king's brother, he could speak to Israel in such terms of reprimand,

B. "in line with this verse: A rich man answers impudently (Prov. 18:23)."

The contrastive verse once more focuses attention on listening, and that is the link to the base verse. The implicit proposition is announced in that same verse: If you listen, you prosper, and if not, you lose out, so XIV:III.1. No. 2 leads us directly into our base verse, commenting on the language that is used. No. 3, 4 then amplify that point by comparing Jeremiah and Isaiah. These form a secondary amplification of the theme; the proposition derives from No. 1. The category once more is the Propositional Form.

XIV:IV

1. A. Said R. Levi, "The matter may be compared to the case of a noble lady who [as her dowry] brought into the king two myrtles and lost one of them and was distressed on that account.

B. "The king said to her, 'Take good care of this other one as if you were taking care of the two of them.'

C. "So too, when the Israelites stood at Mount Sinai, they said, Everything that the Lord has spoken we shall do and we shall hear (Ex. 24:7). They lost the we shall do by making the golden calf.

D. "Said the Holy One, blessed be he, be sure to take care of the we shall listen as if you were taking care of both of them.'

E. "When they did not listen, the Holy One, blessed be he, said to them, Hear the word of the Lord, O House of Jacob, [and all the families of the House of Israel. Thus says the Lord: "What wrong did your fathers find in me that they went far from me and went after worthlessness and became worthless? They did not say, "Where is the Lord who brought us up from the Land of Egypt, who led us in the wilderness, in a land of deserts and pits, in a land of drought and deep darkness, in a land that none passes through, where no man dwells?"] (Jer. 2:4-6)."

2. A. [A further comment on the verse, Hear the word of the Lord (Jer. 2:4-6):] before you have to listen to the words of Jeremiah.

B. Listen to the words of the Torah, before you have to listen to the words of the prophet.

C. Listen to the words of prophecy before you have to listen to words of rebuke.

D. Listen to words of rebuke before you have to listen to words of reprimand.

E. Listen to words of reprimand before you have to listen to the sound of the horn and the pipe (Dan. 3:15).

F. Listen in the land before you have to listen abroad.

G. Listen while alive, before you have to listen when dead.

H. Let your ears listen before your bodies have to listen.

I. Let your bodies listen before your bones have to listen: Dry bones, hear the word of the Lord (Ez. 37:4).

3. A. R. Aha in the name of R. Joshua b. Levi, "Nearly eight times in Egypt the Israelites [Braude and Kapstein, p. 270:] stood shoulder to shoulder].

B. "What is the scriptural verse that indicates it? Come, let us take counsel against him (Ex. 1:10).

C. "On that account [God] took the initiative for them and redeemed them: And I came down to save him from the hand of the Egyptians (Ex. 3:8)."

4. A. R. Abin, R. Hiyya in the name of R. Yohanan: "It is written, My mother's sons were displeased with me, they sent me to watch over the vineyards; so I did not watch over my own vineyard (Song 1:6).

B. "What brought it about that I watched over the vineyards? It is because I did not watch over my own vineyard.

C. "What brought it about that in Syria I separate dough-offering from two loaves? It is because in the

Land of Israel I did not properly separate dough-offering from one loaf.

D. "I thought that I should receive a reward on account of both of them, but I receive a reward only on account of one of them.

E. "What brought it about that in Syria I observe two days for the festivals? It is because in the Land of Israel I did not properly observe one day for the festivals.

F. "I thought that I should receive a reward on account of both of them, but I receive a reward only on account of one of them."

G. R. Yohanan would recite the following verse of Scripture in this connection: And I also gave them ordinances that were not good (Ez. 20:25).

This is a classic example of the Exegetical Form. The implicit syllogism is stated through a systematic exegesis of the components of the base verse on their own. Formally, we know we are in fresh territory because No. 1 does not begin with the citation of any verse at all, and it clearly does not carry forward any prior discussion. So it stands at the head of a unit composed on a different formal paradigm from the foregoing ones. No. 1 presents a powerful comment on our base-verse. The proposition is that when Israel listens, they prosper, and when they do not listen, they lose out, just as before. But God is bound by reason and so expects man to be, hence, "What wrong...?" No. 2 moves in its own direction, but its contrast between listening to A so that you will not have to listen to B makes its point with great power as well. The relevance of Nos. 3, 4 is hardly self-evident. Speculation that these items illustrate entries on the catalogue of No. 2 is certainly not groundless. And No. 4 is explicit that obeying ("listening") yields rewards, and not obeying, penalties.

XIV:V

1. A. It is written, Thus said the Lord, What wrong did your fathers find in me that they went far from me

and went after worthlessness and became worthless? (Jer. 2:5)

B.   Said R. Isaac, "This refers to one who leaves the scroll of the Torah and departs. Concerning him, Scripture says, What wrong did your fathers find in me that they went far from me.

C.   "Said the Holy One, blessed be he, to the Israelites, 'My children, your fathers found no wrong with me, but you have found wrong with me.

D.   "'The first Man found no wrong with me, but you have found wrong with me.'

E.   "To what may the first Man be compared?

F.   "To a sick man, to whom the physician came. The physician said to him, 'Eat this, don't eat that.'

G.   "When the man violated the instructions of the physician, he brought about his own death.

H.   "[As he lay dying,] his relatives came to him and said to him, 'Is it possible that the physician is imposing on you the divine attribute of justice?'

I.   "He said to them, 'God forbid. I am the one who brought about my own death. This is what he instructed me, saying to me, 'Eat this, don't eat that,' but when I violated his instructions, I brought about my own death.

J.   "So too all the generations came to the first Man, saying to him, 'Is it possible that the Holy One, blessed be he, is imposing the attribute of justice on you?'

L.   "He said to them, 'God forbid. I am the one who has brought about my own death. Thus did he command me, saying to me, Of all the trees of the garden you mate eat, but of the tree of the knowledge of good and evil you may not eat (Gen. 2:17). When I violated his instructions, I brought about my own death, for it is written, On the day on which you eat it, you will surely die (Gen. 2:17).'

M.   "[God's speech now continues:] 'Pharaoh found no wrong with me, but you have found wrong with me.'

N.   "To what may Pharaoh be likened?

O.   "To the case of a king who went overseas and

went and deposited all his possessions with a member of his household. After some time the king returned from overseas and said to the man, 'Return what I deposited with you.'

P. "He said to him, 'I did not such thing with you, and you left me nothing.'

Q. "What did he do to him? He took him and put him in prison.

R. "He said to him, 'I am your slave. Whatever you left with me I shall make up to you.'

S. "So, at the outset, said the Holy One, blessed be he, to Moses, Now go and I shall send you to Pharaoh (Ex. 3:10).

T. "That wicked man said to him, Who is the Lord that I should listen to his voice? I do not know the Lord (Ex. 2:5).

U. "But when he brought the ten plagues on him, The Lord is righteous and I and my people are wicked (Ex. 9:27).

V. "[God's speech now continues:] 'Moses found no wrong with me, but you have found wrong with me.'

W. "To what may Moses be compared?

X. "To a king who handed his son over to a teacher, saying to him, 'Do not call my son a moron."

Y. What is the meaning of the word moron?

Z. Said R. Reuben, "In the Greek language they call an idiot a moron."

AA. [Resuming the discourse:] "One time the teacher belittled the boy and called him a moron. Said the king to him, 'With all my authority I instructed you, saying to you, Do not call my son a fool,' and yet you have called my son a fool. It is not the calling of a smart fellow to go along with fools. [You're fired!]'

BB. "Thus it is written, And the Lord spoke to Moses and to Aaron and commanded them concerning the children of Israel (Ex. 6:13).

CC. "What did he command them? He said to them, 'Do not call my sons morons.' But when they rebelled them at the waters of rebellion, Moses said to them, Listen, I ask, you morons (Num. 20:10).

DD. "Said the Holy One, blessed be he, to them,

'With all my authority I instructed you, saying to you, Do not call my sons fools,' and yet you have called my sons fools. It is not the calling of a smart fellow to go along with fools. [You're fired!]'

EE. "What is written is not You [singular] therefore shall not bring, but you [plural] therefore shall not bring (Num. 20:12). [For God said,] 'Neither you nor your brother nor your sister will enter the Land of Israel.'

FF. "[God's speech now continues:] Said the Holy One, blessed be he, to Israel, 'Your fathers in the wilderness found no wrong with me, but you have found wrong with me.'

GG. "'I said to them, One who makes an offering to other gods will be utterly destroyed (Ex. 22:19), but they did not do so, but rather, They prostrated themselves to it and worshipped it (Ex. 32:8).

HH. "After all the wicked things that they did, what is written, And the Lord regretted the evil that he had considered doing to his people (Ex. 32:14)."

2.   A.   Said R. Judah bar Simon, "Said the Holy One, blessed be he, to Israel, 'Your fathers in the wilderness found no wrong with me, but you have found wrong with me.'

B.   "'I said to them, For six days you will gather [the Mana] and on the seventh day it is a Sabbath, on which there will be no collecting of Mana (Ex. 16:26).

C.   "'But they did not listen, but rather: And it happened that on the seventh day some of the people went out to gather Mana and did not find it (Ex. 16:27).

D.   "Had they found it, they would have gathered it [and violated his wishes, so he did not give Mana on the seventh day, therefore avoiding the occasion of making them sin].'"

We have yet another perfect example of the Exegetical Form. The sustained and powerful story amplifies the statement, What wrong did your fathers find in me. The point is that the fathers found no fault with God, which makes the

actions of Jeremiah's generation all the more inexplicable.
The movement from the first Man to Pharaoh, then Moses
and Aaron, leads then to Israel, and the complaint is remarkably apt: it has to do with the forty years in the wilderness, to which Jeremiah makes reference! So the story-teller
has dealt with both parts of the complaint. First, the fathers
found no fault with their punishment, that is, the forty years
they were left to die in the wilderness, and, second, the forty
years were a mark of grace. So complaining against God is
without rhyme or reason. I cannot imagine a better example
of a sustained amplification, through exegesis of intersecting
verses, parables, and syllogisms, of the basic proposition.
While implicit, that proposition could not come to more explicit demonstration than it does in this exquisite composition.

> XIV:VI
> 1. A. ...they went far from me and went after
> worthlessness and became worthless? (Jer. 2:5)
> B. Said R. Phineas in the name of R. Hoshaiah,
> "For they would drive out those who did return to
> God.
> C. "That is in line with this verse of Scripture:
> Therefore I chased him away from me (Neh. 13:28),
> [Braude and Kapstein, p. 272 add: they chased away
> and made go far from me those who would have re-
> turned to me]."

The exegetical form characterizes this exposition of a
further clause in the base verse. The exegesis of a clause of
the base verse imparts to the message a still deeper dimension. The basic proposition seems to me the same as before.

> XIV:VI
> 1. A. ...and went after worthlessness and became
> worthless? (Jer. 2:5):
> B. Said R. Isaac, "The matter may be compared

to the case of a banker, against whom a debit was is-
sued, and he was afraid, saying, 'Is it possible that the
debit is for a hundred gold coins or two hundred gold
coins.'

C.   "Said the creditor to him, 'Do not fear, it covers only a kor of bran and barley, and in any event it's
already been paid off.'

D.   "So said the Holy One, blessed be he, to Israel, My children, as to the idolatry after which you lust,
it is nothing of substance, but they are naught, a work
of delusion (Jer. 10:15).

E.   "But not like these is the portion of Jacob, for
he is the creator of all things, Israel are the tribes of his
inheritance; the Lord of hosts is his name (Jer. 10:16)."

The conclusion turns the final clause on its head.
Since the Israelites went after what was worthless, it is easy
for God to forgive them, and God does forgive them. This is
fresh, but it does not change the formal pattern: the base
verse is systematically worked out.

Clearly, the entire Pisqa' works out its implicit proposition through first the intervention of a contrastive verse,
which imparts to the base verse the fundamental proposition
to be expounded, and then the systematic exposition of the
base verse, which reads the implicit proposition into — but
also in terms of — that verse. We proceed to the second of
the three test-Pisqa'ot.

XXII:I
1.   A.   It is written, Will you not revive us again [that
your people may rejoice in you? Show us your steadfast
love, O Lord, and grant us your salvation] (Ps. 85:6-7):

B.   Said R. Aha, "May your people and your city
rejoice in you."

2.   A.   And Sarah said, God has made joy for me;
everyone who hears will rejoice with me (Gen. 21:6):

B.   R. Yudan, R. Simon, R. Hanin, R. Samuel bar
R. Isaac: "If Reuben is happy, what difference does it

make to Simeon? So too, if Sarah was remembered, what difference did it make to anyone else? For lo, our mother Sarah says, everyone who hears will rejoice with me (Gen. 21:6).

C. "But this teaches that when our mother, Sarah, was remembered, with her many barren women were remembered, with her all the deaf had their ears opened, with her all the blind had their eyes opened, with her all those who had lost their senses regained their senses. So everyone was saying, 'Would that our mother, Sarah, might be visited a second time, so that we may be visited with her!'

D. [Explaining the source common joy,] R. Berekhiah in the name of R. Levi said, "She added to the lights of the heavens. The word making ['God has made joy'] is used here and also in the following verse: And God made the two lights (Gen. 1:16). Just as the word making used elsewhere has the sense of giving light to the world, so the word making used here has the sense of giving light to the world."

E. "The word 'making' ['God has made joy'] is used here and also in the following verse: And he made a release to the provinces (Est. 2:18).

F. "Just as the word 'making;' used there indicates that a gift had been given to the entire world, so the word 'making;' used there indicates that a gift had been given to the entire world."

3. A. R. Berekhiah in the name of R. Levi: "You find that when our mother, Sarah, gave birth to Isaac, all the nations of the world said, 'God forbid! It is not Sarah that has given birth to Isaac, but Hagar, handmaiden of Sarah, is the one who gave birth to him.'

B. "What did the Holy One, blessed be he, do? He dried up the breasts of the nations of the world, and their noble matrons came and kissed the dirt at the feet of Sarah saying to her, 'Do a religious duty and give suck to our children.'

C. "Our father, Abraham, said to her, 'This is not a time for modesty, but [now, go forth, and] sanctify the name of the Holy One, blessed be he, by sitting [in public] in the market place and there giving suck to children.'

D. "That is in line with the verse: Will Sarah give such to children (Gen. 21:7).

E. "What is written is not, to a child, but, to children.

F. "And is it not an argument a fortiori: if in the case of a mortal, to whom rejoicing comes, the person rejoices and gives joy to everyone, when the Holy One, blessed be he, comes to give joy to Jerusalem, all the more so!

G. "I will greatly rejoice in the Lord [my soul shall exult in my God; for he has clothed me with the garments of salvation, he has covered me with the robe of righteousness, as a bridegroom decks himself with a garland, and as a bride adorns herself with her jewels. For as the earth brings forth its shoots, and as a garden causes what is sown in it to spring up, so the Lord God will cause righteousness and praise to spring forth before all the nations] (Isaiah 61:10-11)."

The implicit syllogism maintains that when Jerusalem rejoices, everyone will have reason to join in. That point links the clause, "praise to spring forth before all the nations" to the statement, I will greatly rejoice in the Lord. It is at No. 2 that the proposition emerges, even though the contrastive verse, Ps. 85:6-7, comes first. I do not regard the pericope as a good example of the contrast verse-base verse form, even though the implicit proposition is very powerfully expounded.

XXII:II

1. A. This is the day which the Lord has made; let us rejoice and be glad in it (Ps. 118:24):

B. Said R. Abin, "But do we not know in what to rejoice, whether in the day or in the Holy One, blessed be he? But Solomon came along and explained, We shall rejoice in you: in you, in your Torah, in you, in your salvation."

2.   A.   Said R. Isaac, "In you (BK) [the Hebrew letters of which bear the numerical value of twenty-two, hence:] — in the twenty-two letters which you have used in writing the Torah for us.

B.   "The B has the value of two, and the K of twenty."

3.   A.   For we have learned in the Mishnah:

B.   If one has married a woman and lived with her for ten years and not produced a child, he is not allowed to remain sterile [but must marry someone else]. If he has divorced her, he is permitted to marry another. The second is permitted to remain wed with her for ten years. If she had a miscarried, one counts from the time of the miscarriage. The man bears the religious duty of engaging in procreation but the woman does not. R. Yohanan b. Beroqah says, "The religious duty pertains to them both, for it is said, And God blessed them (Gen. 1:28)" [M. Yeb. 15:6].

4.   A.   There was a case in Sidon of one who married a woman and remained with her for ten years while she did not give birth.

B.   They came to R. Simeon b. Yohai to arrange for the divorce. He said to her, "Any thing which I have in my house take and now go, return to your father's household."

C.   Said to them R. Simeon b. Yohai, "Just as when you got married, it was in eating and drinking, so you may not separate from one another without eating and drinking."

D.   What did the woman do? She made a splendid meal and gave the husband too much to drink and then gave a sign to her slave-girl and said to her, "Bring him to my father's house."

E.   At midnight the man woke up. He said to them, "Where am I?"

F.   She said to him, "Did you not say to me, 'Any thing which I have in my house, take and now go, return to your father's household.' And that is how it is: I have nothing more precious than you."

G. When R. Simeon b. Yohai heard this, he said a prayer for them, and they were visited [with a pregnancy].

H. The Holy One, blessed be he, visits barren women, and the righteous have the same power.

I. "And is it not an argument a fortiori: if in the case of a mortal, to whom rejoicing comes, the person rejoices and gives joy to everyone, when the Holy One, blessed be he, comes to give joy to Jerusalem, all the more so! And when Israel looks forward to the salvation of the Holy One, blessed be he, all the more so!

J. "I will greatly rejoice in the Lord [my soul shall exult in my God; for he has clothed me with the garments of salvation, he has covered me with the robe of righteousness, as a bridegroom decks himself with a garland, and as a bride adorns herself with her jewels. For as the earth brings forth its shoots, and as a garden causes what is sown in it to spring up, so the Lord God will cause righteousness and praise to spring forth before all the nations] (Isaiah 61:10-11)."

The contrastive verse at No. 1 expresses a rather general interest in the theme of rejoicing. No. 2 carries forward the opening element. The implicit syllogism is that when one rejoices, so does the other, however, and that is the main point of Nos. 1, 2, and is made explicit. No. 3 leads us into No. 4, which is the goal of the framer of the whole, since 4.I states precisely what the syllogism wishes to maintain.

XXII:III

1. A. The matter may be compared to the case of a noble lady, whose husband, sons, and sons-in-law went overseas. They told her, "Your sons are coming."

B. She said to them, "My daughters-in-law will rejoice."

C. "Here come your sons-in-law!"

D. "My daughters will rejoice."

E. When they said to her, "Here comes your husband," she said to them, "Now there is occasion for complete rejoicing."

    F.   So to, the former prophets say to Jerusalem, "Your sons come from afar (Is. 60:4)."

    G.   And she says to them, "Let Mount Zion be glad (Ps. 48:12)."

    H.   "Your daughters are carried to you on uplifted arms (Is. 60:4)."

    I.   "Let the daughters of Judah rejoice (Ps. 48:12)."

    J.   But when they say to her, "Behold your king comes to you (Zech. 9:9)," then she will say to him, "Now there is occasion for complete rejoicing."

    K.   I will greatly rejoice in the Lord [my soul shall exult in my God; for he has clothed me with the garments of salvation, he has covered me with the robe of righteousness, as a bridegroom decks himself with a garland, and as a bride adorns herself with her jewels. For as the earth brings forth its shoots, and as a garden causes what is sown in it to spring up, so the Lord God will cause righteousness and praise to spring forth before all the nations] (Isaiah 61:10-11)

The rhetorical pattern shifts. There is no pretense at commencing with a contrastive verse. The parable forces our attention on the base verse, with its statement, I in particular shall rejoice. So we deal with an exegetical form, in which the parabolic medium is used for the delivery of the exegetical message. The next component of the Pisqa' follows suit.

XXII:IV

1.   A.   The matter may be compared to the case of an orphan-girl who was raised in a palace. When the time came for her to be married, they said to her, "Do you have [for a dowry] anything at all?"

    B.   She said to them, "I do indeed: I have an inheritance from father and I have an inheritance from my grandfather."

    C.   So Israel has the merit left to them by Abraham, and they have the inheritance of our father Jacob:

    D.   He has clothed me with garments of salvation

(Is. 61:10) on account of the merit left by our father, Jacob: And the hides of the offspring of goats she wrapped on his hands (Gen. 27:16).

E. He has covered me with the robe of right-eousness (Is. 61:10) refers to the merit left by our father, Abraham: I have known him to the end that he may command his children...to do righteousness (Gen. 16:19).

F. ...as a bridegroom decks himself with a gar-land, and as a bride adorns herself with her jewels (Isaiah 61:10-11):

G. You find that when the Israelites stood at Mount Sinai, they bedecked themselves like a bride, opening one and closing another eye [as a sign of mod-esty (Mandelbaum), and that merit the Israelites be-queathed to their children as well].

The next stage in the unfolding of discourse, that is the exposition of the clauses of our base verse leads to yet another parable. The parable now underlines the Israelites' merit in expecting God's renewed relationship with them, this time deriving from Abraham, Jacob, and the whole of Israel at Sinai. The formal character of the parable is familiar in our document: first the general statement of matters, then the specific restatement in terms of Israel in particular.

The final component of the Pisqa' — third in line in formal types — presents us with a different rhetorical pattern entirely. In what follows, the base verse of our Pisqa' plays no important role at all. Rather, the pericope is built upon a syl-logism proved through a set of examples, that is, an exercise in list-making science. The syllogism is explicit, not implicit, and it has no important relationship to the Pisqa' at hand. The pericope is tacked on at the end only because our base verse occurs in it. And yet, it must be added, the syllogism of the list is in general entirely congruent with the implicit syllo-gism before us.

XXII:V

1. A. In ten passages the Israelites are referred to as a bride, six by Solomon, three by Isaiah, and one by Jeremiah:

B. Six by Solomon: Come with me from Lebanon, my bride (Song 4:8), you have ravished my heart, my sister, my bride (Song 4:9), how beautiful is your love, my sister, my bride (Song 4:10), your lips drip honey, my bride (Song 4:11), a locked garden is my sister, my bride (Song 4:12), and I am come into my garden, my sister my bride (Song 5:1).

C. Three by Isaiah: You shall surely clothe you with them as with an ornament and gird yourself with them as a bride (Is. 49:18), the present verse, as a bridegroom decks himself with a garland, and as a bride adorns herself with her jewels (Isaiah 61:10-11), and As the bridegroom rejoices over the bride (Is. 62:5).

D. One by Jeremiah: The voice of joy and the voice of gladness, the voice of the bridegroom and the voice of the bride (Jer. 33:11).

E. Corresponding to the ten passages in which Israel is spoken of as a bride, there are ten places in Scripture in which the Holy One clothed himself in a garment appropriate to each occasion:

F. On the day on which he created the world, the first garment which the Holy One, blessed be he, put on was one of glory and majesty: You are clothed with glory and majesty (Ps. 104:1).

G. The second garment, one of power, which the Holy One, blessed be he, put on was to exact punishment for the generation of the flood: the Lord reigns, he is clothed with power (Ps. 93:1).

H. The third garment, one of strength, which the Holy One, blessed be he, put on was to give the Torah to Israel: the Lord is clothed, he has girded himself with strength (Ps. 93:1).

I. The fourth garment, a white one, which the Holy One, blessed be he, put on was to exact punishment from the kingdom of Babylonia: his raiment was as white snow (Dan. 7:9).

J. The fifth garment, one of vengeance, which

the Holy One, blessed be he, put on was to exact
vengeance from the kingdom of Media: He put on
garments of vengeance for clothing and was clad with
zeal as a cloak (Is. 59:17). Lo, here we have two [venge-
ance, zeal].

K. The seventh garment, one of righteousness
and vindication, which the Holy One, blessed be he,
put on was to exact vengeance from the kingdom of
Greece: He put on righteousness as a coat of mail and a
helmet of deliverance upon his head (Is. 59:17). Here
we have two more [coat of mail, helmet].

L. The ninth garment, one of red, which the
Holy One, blessed be he, put on was to exact vengeance from the kingdom of Edom [playing on the letters
that spell both Edom and red]: Why is your apparel red
(Is. 63:2).

M. The tenth garment, one of glory, which the
Holy One, blessed be he, put on was to exact vengeance from Gog and Magog: This one that is the most
glorious of his apparel (Is. 63:1).

N. Said the community of Israel before the Holy
One, blessed be he, "Of all the garments you have none
more beautiful than this, as it is said, the most glorious
of his apparel (Is. 63:1)."

The composition has been worked out in its own
terms and is inserted here only because of the appearance of
our base verse as a proof-text.

III.   PESIQTA DERAB KAHANA 27 = LEVITI-
CUS RABBAH 30

Now that we have worked out way through two
Pisqa'ot that are distinctive to Pesiqta deRab Kahana, we turn
to one of those that are shared with Leviticus Rabbah. The
point for my argument is simple. If documentary lines register, then we should be able to show that a given Pisqa' conforms to the preferences of one of the two distinct docu-

ments in which it occurs. If, specifically, my hypothesis concerning the rhetorical singularity of Pesiqta deRab Kahana is sound, then we should find the formal patterns that serve the one document out of phase with those that serve the other document.

What is particular to the rhetorical plan of Pesiqta deRab Kahana, specifically, is the Propositional Form, in which the implicit syllogism is both defined and then stated through the intervention of an contrastive verse into the basic proposition established by the base verse. My analysis of the rhetorical plan of Leviticus Rabbah repeatedly produced the observation that the intersecting verse in that document was subjected to systematic and protracted exegesis *in its own terms* and not in terms of the proposition to be imputed, also, to the base verse at the end. By contrast, in Pesiqta deRab Kahana the contrastive verse, which forms the counterpart to what I called the intersecting verse in Leviticus Rabbah, is not subjected to sustained and systematic exegesis in its own terms. Quite to the contrary, as we have now seen many times, the contrastive verse serves for the sole purpose of imposing upon the base verse a very particular proposition, which then is repeated through a sequence of diverse contrastive verses, on the one side, and also through a sustained reading of the successive components of the base verse, on the other. We come then to a shared Pisqa' and pay close attention to how the contrastive/intersecting verse is treated.

XXVII:I

1. A. R. Abba bar Kahana commenced [discourse by citing the following verse]: Take my instruction instead of silver, [and knowledge rather than choice gold] (Prov. 8:10)."

B. Said R. Abba bar Kahana, "Take the instruction of the Torah instead of silver.

C. "Take the instruction of the Torah and not silver.

D. "Why do you weigh out money? Because there is no bread (Is. 55:2).

E. "'Why do you weigh out money to the sons of Esau [Rome]? [It is because] there is no bread, because you did not sate yourselves with the bread of the Torah.

F. "And [why] do you labor? Because there is no satisfaction (Is. 55:2).

G. "Why do you labor while the nations of the world enjoy plenty? Because there is no satisfaction, that is, because you have not sated yourselves with the bread of the Torah and with the wine of the Torah.

H. "For it is written, Come, eat of my bread, and drink of the wine I have mixed (Prov. 9:5)."

2. A. R. Berekhiah and R. Hiyya, his father, in the name of R. Yosé b. Nehorai: "It is written, I shall punish all who oppress him (Jer. 30:20), even those who collect funds for charity [and in doing so, treat people badly], except [for those who collect] the wages to be paid to teachers of Scripture and repeaters of Mishnah traditions.

B. "For they receive [as a salary] only compensation for the loss of their time, [which they devote to teaching and learning rather than to earning a living].

C. "But as to the wages [for carrying out] a single matter in the Torah, no creature can pay the [appropriate] fee in reward."

3. A. It has been taught on Tannaite authority: On the New Year, a person's sustenance is decreed [for the coming year],

B. except for what a person pays out [for food in celebration] of the Sabbath, festivals, the celebration of the New Month,

C. and for what children bring to the house of their master [as his tuition].

D. If he adds [to what is originally decreed], [in Heaven] they add to his [resources], but if he deducts [from what he should give], [in Heaven] they deduct [from his wealth]. [Margulies, Vayyiqra Rabbah, p. 688,

n. to 1. 5, links this statement to Prov. 8:10.]

4. A. R. Yohanan was going up from Tiberias to Sepphoris. R. Hiyya bar Abba was supporting him. They came to a field. He said, "This field once belonged to me, but I sold it in order to acquire merit in labor in the Torah."

B. They came to a vineyard, and he said, "This vineyard once belonged to me, but I sold it in order to acquire merit in labor in the Torah."

C. They came to an olive grove, and he said, "This olive grove once belonged to me, but I sold it in order to acquire merit in labor in the Torah."

D. R. Hiyya began to cry.

E. Said R. Yohanan, "Why are you crying?"

F. He said to him, "It is because you left nothing over to support you in your old age."

G. He said to him, "Hiyya, my disciple, is what I did such a light thing in your view? I sold something which was given in a spell of six days [of creation] and in exchange I acquired something which was given in a spell of forty days [of revelation].

H. "The entire world and everything in it was created in only six days, as it is written, For in six days the Lord made heaven and earth (Ex. 20:11)

I. "But the Torah was given over a period of forty days, as it was said, And he was there with the Lord for forty days and forty nights (Ex. 34:28). [Leviticus Rabbah adds: And it is written, And I remained on the mountain for forty days and forty nights (Deut. 9:9).]"

5. A. When R. Yohanan died, his generation recited concerning him [the following verse of Scripture]: If a man should give all the wealth of his house for the love (Song 8:7), with which R. Yohanan loved the Torah, he would be utterly destitute (Song 8:7).

B. When R. Abba bar Hoshaiah of Tiria died, they saw his bier flying in the air. His generation recited concerning him [the following verse of Scripture]: If a man should give all the wealth of his house for the love,

with which the Holy One, blessed be he, loved Abba
bar Hoshaiah of Tiria, he would be utterly destitute
(Song 8:7).

C. When R. Eleazar b. R. Simeon died, his generation recited concerning him [the following verse of
Scripture]: Who is this who comes up out of the wilderness like pillars of smoke, perfumed with myrrh and
frankincense, with all the powders of the merchant?
(Song 3:6).

D. What is the meaning of the clause, With all the
powders of the merchant?

E. [Like a merchant who carries all sorts of de-
sired powders,] he was a master of Scripture, a repeater
of Mishnah traditions, a writer of liturgical supplica-
tions, and a poet.

6. A. Another interpretation of the verse, Take my
instruction instead of silver, [and knowledge rather than
choice gold] (Prov. 8:10): Said R. Abba bar Kahana,
"On the basis of the reward paid for one act of taking,
you may assess the reward for [taking] the palm branch
[on the festival of Tabernacles].

B. "There was an act of taking in Egypt: You will
take a bunch of hyssop (Ex. 12:22).

C. "And how much was it worth? Four manehs.,
maybe five.

D. "Yet that act of taking is what stood up for Israel [and so made Israel inherit] the spoil of Egypt, the
spoil at the sea, the spoil of Sihon and Og, and the spoil
of the thirty-one kings.

E. "Now the palm-branch, which costs a person
such a high price, and which involves so many religious
duties — how much the more so [will a great reward be
forthcoming on its account]!"

F. Therefore Moses admonished Israel, saying to
them, [On the fifteenth day of the seventh month,
when you have gathered in the produce of the land, you
shall keep the feast of the Lord seven days...] And you
shall take on the first day [the fruit of goodly trees,
branches of palm trees and boughs of leafy trees and
willows of the brook; and you shall rejoice before the

Lord your God seven days. You shall keep it as a feast to the Lord seven days in the year; it is a statute for ever throughout your generations; you shall keep it in the seventh month. You shall dwell in booths for seven days; all that are native in Israel shall dwell in booths, that your generations may know that I made the people of Israel dwell in booths when I brought them out of the land of Egypt: I am the Lord your God (Leviticus 23:39-43).

The notion of an implicit syllogism seems to me not to apply at all, since the point of interest of No. 1 is simply that study of the Torah is the source of Israel's sustenance. The theme of the intervening passages is established at 1.B, namely, Torah and the value and importance of study of Torah. Nos. 2, 3, 4, and 5 all present variations on amplifications of that theme. No. 2 makes that same point. No. 3 complements it, as do Nos. 3, 4, 5. Only at No. 6 do we revert to the intersecting verse/contrastive verse, which is now brought to bear upon our base verse to make the point that the reward for "taking" is considerable, hence the taking of the fruit of goodly trees will produce a reward. That point is totally out of phase with the syllogism of Nos. 1-5, and therefore the rhetorical program at hand is not one in which the contrastive verse is interpreted solely and finally to impute meaning to the base verse and so to yield an implicit proposition. The rhetorical plan yields two points, one about the study of the Torah, which is irrelevant to our base verse, the other about the reward for taking the species of the Festival, which is, then the main point. As I said above, it is only at No. 6 that Lev. 23:39 — with stress on the word "take" — recurs.

XXVII:II

1.   A.   You show me the path of life, [in your presence] there is fullness of joy (Ps. 16:11).

B.   Said David before the Holy One, blessed be he, "Lord of the ages, show me the open gateway to the life of the world to come."

    C.   R.. Yudan and R. Azariah:

    D.   R. Yudan said, "David said before the Holy One, blessed be he, 'Lord of the ages, Show me the path of life.'

    E.   "Said the Holy One, blessed be he, to David, 'If you seek life, look for fear, as it is said, The fear of the Lord prolongs life (Prov. 10:27)."

    F.   R. Azariah said, "[The Holy One, blessed be he], said to David, 'If you seek life, look for suffering (YYSWRYN), as it is said, The reproofs of discipline (MWSR) are the way of life (Prov. 6:23)." [Leviticus Rabbah adds: Rabbis say, "The Holy One, blessed be he, said to David, 'David, if you seek life, look for Torah,' as it is said, It is a tree of life to those that hold fast to it (Prov. 3:18)." R. Abba said, "David said before the Holy One, blessed be he, 'Lord of the ages, Show me the path of life.' Said to him the Holy One, blessed be he, 'Start fighting and exert yourself! Why are you puzzled? [Lieberman, in Margulies, Vayyiqra Rabbah, p. 880, to p. 692]. Work and eat: Keep my commandments and live (Prov. 4:4)."]

2.   A.   The fullness (SWB') of joy in your presence (Ps. 16:11):

    B.   Satisfy (SB'NW) us with five joys in your presence: Scripture, Mishnah, Talmud, Supplements, and Lore.

3.   A.   Another matter: In your presence is the fullness of joy (Ps. 16:11):

    B.   Read not fullness (SWB') but seven (SB'). These are the seven groups of righteous men who are going to receive the face of the Presence of God.

    C.   And their face is like the sun, moon, firmament, stars, lightning, lilies, and the pure candelabrum that was in the house of the sanctuary.

    D.   How do we know that it is like the sun? As it is said, Clear as the sun (Song 6:10).

    E.   How do we know that it is like the moon? As it is said, As lovely as the moon (Song 6:10).

F. How do we know that it is like the firmament? As it is said, And they that are wise shall shine as the brightness of the firmament (Dan. 12:3).

G. How do we know that it is like the stars? As it is said, And they that turn the many to righteousness as the stars forever and ever (Dan. 12:3).

H. And how do we know that it is like the lightning? As it is said, Their appearance is like torches, they run to and fro like lightning (Nah. 2:5).

I. How do we know that it is like lilies? As it is said, For the leader: upon the lilies (Ps. 69:1).

J. How do we know that it will be like the pure candelabrum of the house of the sanctuary? As it is said, And he said to me, What do you see? And I said, I looked and behold [there was] a candelabrum all of gold (Zech. 4:2).

4. A. At your right hand is bliss for evermore (Ps. 16:11).

B. Said David before the Holy One, blessed be he, "Lord of the ages, now who will tell me which group [among those listed above] is the most beloved and blissful of them all?"

C. There were two Amoras [who differed on this matter]. One of them said, "It is the group that comes as representative of the Torah and commandments, as it is said, With a flaming fire at his right hand (Deut. 33:2)."

D. And the other said, "This refers to the scribes, the Mishnah repeaters, and those who teach children in their fear, who are going to sit at the right hand of the Holy One, blessed be he.

E. "That is in line with the following verse of Scripture: I keep the Lord always before me, because he is at my right hand, I shall not be moved (Ps. 16:8)."

5. A. Another matter concerning the verse You show me the path of life, in your presence there is fullness of joy, in your right hand are pleasures for evermore (Ps. 16:11): In your presence there is fullness (SWB') of joy (Ps. 16:11):

B. [Leviticus Rabbah adds: Read only "seven (SB') joys."] These are the seven religious duties associated with the Festival [Tabernacles].

C. These are they: the four species that are joined in the palm branch, [the building of] the Tabernacle, [the offering of] the festal sacrifice, [the offering of] the sacrifice of rejoicing.

6. A. If there is the offering of the sacrifice of rejoicing, then why is there also the offering of the festal sacrifice? And if there is [the offering of] the festal sacrifice, then why also is there [the offering of] the sacrifice of rejoicing?

B. Said R. Abin, "The matter may be compared to two who came before a judge. Now we do not know which one of them is the victor. But it is the one who takes the palm branch in his hand who we know to be the victor.

C. "So is the case of Israel and the nations of the world. The [latter] come and draw an indictment before the Holy One, blessed be he, on the New Year, and we do not know which party is victor.

E. "But when Israel goes forth from before the Holy One, blessed be he, with their palm branches and their citrons in their hands, we know that it is Israel that are the victors."

F. Therefore Moses admonishes Israel, saying to them, [On the fifteenth day of the seventh month, when you have gathered in the produce of the land, you shall keep the feast of the Lord seven days...] And you shall take on the first day [the fruit of goodly trees, branches of palm trees and boughs of leafy trees and willows of the brook; and you shall rejoice before the Lord your God seven days. You shall keep it as a feast to the Lord seven days in the year; it is a statute for ever throughout your generations; you shall keep it in the seventh month. You shall dwell in booths for seven days; all that are native in Israel shall dwell in booths, that your generations may know that I made the people of Israel dwell in booths when I brought them out of the land of Egypt: I am the Lord your God (Leviticus 23:39-43).

G.

The intersecting verse — Ps. 16:11 — leads us to the base verse, after a long and majestic sequence of exegeses of the three elements of the intersecting verse. But the implicit syllogism associated with the base verse does not form the sole and principal interest of the exegesis of the intersecting verse/contrastive verse. When we do reach the base verse, the connection turns out to be tight and persuasive. The original repertoire of key words — Torah, commandments, and the like — is reviewed. Nos. 5-6 go over the same verse with respect to Israel, introducing the matter of the New Year, Day of Atonement, and Festival. Then each clause suitably links to the several themes at hand. 6 of course is tacked on, since the composition concludes properly with No. 5, at which point the intersecting verse has reached the base verse.

XXVII:III

1.   A.   He will regard the prayer of the destitute [and will not despise their supplication] (Ps. 102:17):

B.   Said R. Reuben, "We are unable to make sense of David's character. Sometimes he calls himself king, and sometimes he calls himself destitute.

C.   "How so? When he foresaw that righteous men were going to come from him, such as Asa, Jehoshaphat, Hezekiah, and Josiah, he would call himself king as it is said, Give the king your judgments, O God (Ps. 72:1).

D.   "When he foresaw that wicked men would come forth from him, for example, Ahaz, Manasseh, and Amon, he would call himself destitute, as it is said, A prayer of one afflicted, when he is faint [and pours out his complaint before the Lord] (Ps. 102:1)."

2. A. R. Alexandri interpreted the cited verse He will regard the prayer of the destitute [and will not despise their supplication] (Ps. 102:17) to speak of a worker: "[Margulies, ad loc., explains: The one afflicted is the worker. The word for faint, 'TP, bears the meaning, cloak oneself, hence in prayer. The worker then has delayed his prayer, waiting for the overseer to leave, at which point he can stop and say his prayer. So he postpones his prayer.] [So Alexandri says], "Just as a worker sits and watches all day long for when the overseer will leave for a bit, so he is late when he says [his prayer], [so David speaks at Ps. 102:1: Hear my prayer, O Lord; let my cry come to you]."

B. "That [interpretation of the word 'TP] is in line with the use in the following verse: And those that were born late belonged to Laban (Gen. 30:42)."

C. What is the meaning of those that were born late?

D. R. Isaac bar Haqolah said, "The ones that tarried."

3. A. [Another interpretation: He will regard the prayer of the destitute [and will not despise their supplication] (Ps. 102:17):] Said R. Simeon b. Laqish, "As to this verse, the first half of it is not consistent with the second half, and vice versa.

B. "If it is to be, 'He will regard the prayer of the destitute [individual],' he should then have said, 'And will not despise his supplication.'

C. "But if it is to be, 'He will not despise their supplication,' then he should have said, 'He will regard the prayer of those who are destitute.'

D. "But [when David wrote,] He will regard the prayer of the individual destitute, this [referred to] the prayer of Manasseh, king of Judah.

E. "And [when David wrote,] He will not despise their supplication, this [referred to] his prayer and the prayer of his fathers.

F. "That is in line with the following verse of Scripture: And he prayed to him, and he was entreated (Y'TR) of him (2 Chron. 33:13)."

G. What is the meaning of the phrase, He was entreated of him?

H. Said R. Eleazar b. R. Simeon, "In Arabia they call a breach an athirta [so an opening was made for his prayer to penetrate to the Throne of God]" (Slotki, p. 385, n. 3).

I. And he brought him back to Jerusalem, his kingdom (2 Chron. 33:13).

J. How did he bring him back?

K. R. Samuel b. R. Jonah said in the name of R. Aha, "He brought him back with a wind.

L. "That is in line with the phrase [in The Prayer], He causes the wind to blow."

M. At that moment: And Manasseh knew that the Lord is God (2 Chron. 33:13). Then Manasseh said, "There is justice and there is a judge."

4. A. R. Isaac interpreted the verse He will regard the prayer of the destitute [and will not despise their supplication] (Ps. 102:17)to speak of these generations which have neither king nor prophet, neither priest nor Urim and Thummim, but who have only this prayer alone.

B. "Said David before the Holy One, blessed be he, 'Lord of the ages, "Do not despise their prayer. Let this be recorded for a generation to come ' (Ps. 102:18).

C. "On the basis of that statement, [we know that] the Holy One, blessed be he, accepts penitents.

D. "So that a people yet unborn may praise the Lord (Ps. 102:18).

E. "For the Holy One, blessed be he, will create them as a new act of creation."

5. A. Another interpretation: Let this be recorded for a generation to come (Ps. 102:18):

B. This refers to the generation of Hezekiah, [Leviticus Rabbah adds: which was tottering toward death].

C. So that a people yet unborn may praise the Lord (Ps. 102:18): for the Holy One, blessed be he, created them in a new act of creation.

6. A. Another interpretation: Let this be recorded for a generation to come (Ps. 102:18):

B. This refers to the generation of Mordecai and Esther, which was tottering toward death.

C. So that a people yet unborn may praise the Lord (Ps. 102:18): for the Holy One, blessed be he, created them in a new act of creation.

7. A. Another interpretation: Let this be recorded for a generation to come (Ps. 102:18):

B. This refers to these very generations [in our own day], which are tottering to death.

C. So that a people yet unborn may praise the Lord (Ps. 102:18):

D. For the Holy One, blessed be he, is going to create them anew, in a new act of creation.

8. A. What do we have to take [in order to reach that end]? Take up the palm branch and citron and praise the Holy One, blessed be he.

B. Therefore Moses admonishes Israel, saying, [On the fifteenth day of the seventh month, when you have gathered in the produce of the land, you shall keep the feast of the Lord seven days...] And you shall take on the first day [the fruit of goodly trees, branches of palm trees and boughs of leafy trees and willows of the brook; and you shall rejoice before the Lord your God seven days. You shall keep it as a feast to the Lord seven days in the year; it is a statute for ever throughout your generations; you shall keep it in the seventh month. You shall dwell in booths for seven days; all that are native in Israel shall dwell in booths, that your generations may know that I made the people of Israel dwell in booths when I brought them out of the land of Egypt: I am the Lord your God (Leviticus 23:39-43).

This is a fine example of how the framers of a pericope of the intersecting verse/base verse classification dwell on the intersecting verse and provide an ample picture of its diverse meanings. The difference between this rhetorical pattern and the one dominant in Pesiqta deRab Kahana proves blatant, since the implicit syllogism to be imputed to the base verse is simply not to be found in any aspect of the intersecting verse/contrastive verse — not at any point! The established pattern — the tripartite exegesis of Ps. 102:17, 18 — is worked out at Nos. 1 (supplemented by Nos. 2 and 3), then Nos. 4-7. Until the very final lines, No. 8, we have no reason at all to associate the exegesis of Ps. 102:17-18 with the theme of the Festival. On the contrary, all of the materials stand autonomous of the present "base verse," and none of them hints at what is to come at the end.

XXVII:IV

1. A. Let the field exult and everything in it. [Then shall all the trees of the wood sing for joy before the Lord, for he comes, for he comes to judge the earth] (Ps. 96:12-13):

B. Let the field exult refers to the world, as it is said, And it came to pass, when they were in the field (Gen. 4:8) [and determined to divide up the world between them].

C. And everything in it refers to creatures.

D. That is in line with the following verse of Scripture: The earth is the Lord's, and all that is in it (Ps. 24:1).

E. Then shall all the trees of the wood sing for joy (Ps. 96:12).

F. Said R. Aha, "The forest and all the trees of the forest.

G. "The forest refers to fruit-bearing trees.

H. "And all the trees of the forest encompasses those trees that do not bear fruit."

I. Before whom? Before the Lord (Ps. 96:14).

J. Why? For he comes on New Year and on the Day of Atonement.

K. To do what? To judge the earth. He will judge the world with righteousness, and the peoples with his truth (Ps. 96:13).

Ps. 96:12-14 supplies direct connections to the theme
of Tabernacles, with its reference to trees of the wood, exul-
tation and rejoicing, judgment, and the like. These topics are
explicitly read into the intersecting verse at the end, but I am
inclined to see the whole as a single and unified construction,
with 1.F-H as an interpolated comment. But the base verse
makes no appearance at all, on the one side, and among the
holy days mentioned, The Festival is not one. So the passage
is included for less than self-evident reasons.

XXVII:V

1. A. I wash my hands in innocence [and go about
your altar, O Lord, singing aloud a song of thanksgiving, and telling all your wondrous deeds] (Ps. 26:6-7):

B. [What I require I acquire] through purchase,
not theft.

C. [Leviticus Rabbah adds:] For we have learned
there: A stolen or dried up palm branch is invalid. And
one deriving from an asherah or an apostate town is invalid (M. Suk. 3:1A-B).

D. And go about your altar, O Lord (Ps. 26:7).

E. That is in line with what we have learned
there: Every day they circumambulate the altar one
time and say, "We beseech you, O Lord, save now. We
beseech you, O Lord, make us prosper now [Ps.
118:25]. R. Judah says, "I and him, save now." On that
day they circumambulate the altar seven times (M. Suk.
4:5).

2. A. Singing aloud a song of thanksgiving (Ps. 26:7)
— this refers to the offerings.

B. And telling all your wondrous deeds (Ps.
26:7):

C. Said R. Abun, "This refers to the Hallel
Psalms [Ps. 113-118], which contain [praise for what
God has done] in the past, also [what he has done] during these generations, as well as what will apply to the
days of the Messiah, to the time of Gog and Magog,

and to the age to come.

    D. "When Israel went forth from Egypt (Ps. 114:1) refers to the past.

    E. "Not for us, O Lord, not for us (Ps. 115:1) refers to the present generations.

    F. "I love for the Lord to hear (Ps. 116:1) refers to the days of the Messiah.

    G. "All the nations have encompassed me (Ps. 118:10) speaks of the time of Gog and Magog.

    H. "You are my God and I shall exalt you (Ps. 118:28) speaks of the age to come."

I see no formal counterpart in Pesiqta deRab Kahana's other Pisqa'ot — those not shared with Leviticus Rabbah — to this rather odd composition. The elements are quite discrete and in no way convey demonstrations of a single syllogism, quite the opposite. No. 1 makes a point distinct from No. 2. "The innocence" of Ps. 26:6 refers to the fact that one must not steal the objects used to carry out the religious duty of the waving of the palm branch at Tabernacles. I assume that the allusion to Tabernacles in Ps. 26:6-7 is found in the referring to circumambulating the altar, such as is done in the rite on that day, as 1.C makes explicit. No. 2 then expands on the cited verse in a different way. To be sure, the Hallel Psalms are recited on Tabernacles, but they serve all other festivals as well. Only No. 1 therefore relates to the established context of Lev. 23:40. It follows that the exegeses of Ps. 26:6-7 were assembled and only then utilized — both the relevant and also the irrelevant parts — for the present purpose. The syllogisms are worked out in terms that are otherwise alien to our document.

    Now we reach the more familiar territory of the clause by clause exegesis of the base verse, with the syllogism imputed through the reading of each of those discrete components. But the intersecting verse/contrastive verse exercises have not yielded a single and paramount syllogism. If my thesis is correct, that the rhetorical preferences of Leviticus Rabbah dominate here and those of Pesiqta deRab Kahana make no impact, then we should uncover no cogent syllogism read consistently into one component after another of the base verse. Rather, we should anticipate quite the opposite, namely, a diverse program of syllogisms, all of them relevant to the established theme, but none of them deeply engaged with any other of them in the set.

For the effect of the contrastive verse/base verse construction is to produce a single syllogism, which then serves to impart to the base verse the meaning that will be discovered everywhere, in each of its details. If we have not been given a syllogism on the foundation of the contrast between the external verse and the base verse, then we also should have no syllogism to emerge from each of the components of the base verse, and a diversity of (thematically appropriate, but syllogistically diverse) propositions should emerge. We shall now see that that is the case. Let me state with emphasis the operative criterion together with the reason for it: *We have been given no implicit syllogism stated through the intervention of an contrastive verse into the basic proposition established by the base verse. We therefore shall discover no implicit syllogism stated through a systematic exegesis of the components of the base verse on their own.*

XXVII:VI

1. A. And you will take for yourselves (Lev. 23:40):

B. R. Hiyya taught, "The act of taking must be accomplished by each and every one of you."

C. "For yourselves" — for every one of you. They must be yours and not stolen.

2. A. Said R. Levi, "One who takes a stolen palm branch — to what is he comparable? To a thief who sat at the cross roads and mugged passersby.

B. "One time a legate came by, to collect the

taxes for that town. [The thug] rose before him and mugged him and took everything he had. After some time the thug was caught and put in prison. The legate heard and came to him. He said to him, 'Give back what you grabbed from me, and I'll argue in your behalf before the king.'

C. "He said to him, 'Of everything that I robbed and of everything that I took, I have nothing except for this rug that is under me, and it belongs to you.'

D. "He said to him, 'Give it to me, and I'll argue in your behalf before the king.'

E. "He said to him, 'Take it.'

F. "He said to him, 'You should know that tomorrow you are going before the king for judgment, and he will ask you and say to you, "Is there anyone who can argue in your behalf," and you may say to him, "I have the legate, Mr. So-and-so, to speak in my behalf," and he will send and call me, and I shall come and argue in your behalf before him.'

G. "The next day they set him up for judgment before the king. The king asked him, saying to him, 'Do you have anyone to argue in your behalf?'

H. "He said to him, 'I have a legate, Mr. So-and-so, to speak in my behalf.'

I. "The king sent for him. He said to him, 'Do you know anything to say in behalf of this man?'

J. "He said to him, 'I do indeed have knowledge. When you sent me to collect the taxes of that town, he rose up before me and mugged me and took everything that I had. That rug that belongs to me gives testimony against him.'

K. "Everyone began to cry out, saying, 'Woe for this one, whose defense attorney has turned into his prosecutor.'

L. "So a person acquires a palm branch to attain merit through it. But if it was a stolen one, [the branch] cries out before the Holy One, blessed be he, 'I am stolen! I am taken by violence.'

M. "And the ministering angels say, 'Woe for this one, whose defense attorney has turned into his prosecutor!'"

The theme of the preceding, the prohibition against using a stolen palm branch, is given two further treatments. Except in a formal way none of this pretends to relate to the specific verses of Lev. 23:40ff., nor do we find an intersecting verse.

XXVII:VII
1. A. On the fifteenth day of the seventh month, when you have gathered the produce of the land, you shall keep the feast of the Lord seven days;] on the first day [shall be a solemn rest] (Lev. 23:40).

B. This in fact is the fifteenth day, yet you speak of the first day!

C. R. Mana of Sheab and R. Joshua of Sikhnin in the name of R. Levi said, "The matter may be compared to the case of a town which owed arrears to the king, so the king went to collect [what was owing]. [When he had reached] ten mils [from the town], the great men of the town came forth and praised him. He remitted a third of their [unpaid] tax. When he came within five mils of the town, the middle-rank people came out and acclaimed him, so he remitted yet another third [of what was owing to him]. When he entered the town, men, women, and children, came forth and praised him. He remitted the whole [of the tax].

D. "Said the king, 'What happened happened. From now on we shall begin keeping books [afresh].'

E. "So on the eve of the New Year, the Israelites repent, and the Holy One, blessed be he, remits a third of their [that is, Israel's] sins. On the ten days of repentance from the New Year to the Day of Atonement outstanding individuals fast, and the Holy One, blessed be he, remits most of their [that is, Israel's] sins. On the Day of Atonement all Israel fasts, so the Holy One, blessed be he, forgives them for all their sins [Leviticus Rabbah: says to Israel, 'What happened happened. From now on we shall begin keeping books afresh].'"

2. A. Said R. Aha, "For with you there is forgive-

ness (Ps. 80:4). From the New Year forgiveness awaits you.

B. "Why so long? So that you may be feared (Ps. 80:4). To put your fear into creatures.

C. "From the Day of Atonement to the Festival, all the Israelites are kept busy with doing religious duties. This one takes up the task of building his tabernacle, that one preparing his palm branches. On the first day of the Festival, all Israel they take their palm branches and citrons in their hand and praise the Holy One, blessed be he. The Holy One, blessed be he, says to them, 'What happened happened. From now on we shall begin keeping books [afresh].'"

D. Therefore Scripture says, On the first day. What is the sense of the first day? It is first in the task of reckoning sins [done in the future[, that is, from the first day of the festival.

Nos. 1 and 2 go over the same matter. It seems to me that Ahab's version puts into concrete terms the basic point of Levi's. 2.D is out of place, since it ignores the antecedent materials and takes as its proof text a formula in no way important in the preceding. There can be no doubt that we have an implicit syllogism, which is that the Festival is an occasion for forgiveness, and that that fact derives from the wording of the base verse. If we were in a composition particular to Pesiqta deRab Kahana, we should now expect further expositions of other clauses of the base verse to demonstrate this same proposition — an important and powerful one. But that is not what we shall now find.

XXVII:VIII

1. A. On the first day (Lev. 23:40):

B. By day and not by night.

C. On the ... day — even on the Sabbath.

D. On the first day — only the first day [of the Festival] overrides the restrictions [of Sabbath rest. When the Sabbath coincides with other than the first day of the Festival, one does not carry the palm branch.]

2. A. [And you shall take . . .] the fruit of a goodly tree [branches of palm trees and boughs of leafy trees and willows of the brook] (Lev. 23:40).

B. R. Hiyya taught, "A tree: the taste of the wood and fruit of which is the same. This is the citron."

C. Goodly (HDR): Ben Azzai said, "[Fruit] that remains [HDR] on its tree from year to year."

D. Aqilas the proselyte translated [HDR] as, "That which dwells by water (Greek: hudor)."

E. Branches of a palm tree (Lev. 23:40): R. Tarfon says, "[As to branch of palm tree (KPWT)], it must be bound. If it was separated, one has to bind it up."

F. Boughs of leafy trees: The branches of which cover over the wood. One has to say, "This is the myrtle."

G. Willows of the brook: I know only that they must come from a brook. How do I know that those that come from a valley or a hill [also are valid]? Scripture says, "And willows of a brook."

H. Abba Saul says, "'And willows of the brook' refers to the requirement that there be two, one willow for the palm branch, and a willow for the sanctuary."

I. R. Ishmael says, "'The fruit of goodly trees' indicates one; 'branches of palm tree' also one; 'boughs of leafy trees,' three; 'willows of the brook,' two. Two [of the myrtles] may have the twigs trimmed at the top, and one may not."

J. R. Tarfon says, "Even all three of them may be trimmed."

We have a mass of exegetical materials, linking laws of the Festival to the verses of Scripture at hand. There is no pretense of interest an any implicit syllogism. Quite to the contrary, we might as well be in the deepest heart of Sifra or Sifré to Numbers, with their rather discrete exposition of verses, clause by clause. No. 1 conducts an inquiry into law, and No. 2 provides a word-for-word exegesis of the cited verse. ages such as the present one in Pesiqta deRab Kahana are few and far between.

XXVII:IX

1. A. R. Aqiba says, "The fruit of goodly (HDR) trees refers to the Holy One, blessed be he, concerning whom it is written, You are clothed with glory and majesty (HDR) (Ps. 104:1).

   B. "Branches of palm trees refers to the Holy One, blessed be he, concerning whom it is written, The Righteous One shall flourish like a palm tree (Ps. 92:13).

   C. "Boughs of leafy trees refers to the Holy One, blessed be he, concerning whom it is written, And he stands among the leafy trees (Zech. 1:8).

   D. "And willows of the brook refers to the Holy One, blessed be he, concerning whom it is written, Extol him who rides upon the willows, whose name is the Lord (Ps. 68:5)."

2. A. Another interpretation: The fruit of goodly (HDR) trees (Lev. 23:40):

   B. This refers to Abraham, whom the Holy One, blessed be he, honored (HDR) with a goodly old age,

   C. as it is said, And Abraham was an old man, coming along in years (Gen. 24:1).

   D. [Leviticus Rabbah adds:] And it is written, And you will honor (HDR) the face of an old man (Lev. 19:32).

   E. Branches (KPWT) of palm trees (Lev. 23:40):

   F. This refers to Isaac, who was tied (KPWT) and bound upon the altar.

   G. And boughs of leafy trees (Lev. 23:40):

   H. This refers to Jacob. Just as a myrtle is rich in leaves, so Jacob was rich in children.

   I. Willows of the brook (Lev. 23:40):

   J. This refers to Joseph. Just as the willow wilts before the other three species do, so Joseph died before his brothers did.

3. A. Another interpretation: The fruit of goodly

tree (Lev. 23:40):

B. This refers to Sarah, whom the Holy One, blessed be he, honored with a goodly old age, as it is said, And Abraham and Sarah were old (Gen. 18:11).

C. Branches of palm trees (Lev. 23:40): this refers to Rebecca. Just as a palm tree contains both edible fruit and thorns, so Rebecca produced a righteous and a wicked son [Jacob and Esau].

D. Boughs of leafy trees (Lev. 23:40): this refers to Leah. Just as a myrtle is rich in leaves, so Leah was rich in children.

E. And willows of the brook (Lev. 23:40): this refers to Rachel. Just as the willow wilts before the other three species do, so Rachel died before her sister.

4. A. Another interpretation: The fruit of goodly trees (Lev. 23:40) refers to the great Sanhedrin of Israel, which the Holy One, blessed be he, honored (HDR) with old age, as it is said, You will rise up before old age (Lev. 19:32).

B. Branches (KPWT) of palm trees (Lev. 23:40): this refers to disciples of sages, who compel (KWPYN) themselves to study Torah from one another.

C. Boughs of leafy trees refers to the three rows of disciples who sit before them.

D. And willows of the brook (Lev. 23:40): this refers to the court scribes, who stand before them, one on the right side, the other on the left, [and write down the opinions of those who vote to acquit and those who vote to convict].

5. A. Another interpretation: The fruit of goodly trees refers to Israel.

B. Just as a citron has both taste and fragrance, so in Israel are people who have [the merit of both] Torah and good deeds.

C. Branches of palm trees (Lev. 23:30): refers to Israel. Just as a palm has a taste but no fragrance, so in Israel are people who have [the merit of] Torah but not of good deeds.

D. Boughs of leafy tree refers to Israel. Just as a

myrtle has a fragrance but no taste, so in Israel are people who have the merit of good deeds but not of Torah.

E.   Willows of the brook refers to Israel. Just as a
willow has neither taste nor fragrance, so in Israel are
those who have the [merit] neither of Torah nor of
good deeds.

F.   Said the Holy One, blessed be he, "Utterly to
destroy them is not possible.

G.   "Rather, let them all be joined together in a
single bond, and they will effect atonement for one another.

H.   "And if you have done so, at that moment I
shall be exalted."

I.   Therefore Moses admonishes Israel: [On the
fifteenth day of the seventh month, when you have
gathered in the produce of the land, you shall keep the
feast of the Lord seven days...] And you shall take on
the first day [the fruit of goodly trees, branches of palm
trees and boughs of leafy trees and willows of the
brook; and you shall rejoice before the Lord your God
seven days. You shall keep it as a feast to the Lord
seven days in the year; it is a statute for ever throughout
your generations; you shall keep it in the seventh
month. You shall dwell in booths for seven days; all
that are native in Israel shall dwell in booths, that your
generations may know that I made the people of Israel
dwell in booths when I brought them out of the land of
Egypt: I am the Lord your God (Leviticus 23:39-43).

The base text is systematically read in line with intersecting verses referring to God. The species are read as sym-
bolizing, in sequence, God, the patriarchs and matriarchs, Torah institutions, and Israel. The powerful result of the exegesis at Nos. 2, 3, is to link the species of the Festival to the patriarchs and matriarchs of Israel. It is continuous with the
foregoing, linking the species to God, and with what is to follow, as the species will be compared to Israel's leadership, on
the one side, as well, finally, to ordinary people, on the other.

The reading of the symbols of the Festival at No. 4 as a parable of Israel's life continues, as noted above, now with reference to the (imaginary) national government. The final exegesis reaches its climax here, concluding, then, with the redactional subscript. The composition follows a single program, beginning to end, as it rehearses the several intersecting realms of Judaic symbol systems. Always at the climax come Torah and good deeds. The base verse in the present composition yields diverse propositions and the notion of an implicit syllogism stated through a systematic exegesis of the components of the base verse on their own has no bearing upon this interesting composition.

> XXVII:X
> 1. A. R. Berekhiah in the name of R. Levi: "[God speaks], 'Through the merit [attained in fulfilling the commandment], And you will take for yourself on the first day . . . (Lev. 23:40), lo, I shall be revealed to you first; I shall exact punishment for you from the first one; I shall build for you first; and bring to you the first one.'"
>   B. "I shall be revealed for you first, as it is said, I the Lord am first (Is. 41:4).
>   C. "I shall exact punishment for you from the first one refers to the wicked Esau, as it is written, And the red one came forth first (Gen. 24:24).
>   D. "And I shall build for you first refers to the house of the sanctuary, concerning which it is written, You throne of glory, on high from the first (Jer. 17:12).
>   E. "And I shall bring to you the first one, namely, the king messiah, concerning whom it is written, The first to Zion I shall give (Is. 41:27)."

The eschatological-salvific character of the Festival is now spelled out in specific detail. Esau, that is, Rome, will be punished, the Temple will be rebuilt, and the Messiah will come, all by virtue of the merit attained in observing the Festival. That all this is fresh and without preparation in the prior components of the Pisqa' requires no demonstration.

IV.   THE SHARED PISQA'/PARASHAH: WHERE DOES IT BELONG?

The upshot may be stated very simply. The formal analysis of the characteristic rhetorical plan of Pesiqta deRab Kahana shows definitive traits: a Pisqa' aims at arguing a single, cogent syllogism, and this is in two rhetorical forms. A Pisqa' in Pesiqta deRab Kahana systematically presents a single syllogism, which is expressed through, first the contrast of an external verse with the base verse — hence, the Propositional Form, in which the implicit syllogism is stated through the intervention of an contrastive verse into the basic proposition established by the base verse, and then through the a systematic exegesis of the components of the base verse on their own, hence through the Exegetical Form. In Leviticus Rabbah's parashah 30 which is also Pesiqta deRab Kahana's Pisqa', we find neither of these forms. Since these forms otherwise characterize our document, that is, Pesiqta deRab Kahana, it follows that Pisqa' 27 does not fit well with the rhetorical program of Pesiqta deRab Kahana, so far as the materials distinctive to our document, viewed whole, define that program.

What is striking is that both components that prove relevant, the intersecting verse-base verse construction of Leviticus Rabbah = the Propositional Form made up of the contrastive verse-base verse construction of Pesiqta deRab Kahana, and also the Exegetical Form shared between both documents, with its clause by clause exegesis of the base verse, prove remarkably disparate.

Since we have traveled a considerable distance from our point of departure, let me now briefly state the results of this exercise.

A. PESIQTA DERAB KAHANA'S AUTHORSHIP RE-
SORTED TO THREE RHETORICAL PATTERNS:

1. The Propositional Form: The implicit syllogism is
stated through the intervention of an contrastive verse into
the basic proposition established by the base verse.
2. The Exegetical Form: The implicit syllogism is
stated through a systematic exegesis of the components of
the base verse on their own.
3. The Syllogistic List: The syllogism is explicit, not
implicit, and is proven by a list of probative examples.

B. THE NATURE OF THESE RHETORICAL PREFERENCES
ALSO SUGGESTS THAT THE ORDER IN WHICH THESE TYPES
OF FORMS OCCUR WILL BE AS JUST NOW GIVEN, FIRST THE
SYLLOGISM GENERATED BY THE INTERSECTION OF THE
CONTRASTING AND BASE VERSES, THEN THE SYLLOGISM
REPEATED THROUGH A SYSTEMATIC READING OF THE
BASE VERSE ON ITS OWN, FINALLY, WHATEVER MISCELLA-
NIES THE FRAMERS HAVE IN HAND (OR LATER COPYISTS
INSERT).

C. WHEN WE COMPARE OUR DOCUMENT WITH AN-
OTHER BY EXAMINING A PISQA' OF PESIQTA DERAB KA-
HANA THAT IS NOT UNIQUE TO THAT COMPOSITION BUT IS
SHARED WITH LEVITICUS RABBAH, WE SEE THAT THE DE-
FINITIVE RHETORICAL TRAITS OF OUR DOCUMENT ALSO
PROVE DISTINCTIVE — AND DIFFER FROM THE RHETORI-
CAL PLAN ELSEWHERE SHOWN TO CHARACTERIZE THAT
OTHER DOCUMENT.

Rhetorical analysis has yielded the proposition that Pesiqta deRab Kahana consists of twenty-eight syllogisms, each

presented in a cogent and systematic way by the twenty-eight Pisqa'ot, respectively. Each Pisqa' contains an implicit proposition, and that proposition may be stated in a simple way. It emerges from the intersection of an external verse with the base verse that recurs through the Pisqa', and then is restated by the systematic dissection of the components of the base verse, each of which is shown to say the same thing as all the others.

The Pisqa' shared with Leviticus Rabbah violates the rhetorical plan characteristic of the twenty-four Pisqa'ot that are unique to Pesiqta deRab Kahana but (as I have shown elsewhere) it conforms with great precision to the rhetorical plan characteristic of all of the parashiyyot of Leviticus Rabbah.

Pisqa'ot of Pesiqta deRab Kahana that are shared with Leviticus Rabbah conform to the rhetorical plan of that Leviticus Rabbah and therefore are primary to Leviticus Rabbah and secondary to Pesiqta deRab Kahana. The reason that the authorship of the latter document has made use of these materials requires explanation as part of the larger syllogistic program of Pesiqta deRab Kahana. Now let us follow the same problem: the shared Pisqa'ot of Pesiqta deRab Kahana and Pesiqta Rabbati.

3.

THE SHARED PISQA' IN PESIQTA DERAB KAHANA AND PESIQTA RABBATI

I.   INTRODUCTION

The form-analytical description of the rhetorical program of a given document establishes clear definitions of the
formal preferences of an authorship — those who compiled
the compositions and composites, perhaps also writing them
for that particular document. That fact is established in Chapter One. If those results are to compel assent, they have to be
tested against other data. But where to continue the exercise?

Were we to take the easy way, we should compare the
formal preferences of Leviticus Rabbah with those of Genesis Rabbah (a work already done, in fact).[2] Those documents
clearly part company from one another, so that were we given
an unidentified Parashah of one or another of the two, we
should have little difficulty in assigning it to its correct documentary home. Variations in readings do not affect that
judgment. And the proportion of the two compilations that is
comprised by autonomous, free-ranging compositions or

---

[2] *Comparative Midrash: The Plan and Program of Genesis Rabbah and Leviticus
Rabbah.* Atlanta, 1986: Scholars Press for Brown Judaic Studies.

composites is negligible, within the qualification established in Chapter One concerning the relationship of Leviticus Rabbah to Pesiqta deRab Kahana. There we have a relationship of intimacy, by reason of the shared rhetorical form, intersecting-verse/base-verse composites. Yet faced with composites shared by both documents, on form-analytical grounds we could easily differentiate the Parashiyyot primary to Leviticus Rabbah from the Pisqa'ot of Pesiqta deRab Kahana. Now we ask, can we repeat the same exercise, with a different document — one that intersects with a familiar compilation? We can indeed, and for that purpose we turn to Pesiqta Rabbati, which carries on a rhetorical tradition beginning with Leviticus Rabbah and continued in Pesiqta deRab Kahana. Here once more, we pursue the project of defining precisely what makes a document distinctive, and that with little regard to the state of the manuscript tradition, on the one side, and to the presence of free-standing pericopes, on the other.

The operative unit is at part x; parts i-ix set the stage.

II. THE LITERARY STRUCTURES OF PESIQTA RABBATI

Documents are defined by their selections of rhetoric, topic, and logic of coherent discourse. Within the rhetorical component of the definitive traits falls the literary structure characteristic of one document and not some other. A literary structure is a set of rules that dictate to an authorship recurrent conventions of expression, organization, or proportion that are extrinsic to the message of the author or authorship. The conventions at hand bear none of the particular burden of the author's personal and particular message, so they are not idiosyncratic. They convey in their context the larger world-view expressed within the writing in which they are used, so they prove systemic and public. That is because a literary structure conforms to rules that impose upon the individual writer a limited set of choices about how he will convey whatever message he has in mind. Or the formal convention will limit an editor or redactor to an equally circumscribed set of alternatives about how to arrange received materials. These conventions then form a substrate of the literary culture that preserves and expresses the world view and way of life of the system at hand.

A structure in a formalized literature such as the Rabbinic sages produced thus will dictate the way in which diverse topics or ideas come to verbal expression. It follows that we cannot know that we have a structure if the text under analysis does not repeatedly resort to the presentation of its message through that disciplined syntactic pattern (or other structure that organizes fixed components of discourse, e.g., materials taken from some other and prior document), external to its message on any given point. And, it follows, quite self-evidently, that we do know that we have a structure when the text in hand repeatedly follows recurrent conventions of expression, organization, or proportion extrinsic to the message of the author. The adjective "recurrent" therefore constitutes a redundancy when joined to the noun "structure." For a structure — in our context, a persistent syntactic pattern, rhetorical preference, logical composition — by definition recurs and characterizes a variety of passages. Like Pesiqta deRab Kahana, Pesiqta Rabbati is comprised and so defined by a determinate set of large-scale literary structures.

How do we know that fact? It is because, when we divide up the undifferentiated columns of words and sentences and point to the boundaries that separate one completed unit of thought or discourse from the next such completed composition, we produce rather sizable statements conforming to a single set of syntactic and other formal patterns. On the basis of what merely appears to us to be pat-

terned or extrinsic to particular meaning and so entirely formal, we cannot allege that we have in hand a fixed, literary
structure. Such a judgment would prove subjective. Nor shall
we benefit from bringing to the text at hand recurrent syntactic or grammatical patterns shown in other texts, even of the
same canon of literature, to define conventions for commu-
nicating ideas in those other texts. Quite to the contrary, we
find guidance in a simple principle: *A text has to define its own
structures for us.*

Its authors do so by repeatedly resorting to a given set
of linguistic patterns and literary conventions — and no others. On the basis of a survey of recurrent choices, we may account for the "why this, not that" of literary forms. On that
same basis of inductive evidence alone we test the thesis that
the authors at hand adhere to a fixed canon of literary forms.
If demonstrably present, we may conclude that these forms
will present an author or editor with a few choices on how
ideas are to be organized and expressed in intelligible —
again, therefore, public — compositions. When, as in the present exercise, we draw together and compare two distinct
documents, each one to begin with has to supply us with evidence on its own literary structures. We conduct a survey in
detail for our sample of Pesiqta Rabbati and then review the
findings already in hand for Pesiqta deRab Kahana.

So we look for large-scale patterns and point to such
unusually sizable compositions as characteristic. Why? Because they recur and define discourse, Pisqa' by Pisqa'. Indeed, as we shall now see, a given Pisqa' is made up of a
large-scale literary structure, which in a moment I shall describe in detail. In all, what I mean when I claim that Pesiqta
Rabbati, like Pesiqta deRab Kahana, is made up of large-scale
literary structures is simple. When we divide a given Pisqa', or
chapter, of Pesiqta Rabbati into its sub-divisions, we find
these sub-divisions stylistically cogent and well-composed,

always conforming to the rules of one out of three possible formal patterns. To identify the structures of the document before us, we had best move first to the analysis of a single Pisqa'. We seek, within that Pisqa', to identify what holds the whole together. The second step then is to see whether we have identified something exemplary, or what is not an example of a fixed and formal pattern, but a phenomenon that occurs in fact only once or at random. For the first exercise, we take up Pisqa' One, and for the second, Two through Five, then Fifteen. I do not cite the texts already translated in the earlier part of this book. A bird's eye view of the whole of Pesiqta Rabbati shows it to be a formally uniform document.

III.   PESIQTA RABBATI PISQA' ONE

First I present the entire Pisqa', then I make my form-analytical remarks.

I:I
1.   A.   May our master instruct us:

B.   In the case of an Israelite who said the blessing for food on the New Moon but forgot and did not make mention of the New Moon [in the recitation of the grace after meals], what does one have to do?

C.   Our masters have taught us:

D   If one has forgotten and not made mention of the New Moon, but, once he has completed reciting the Grace after Meals, remembered on the spot, still having in mind the blessing that he has recited, one does not have to go back to the beginning. But he concludes with a brief blessing at the end, which is as follows: "Blessed are you, Lord, our God, king of the world, who has assigned New Moons to Israel, his people. Blessed are you, Lord, who sanctifies both Israel and the New Moons."

2. A. Simeon b. Abba in the name of R. Yohanan said, "And in reference to the New Moon [in the Grace] one has to say, 'And bestow upon us, Lord our God [the blessing of the festival season].'"

B. Lo, we learn, the New Moons are equivalent to festivals.

C. For it is said, On the day of your rejoicing, and on your festivals, and on your new moons (Num. 10:10).

D. And are New Moons equivalent even to the Sabbath?

E. You may state [the proof of that proposition] as follows:

F. New Moons are equivalent to festivals and the Sabbath. And how do we know that they are, in fact, equivalent to Sabbaths?

G. It is on the basis of what the complementary reading of the prophetic writings [for the New Moon that coincides with the Sabbath] states: ...and month by month at the new moon, week by week on the Sabbath, all mankind shall come to bow down before me (Is. 66:23). [The New Moon is treated as equivalent in importance to the Sabbath.]

The thematic principle of composition is shown by the simple fact that No. 2 has no bearing upon No. 1. The opening unit is autonomous and presents a simple legal question. The liturgical reply does not include a proof-text of any kind. No. 2 then pursues its theological question, on the equivalent importance of the New Moon to the Sabbath. Since no rule of conduct is adduced, the issue is theoretical. Then proof derives from the base-text at hand.

I:II

1. A. Thus did R. Tanhuma commence discourse [citing a Psalm that express sorrow that one cannot go to the Temple on a pilgrim festival]: [As a hind longs for the running streams, so do I long for you, O God.] With my whole being I thirst for God, the living God.

When shall I come to God and appear in his presence? [Day and night, tears are my food; Where is your God?' they ask me all day long. As I pour out my soul in distress, I call to mind how I marched in the ranks of the great to the house of God, among exultant shouts of praise, the clamor of the pilgrims] (Ps. 42:1-4).

B. In respect to this inaugural discourse, [what follows] is the materials that occur at the beginning of the discussion of the passage, After the death of the two sons of Aaron (Lev. 16:1ff).

2. A,. Another matter: With my whole being I thirst for God,

B. specifically [I thirst for the time] when you mete out justice upon the nations of the world,

C. in line with the verse, You shall not curse God [meaning, judges] (Ex. 22:27).

3. A,. Another matter: With my whole being I thirst for God:

B. [I thirst for God specifically, for the time] when you will restore that divinity which you formed of me at Sinai:

C. I said, You are God (Ps. 82:6).

4. A.. Another matter: [With my whole being]I thirst for God:

B. [I thirst for God specifically, for the time] [Mandelbaum:] when You will be cloaked with the power of divinity as You were cloaked in divinity at Sinai]. [Following Braude: I thirst for God specifically for the time when you cloak me in divinity as you cloaked me in divinity at Sinai.]

C. Draw near the end-time and make one alone your divinity in your world: The Lord will be king over the entire earth (Zech. 14:9).

D. That is in line with the exegesis of the statement concerning Jacob: So may God give you dew (Gen. 27:28), [which may be interpreted, May he give you the power of divinity and you take it,] when [therefore] he accepts the power of divinity. [This sustains Braude's reading.]

5. A.. Another matter: With my whole being I thirst for God:

B. who lives and endures for ever and ever.

6. A.. Another matter: With my whole being I thirst for God:

B. who watches over our lives, bringing down rain in its season, and calling up due in its time, for the sake of our lives.

7. A. Another matter: [With my whole being I thirst for God,] the living God.

B. The living God, who lives and endures by his word.

C. Said R. Phineas the priest, son of Hama, "Even though those who carried the promises among the prophets have died, God, who made the promises, lives and endures."

8. A. With my whole being I thirst for God, the living God. When shall I come to God and appear in his presence?

B. Said Israel to him, "Lord of the world, When will you restore to us the glory that we should go up [to the Temple [on the three pilgrim festivals and see the face of the Presence of God?"

C. Said R. Isaac, "Just as they came to see, so they came to be seen, for it is said, 'When shall I come to God and appear in his presence?' "

9. A. Said R. Joshua b. Levi, "Why did they call it 'the Rejoicing of the Place of the Water Drawing'? Because from there they drink of the Holy Spirit" [Gen. R. LXX:VIII.3.E].

10. A. They said, "When will you restore us to that glory!

B. "Lo, how much time has passed since the house of our life [the Temple] was destroyed! Lo, a septennate, lo, a jubilee, lo, seven hundred seventy-seven years [have gone by], and now it is one thousand one hundred and fifty one years [since then].

11. A. When shall I come to God and appear in his presence?

B. He said to them, "My children, in this age how many times a year did you go up for the pilgrim festivals [in each year]? Was it not merely three times a year? But when the end will come, I shall build it, and you will come up not merely three times a year, but every single month [at the new moon], and every Sabbath you will come up."

C. That is in line with this verse: and month by month at the new moon, week by week on the Sabbath, all mankind shall come to bow down before me, says the Lord (Is. 66:22-24). [That is to say, not only on the festivals but on the New Moon and the Sabbath people will bow down before God, just as, at Nos. 8-9, we have said people do on the pilgrim festivals.]

No. 1 is not articulated, but the important contribution is not to be missed. The intersecting verse, which will be fully expounded before being drawn into contact with the base verse, is introduced. The relevance of the intersecting verse cannot be missed. It speaks of the yearning to go to the Temple on a pilgrim festival, and at the end the promise is made that, when the end comes, Israel will go to the Temple not only for pilgrim festivals, but also for the New Moon and the Sabbath. That eschatological reading of the New Moon, in particular, then is fully articulated in the exposition of the intersecting verse. Nos. 2, 3, 4 speak of the I, Israel, yearning to gain that union with divinity that it once enjoyed. No. 5, 6 then speak of God, and No. 7 underlines the continuing validity of the promises made to Israel by the prophets. The prophets are no more, but God will keep the promises announced through them. This leads us directly to Nos. 8, 10-11, which come to the point of the compositor of the whole. Specifically, the New Moon will enter the status of a pilgrim festival -- and that fundamental proposition certainly has the support of the intersecting verse as we have already expounded it. So the whole forms a cogent and stunning statement. Only No. 9 is borrowed, verbatim.

I:III

1. A. Another interpretation of the verse ...and month by month at the new moon, week by week on the Sabbath, all mankind shall come to bow down before me, says the Lord (Is. 66:22-24):

B. How is it possible that all mankind will be able to come to Jerusalem every month and every Sabbath?

C. Said R. Levi, "Jerusalem is going to become equivalent to the Land of Israel, and the Land of Israel equivalent to the entire world.

D. And how will people come every New Month and Sabbath from the end of the world?

E. Clouds will come and carry them and bring them to Jerusalem, where they will say their morning prayers.

F. That is in line with what the prophet says in praise: Who are those, who fly like a cloud (Is. 60:8).

2. A. Another interpretation of the verse ...and month by month at the new moon, week by week on the Sabbath, all mankind shall come to bow down before me, says the Lord (Is. 66:22-24):

B. Now lo if the New Moon coincided with the Sabbath, and Scripture has said, Another interpretation of the verse ...and month by month at the new moon, week by week on the Sabbath, how [is it possible to do so once on the New Moon and once on the Sabbath, for on the occasion on which the two coincide, they can do it only once, not twice]?

C. Said R. Phineas, the priest, son of Hama, in the name of R. Reuben, "They will come twice, once for the purposes of the Sabbath, the other time for the purposes of the New Moon. The clouds will carry them early in the morning and bring them to Jerusalem, where they will recite the morning-prayer, and they will then bring them home.

D. "Who are those, who fly like a cloud (Is. 60:8) refers to the trip in the morning.

E. "And as the doves to the dovecotes (Is. 60:8) refers to the trip in the evening."

3. A. What the verse says is not Israel, but rather all mankind [shall come to bow down before me, says the Lord] (Is. 66:22-24).

B. Said R. Phineas, "What is the meaning of all mankind [Hebrew: all flesh, BSR]?

C. "Whoever has restrained [BSR] his desire in this age will have the merit of seeing the face of the Presence of God.

D. "For it is written, He who closes his eyes from gazing upon evil (Is. 33:15).

E. "And what follows? The king in his beauty will your eyes behold (Is. 33:17).

4. A. Another interpretation of the verse all mankind [shall come to bow down before me, says the Lord] (Is. 66:22-24):

B. Does this apply to all the idolaters?

C. Rather, only those who did not subjugate Israel will the Messiah accept.

We proceed to the clause by clause exposition of our base verse, asking questions that point toward the eschatological theme the compositor wishes to underline. The first question, No. 1, is a practical one. But, we see, the proof text, Is. 60:8, is then drawn in for further service at No. 2. No. 3 proceeds to the issue of all flesh/mankind, of the base-verse, and No. 4 pursues that same matter
-- in all, a cogent and well composed discourse.

I:IV.

1. A. On account of what merit will Israel enjoy all of this glory?

B. It is on account of the merit of dwelling in the Land of Israel.

C. For the Israelites lived in distress among the nations in this world.

D. And so you find concerning the patriarchs of the world without end: concerning what did they go to much trouble? Concerning burial in the Land of Israel.

2. A. Said R. Hanina, "All references to shekels that are made in the Torah are to selas, in the Prophets are to litras, in the Writings are to centenarii."

B. R. Abba bar Yudan in the name of R. Judah bar Simon: "Except for the shekels that Abraham weighed out for Ephron for the burial ground that he purchased from him, which were centenarii [(Mandelbaum:) the word shekel has the same numerical value as centenarii]: The piece of land cost four hundred silver shekels (Gen,. 23:15).

C. "Now take note that he paid for hundred silver centenarii for a burial plot.

D. "So in the case of Jacob, all the gold that he had ever acquired and all the money that he had been given he handed over to Esau in exchange for his right of burial, so that he should not be buried in it.

E. "For it is said, [Joseph spoke to the household of Pharaoh saying, If now I have found favor in your eyes, speak, I pray you, in the ears of Pharaoh, saying, My father made me swearing, saying, I am about to die,] in my tomb which I hewed out for myself in the land of Canaan, there shall you bury me (Gen. 50:4-5).

F. "And so you find that, when he was departing this earth, he imposed on Joseph an oath, saying to him, Do not, I pray you, bury me in Egypt (Gen. 47:29)."

G. Why so?

H. R. Hanina says, "There is a sound reason."

I. R. Yosé says, ""There is a sound reason."

J. Said R. Simeon b. Laqish in the name of R. Eleazar Haqqappar, "It is because the dead [of the Land of Israel] will live in the time of the Messiah, as David has said, I shall go before the Lord in the land of the living (Ps. 116:9).

K. "Now [can his meaning be that people do not die there, and] is it really the case that in the Land of Israel people live [and do not die]? But do people not die there? And is it not the case that outside of the Land of Israel is the land where people live?

L. "But as to the Land of Israel, the corpses are commonly found there, and when David said, In the land of the living, he meant that the dead there will live in the days of the Messiah."

The connection to the foregoing is rather tenuous. The compositor simply introduces the systematic discussion of the value of living in the land by referring obliquely to what has gone before at 1.A-2, and then proceeding to collect materials on the importance to the patriarchs and to David and the Messiah of living in the land. No. 2 is an autonomous entry, parachuted in for good reasons, and these are spelled out. The dead buried in the Land will live again. Discourse continues in I:V, as we now see.

I:V

1. A. R. Yosé asked R. Simeon b. Laqish, "Even will such as Jeroboam son of Nabat rise [from the grave when the Messiah comes]?"

B. He said to him, "Brimstone and salt [will be his fate]."

C. R. Helbo asked R. Ammi, "Even will such as Jeroboam son of Nabat rise [from the grave when the Messiah comes]?"

D. He said to him, "I asked R. Simeon b. Laqish, and he said to me, 'Brimstone and salt [will be his fate].'"

E.   R. Berekhiah asked R. Helbo, "Even will such as Jeroboam son of Nabat rise [from the grave when the Messiah comes]?"

F.   He said to him, "I asked R. Ammi, and he said to me, 'I asked R. Simeon b. Laqish, and he said to me, "Brimstone and salt [will be his fate].""'"

G.   Said R. Berekhiah, "Should we wish to state the mystery, what is the sense of his reply to him, 'Brimstone'?

H.   "Is it not the case that the Holy One, blessed be he, is going to exact punishment of the wicked in Gehenna only with brimstone and salt! But the Temple has been destroyed [with brimstone and salt, which therefore have already been inflicted on those buried in the land, inclusive of Jeroboam, who, having received his punishment, along with the others, therefore will rise from the dead]."

2.   A.   Said R. Judah b. R. Ilai, "For seven years the Land of Israel was burning with brimstone and fire, in line with this verse: The whole land thereof is brimstone and salt and a burning (Deut. 29:22).

3.   A.   Said R. Yosé b. Halafta, "For fifty two years after the destruction of the Temple, no one passed through the Land of Israel,

B.   "in line with this verse, For the mountains will I ake a weeping and a wailing...because they are burned up, so that none passes through..both the fowl of the heavens and the beast are fled and gone (Jer. 9:9).

C.   "Why is this the case? Because it was burning with the fire that had been poured out on it in line with this verse, From on high has he sent fire into my bones (Lam. 1:13)."

4.   A.   Why was this [done] by God? It was to exact punishment from Jeroboam son of Nabat and his fellows through those seven years during which the Land of Israel was burning with fire.

B.   It follows that even Jeroboam ben Nabat and his fellows will live in the time of the Messiah.

C. And what was it that saved them from the judgment of Gehenna and to live [in the resurrection of the dead]?

D. It was the fact that they were buried in the Land of Israel, as it is said, His land will make expiation for his people (Dt. 32:43)..

The foregoing is concluded here, a distinct essay on Jeroboam, which makes the point introduced in I:V that there is distinct merit in living in the Land of Israel. Nos. 2, 3 are separates that have been inserted because they contain facts important for the unfolding argument. No. 4 carries forward the matter begun at No. 1 and underlines the main point.

I:VI

1. A. Said R. Huna the priest, son of Abin, in the name of R. Abba b. Yamina, "R. Helbo and R. Hama bar Hanina [differed].

B. "R. Helbo said, 'He who dies overseas and is buried overseas is subject to distress on two counts, distress because of death, distress because of burial.

C. "'Why? For it is written in connection with Pashhur, And you, Pashhur, and all those who well in your house shall go into captivity, and you shall to Babylonia and there you shall die and there you shall be buried (Jer. 20:6).'

D. "And R. Hama bar Hanina said, 'He who dies overseas, if he comes from overseas and is buried in the land, is subject to distress only by reason of death alone.'"

E. Then how does R. Hama bar Hanina interpret the verse, ...here you shall die and there you shall be buried (Jer. 20:6)?

F. Burial in the Land of Israel achieves atonement for him.

2. A. R. Beroqia and R. Eleazar b. Pedat were walking in a grove [Braude, p. 45], and biers came from abroad. Said R. Beroqia to R. Eleazar, "What good have these accomplished? When they were alive, they aban-

doned [the Land] and now in death they have come back!"

B.   Said R. Eleazar b. Pedat to him, "No, that is not the case. Since they are buried in the Land of Israel, and a clump of earth of the Land of Israel is given over to them, it effects atonement for them,

C.   "as it is said, And his land shall make expiation for his people (Deut. 32:43)."

3.   A.   If that is the case, then have the righteous who are overseas lost out?

B.   No. Why not?

C.   Said R. Eleazar in the name of R. Simai, "God makes for them tunnels in the earth, and they roll like skins and come to the Land of Israel.

D.   "And when they have come to the Land of Israel, God restores their breath to them.

E.   "For it is said, He who gives breath to the people upon it and spirit to them that go through it (Is. 42:5)."

F.   "And there is, furthermore, an explicit verse of Scripture in Ezekiel that makes that point: You shall know that I am the Lord when I open your graves and bring you to the Land of Israel (Ez. 37:13).

G.   "Then: I shall put my spirit in you and you shall live (Ex. 37:14)."

4.   A.   Thus you have learned that [1] those who die in the Land of Israel live in the days of the Messiah, and [2] the righteous who die overseas come to it and live in it.

B.   If that is the case, then will the gentiles who are buried in the Land also live?

C.   No, Isaiah has said, The neighbor shall not say, I too have suffered pain. The people who dwell therein shall be forgiven their sin (Is. 33:24).

D.   The sense is, "My evil neighbors are not going to say, "We have been mixed up [with Israel and will share their fate, so] we too shall live with them."

E.   But that one that was the people dwelling therein [is the one that will live,[and what is that peo-

ple? It is the people that has been forgiven its sin,
namely, those concerning whom it is said, Who is God
like you, who forgives sin and passes over transgression
for the remnant of his inheritance (Mic. 7:18) [which
can only be Israel].

The established topic continues its course; the compositor has introduced further materials on the theme of living and dying in the Land of Israel. The discourse seems continuous; there is no interest in the base text and no intersecting text appears. It is a sustained essay on a topic.

I:VII

1. A. How long are the days of the Messiah?

B. R. Aqiba says, "Forty years, in line with this
verse: And he afflicted you and allowed you to hunger
(Deut. 8:3), and it is written, Make us glad according to
the days in which you afflicted us (Ps. 90:15). Just as
the affliction lasted forty years in the wilderness, so the
affliction here is forty years [with the result that the
glad time is the same forty years]."

C. Said R. Abin, "What verse of Scripture further
supports the position of R. Aqiba? As in the days of
your coming forth from the land of Egypt I will show
him marvelous things (Mic. 7:15)."

D. R. Eliezer says, "Four hundred years, as it is
written, And they shall enslave them and torment them
for four hundred years (Gen. 15:13), and further it is
written, Make us glad according to the days in which
you afflicted us (Ps. 90:15)."

E. R. Berekhiah in the name of R. Dosa the Elder says, "Six hundred years, as it is written, As the days
of a tree shall be the days of my people (Is. 65:22)."

F. "How long are the days of a tree? A sycamore
lasts for six hundred years."

G. R. Eliezer b. R. Yosé the Galilean says, "A
thousand years, as it is written, For a thousand years in
your sight as are but as yesterday when it has passed
(Ps. 90:40), and it is written, The day of vengeance as in

my heart but now my year of redemption is come (Is. 63:4).

H. "The day of the Holy One, blessed be he, is the same as a thousand years for a mortal."

I. R. Joshua says, "Two thousand years, according to the days in which you afflicted us (Ps. 90:15).

J. "For there are no fewer days [as in the cited verse] than two, and the day of the Holy One, blessed be he, is the same as a thousand years for a mortal."

K. R. Abbahu says, "Seven thousand years, as it is said, As a bride groom rejoices over his bride will your God rejoice over you (Is. 62:5), and how long does a groom rejoice over his bride? It is seven days,

L. "and the day of the Holy One, blessed be he, is the same as a thousand years for a mortal."

M. Rabbi says, "You cannot count it: For the day of vengeance that was in my heart and my year of redemption have come (Is. 63:4)."

N. How long are the days of the Messiah? Three hundred and sixty-five thousand years will be the length of the days of the Messiah.

2. A. Then the dead of the Land of Israel who are Israelites will live and derive benefit from them, and all the righteous who are overseas will come through tunnels.

B. And when they reach the land, the Holy One, blessed be he, will restore their breath, and they will rise and derive benefit from the days of the Messiah along with them [already in the land].

C. For it is said, He who spread forth the earth and its offspring gives breath to the people on it (Is. 42:5).

3. A. When will the royal Messiah come?

B. Said R. Eleazar, "Near to the Messiah's days, ten places will be swallowed up, ten places will be overturned, ten places will be wiped out."

C. And R. Hiyya bar Abba said, "The royal Messiah will come only to a generation the leaders of which are like dogs."

D. R. Eleazar says, "It will be in the time of a generation that is worthy of annihilation that the royal Messiah will come."

E. R. Levi said, "Near the time of the days of the Messiah a great event will take place in the world."

The final issue in the messianic essay concerns the time that the days of the Messiah will last. (Braude's translation, p. 46, "How long to the days of the Messiah," is certainly wrong, as the discussion that follows in No. 3, which does raise that question, indicates.) The several theories, along with their proof texts, are laid out in a clear way. No. 2 then reviews familiar ideas. No. 3 then goes over another aspect of the matter. None of this composite has been made up for the purposes of our document. Now to identify the formal program of the document.

1. PESIQTA RABBATI PISQA' ONE I:I

"May our master teach us" — *yelammedenu rabbenu* — introduces a discourse on a matter of law, following a highly conventional and restrictive form: question with the formal introduction, followed by our masters have taught us, with a legal formulation, and then a secondary thematic development. No. 1 presents us with the colloquy, May our master instruct us...our masters have taught us..., followed at No. 2 by a secondary point not generated by the primary colloquy. We note that the theme of the Pisqa' as a whole, the New Moon, does not generate in the legal component of the Pisqa' a thesis that will dominate discourse later on. There is no correlation whatsoever between the legal problem and the thematic exposition that follows. No. 3 likewise pursues its own interests, without intersecting with any point that will follow.

2. PESIQTA RABBATI PISQA' ONE I:II

We should expect to have an intersecting verse fully expounded and then brought into relationship with a base verse. But that anticipated form is not realized. We do have a brief feint in that direction at No. 1, for No. 1 intends to draw into juxtaposition Ps. 42:1-4 and Lev. 16:1ff. We have an allusion to the matter, in that the two verses — intersecting, base — are cited. But then the authorship refers us to another discourse, without copying that other discourse. In a fully realized execution of the intersecting verse/base version construction, we should have not only an exposition of the intersecting verse, which we do have here, but also an explicit introduction, at the outset, of the base verse, which should be Is. 66:22-24. That verse does occur at the end, but no preparation has announced that it is going to be the centerpiece of discussion. The result is an exceedingly defective exercise in which base verse is ignored, even though a powerful message concerning its ultimate meaning is exposed by the intersecting verse.

Nos. 3, 4, 5, 6, 7, 8 cite the intersecting verse, With my whole being I thirst for God, and impute meanings to that verse. Hence the form is simple: citation of a verse, statement of the meaning or application of that verse. No. 9 is tacked on to No. 8 because of thematic reasons. No. 10 continues No. 9. No. 11 pursues the same program of exegesis of what we call the intersecting verse. Then No. 11 brings us back to the lection for the Sabbath that coincides with the New Moon. But that lection has not been cited, so we cannot imagine that we have a sizable exposition of an intersecting verse and then its juxtaposition with a base-verse, simply because the "base verse" in this case is cited only at the end. The theme of a yearning of Israel to union with God is a rather general one. There is no sustained exposition of a proposition that opens the base verse in a fresh way. True, there is a powerful proposition, which is that in the end of time the New Moon will enter the status of a pilgrim festival. But it is difficult for me to see how the formal characteristics of the composition match the cogency of the programmatic intent. The one formal possibility is that I:I is intended to introduce the base verse, the presence of which is then taken for granted in the execution of I:II. But I find no evidence in the document before us that that is the intent. There is no continuity in either form or program between I:I and I:II.

Overall, it suffices to note that in Leviticus Rabbah there will be a full and sustained inquiry into the many meanings of the intersecting verse, and only then the base verse comes into view and its meaning is revised by the intersection. In Pesiqta deRab Kahana, by contrast, the intersecting verse always focuses upon a single point, the point that the authorship wishes to make with reference to the base verse. So the articulation is intellectually economical and disciplined, by contrast to the intellectually promiscuous character of the use of the form in Leviticus Rabbah. In our document, the formal discipline is lost altogether; there is neither a systematic treatment of the intersecting verse nor a highly purposeful intersection, making a single stunning point, such as we note in the two prior compilations, respectively.

3. PESIQTA RABBATI PISQA' ONE I:III

We have now an exposition of the base verse, which is Is. 66:22-24. Formally, we find precisely the formal plan characteristic of the foregoing: citation of a verse, a few words that impute meaning to that verse. Once more we shall notice how our authorship contrasts with that of Pesiqta deRab Kahana. For the exegetical form employed in Pesiqta deRab Kahana, in its syntactic traits identical to the one before us, yields a single message, an implicit syllogism repeated many times over. In our document (as in Leviticus Rabbah), by contrast, the exegetical form permits an authorship to say pretty much whatever it wants on a given theme, and does not impose the requirement to state in yet another, new way an established syllogism. These distinctions become important in Chapter Eleven.

4. PESIQTA RABBATI PISQA' ONE I:IV

I:IV.1-2 seem to me to continue the preceding, that is, I:III.4.

5. PESIQTA RABBATI PISQA' ONE I:V

This subdivision continues the foregoing.

6. PESIQTA RABBATI PISQA' ONE I:VI

This subdivision continues the established theme, the importance of living in the Land of Israel.

7. PESIQTA RABBATI PISQA' ONE I:VII

What I said just now applies here.

IV. THE FORMS OF PESIQTA RABBATI PISQA' ONE

We may now review the results of the form-analysis. We have defined the following formal preferences:

1. LEGAL COLLOQUY:

May our master instruct us...our masters have taught us..., followed by a secondary lesson.

2. EXEGESIS OF A VERSE

A verse is cited and then given a secondary or imputed meaning, e.g., Another matter + verse + a few words that state the meaning of that verse or its concrete application.

3. INTERSECTING-VERSE/BASE-VERSE (HYPOTHETICAL)

We should expect to find a base verse, e.g., Is. 66:22-24, cited, then an intersecting verse, e.g., Ps. 42:1-4, used to impute to the former some more profound meaning than is obvious at the surface. This form, not realized here, is suggested and of course elsewhere validated as a routine option. That is why it must take its place within the formal repertoire, even though our sample does not present us with an instance in which it is used.

V. THE THEMATIC PROGRAM AND PROPOSITION OF PESIQTA RABBATI PISQA' ONE: SYLLOGISM, COLLAGE, OR SCRAPBOOK?

Before proceeding to test our form-analytical hypothesis, we have now to ask whether the Pisqa' at hand presents a cogent statement of its own, or whether it constitutes a collection of thematically joined but syllogistically distinct statements. Let us review the propositions of our Pisqa':

I:I: If one forgot to include a reference to the New Moon in the Grace after Meals. Other rules about the

Grace after Meals for the New Moon. The New Moon is equivalent to a festival.

I:II: Israel thirsts for God, who bestows blessings of a natural order and also will bring salvation. Leading to 8.B: When will you restore the glory of going up on the three pilgrim festivals to see the face of God. Ultimately the New Moon will be equivalent to a pilgrim festival.

I:III: Interpretation of Is. 66:22-24: can people really come to Jerusalem every New Moon and every Sabbath? Other problems in that same framework.

I:IV: On what account will Israel enjoy all this glory? Because of the merit of dwelling in the Land of Israel. The resurrection of those who are buried in the Land.

I:V: More on the resurrection of those who are buried in the Land.

I:VI: More on the resurrection of those who are buried in the Land.

I:VII: Secondary expansion of a detail in the foregoing. More on the resurrection of those who are buried in the Land. When will the Messiah come.

We may now ask whether our Pisqa' forms a highly cogent syllogism, with a proposition systematically proven by each of the components; whether it forms a collage, in which diverse materials seen all together form a cogent statement; or whether it constitutes a scrapbook in which thematically contiguous materials make essentially individual statements of their own. Among these three choices, the second seems to me, in balance, to apply to Pisqa' One. We certainly do not find a single cogent statement, an implicit syllogism repeated over and over in the several components of the Pisqa'. But we do have more than a mere scrapbook on a common theme. For the basic point, the equivalence of the New Moon to a pilgrim festival, is made both at the legal passage, I:I, and the exegetical one, I:II-III. I:IV-VII then form a mere appendix, tacked on without much good reason. So we may judge our Pisqa' to be an imperfectly executed collage, one that, in the aggregate, really does make its point.

VI. THE ORDER OF THE FORMS OF PISQA' ONE

The legal colloquy appears first of all, at I:I. If I:II had worked out an intersecting-verse/base-verse composition, then that would have constituted the form to appear second in sequence. I:III presents an exegesis of the base-verse on its own terms. It follows that as a matter of hypothesis, we should expect the order of types of forms to be, first, a legal colloquy, which will introduce the theme and possibly also the thesis; second, the intersecting verse/base verse form, which will allow the theme, and possibly the thesis, to come to expression in exegetical, rather than legal terms; and, third, the exegetical form, which allows the base verse to be spelled out on its own. Miscellanies then will come at the end. So there would appear to be a preferred order of types of units of discourse.

VII. RECURRENT LITERARY STRUCTURES: TYPES OF UNITS OF DISCOURSE, THEIR OR-DER, AND THEIR COGENCY

A survey of five further Pisqa'ot, not copied here, yields a firm result. We may classify all the large-scale compositions of Pesiqta Rabbati within four literary structures. These are the legal colloquy, which itself follows a fairly restrictive pattern in that the form opens with a narrowly legal question, which moves toward a broader, propositional conclusion; the intersecting-verse/base-verse construction, the exegetical form, and the propositional list. The intersecting-verse/base-verse construction itself is composed of a variety of clearly formalized units, e.g., exegesis of verses of Scripture and the like. The exegetical form, for its part, is remarkably simple, since it invariably consists of the citation of a verse of Scripture followed by a few words that impute to that verse a given meaning; this constant beginning may then be followed by a variety of secondary accretions which themselves exhibit no persistent formal traits. The propositional list is remarkably cogent in both its formal traits and its principle of cogency.

It goes without saying that the order of the types of forms is not fixed. In Pesiqta Rabbati we find one fixed order: the legal colloquy always comes first. But even that form serves diverse purposes, since, as we noted, in some Pisqa'ot it announces a proposition which will be spelled out and restated in exegetical form as well, while in others the legal colloquy introduces a theme but no proposition in connection with that theme. From that point we may find anything and its opposite: propositional lists, then, intersecting-verse/base-verse-compositions, then exegetical statements, or any other arrangement.

The matter of cogency invokes a somewhat more subjective judgment. Yet I find it difficult to discover as a general or indicative trait of Pesiqta Rabbati a sustained effort at making a cogent and single statement. That — as we shall shortly see — indeed does mark Pesiqta de Rab Kahana beginning to end. That fact is suggested by our survey of the cogency of the Pisqa'ot of Pesiqta Rabbati that we have reviewed. Among the three analogies which I proposed — syllogism, collage, or scrapbook — we could invoke all three. That means that the authorship of the document as a whole found itself contented with a variety of types of logical discourse. Some of the Pisqa'ot appeared to treat a single topic, but only in a miscellaneous way. The propositions associated with that topic would scarcely cohere to form a single cogent statement. In that case I found we had a scrapbook. Other Pisqa'ot seemed to wish to draw a variety of statements into juxtaposition so that, while not coherent, when viewed all together, those statements would form a single significant judgment upon a theme, hence, a collage. While I cannot demonstrate beyond a doubt the correctness of my assignment of a given Pisqa' to a given classification, I think that, overall, we are on firm ground in making these assignments: Pisqa' I, collage; Pisqa' II, scrapbook on a single theme; Pisqa' III, syllogism; Pisqa' IV, scrapbook; Pisqa' Five, scrapbook. So we find everything and its opposite. The contrast to Pesiqta Rabbati Pisqa' XV = Pesiqta deRab Kahana Pisqa' V is then stunning: there we see what a Pisqa' looks like when the authorship has made not merely a composite but a single and uniform composition. In a moment we shall see that the entirety of Pesiqta deRab Kahana follows suit.

The conclusion may be stated very briefly. The authorship of Pesiqta Rabbati has made use of a fixed and limited repertoire of large-scale literary structures — four in all. These it has ordered in diverse ways, so the authorship found no important message to be delivered through the sequence in which the types of forms would be utilized. The same authorship pursued a variety of modes of cogent discourse, sometimes appealing to the theme to hold together whatever materials they chose to display, sometimes delivering a rather general message in connection with that theme, and, on occasion, choosing to lay down a very specific syllogism in connection with a theme. These traits revealed by our survey take on significance when we compare Midrash to Midrash, that is to say, Pesiqta Rabbati to Pesiqta deRab Kahana. For it is now self-evident that, confronted with a Pisqa' lacking all identification, we could readily and easily distin-

guish a Pisqa' particular to Pesiqta Rabbati from one shared
with Pesiqta deRab Kahana, and that on more than a single
basis. And, it goes without saying, we should have no difficulty whatsoever in picking out a Pisqa' that may fit into either of the two Pesiqtas from a Pisqa' that would belong to
Sifra, Sifré to Numbers, Genesis Rabbah, Leviticus Rabbah,
The Fathers According to Rabbi Nathan, the Tosefta, the
Mishnah, the Yerushalmi, or the Bavli. Each document exhibits its distinctive and definitive traits of rhetoric and logic.
When we speak of a document, we refer to determinate traits
of rhetoric, logic of coherent discourse, and topic that are
particular to that compilation and not replicated by any other.
On that basis, we may speak of a document bearing its own
definition for the bulk of materials compiled therein.

VIII. THE RHETORICAL PLAN OF PESIQTA DERAB KAHANA

A Pisqa' in Pesiqta deRab Kahana, for its part, systematically presents a single syllogism, which is expressed
through, first the contrast of an external verse with the base
verse — hence, the Propositional Form, in which the implicit
syllogism is stated through the intervention of an contrastive
verse into the basic proposition established by the base verse,
and then through the a systematic exegesis of the components of the base verse on their own, hence through the Exegetical Form.

A. Pesiqta deRab Kahana's authorship resorted to three
rhetorical patterns:

1. The Propositional Form: The implicit syllogism is
stated through the intervention of an contrastive verse into
the basic proposition established by the base verse.

2. The Exegetical Form: The implicit syllogism is stated through a systematic exegesis of the components of the base verse on their own.

3. The Syllogistic List: The syllogism is explicit, not implicit, and is proven by a list of probative examples.

B. The nature of these rhetorical preferences also suggests that the order in which these types of forms occur will be as just now given, first the syllogism generated by the intersection of the contrasting and base verses, then the syllogism repeated through a systematic reading of the base verse on its own, finally, whatever miscellanies the framers have in hand (or later copyists insert).

C. When we compare our document with another by examining a Pisqa' of Pesiqta deRab Kahana that is not unique to that composition but is shared with Leviticus Rabbah, we see that the definitive rhetorical traits of our document also prove distinctive. Chapter One has already covered that ground.

Rhetorical analysis has yielded the proposition that Pesiqta deRab Kahana consists of twenty-eight syllogisms, each presented in a cogent and systematic way by the twenty-eight Pisqa'ot, respectively. Each Pisqa' contains an implicit proposition, and that proposition may be stated in a simple way. It emerges from the intersection of an external verse with the base verse that recurs through the Pisqa', and then is restated by the systematic dissection of the components of the base verse, each of which is shown to say the same thing as all the others.

As to the order of the types of forms, the propositional form always occurs first, and in the Pisqa'ot shared with Leviticus Rabbah, the intersecting verse-base verse form always occurs first. There is a tendency for the intersecting-verse base verse items of Leviticus Rabbah in Pesiqta deRab Kahana to prove somewhat more prolix than those corresponding items in propositional form in our document, for reasons I have already explained. The exegetical form (Leviticus Rabbah: base verse form) always follows the propositional form. No Pisqa' begins with the exegetical form and moves to the propositional form.

This review of the paramount formal traits of the principal divisions — Pisqa'ot — of Pesiqta deRab Kahana has shown both the characteristics of the formal patterns of all twenty-eight Pisqa'ot and also the order in which the formal patterns persistently occur: Pesiqta deRab Kahana is made up of propositional and exegetical compositions, presented in that order, in which an implicit syllogism is created out of the interplay of an intersecting verse and a base verse and then shown to inhere, also, in each of the components of the base verse. Having characterized the two Pesiqtas, I may now compare them and place them into the still larger comparative context defined by the canon in which they occur.

IX. COMPARATIVE MIDRASH [1]: THE RHETORICAL, LOGICAL, AND TOPICAL ASPECT. THE PLAN AND PROGRAM OF PESIQTA DERAB KAHANA AND PESIQTA RABBATI

Pesiqta Rabbati's authorship refers to four forms, the legal colloquy, the intersecting-verse/base-verse construction, the propositional list, and the exegetical form. These follow no fixed and conventional order. Pesiqta deRab Kahana's authorship makes extensive use of the second and the third types of form, much less common use of the fourth and none at all of the legal colloquy, which, in our context, is particular to the later of the two Pesiqtas. Except for the fixed practice of placing the legal colloquy at the outset of discourse, Pesiqta Rabbati's authorship as represented in our sample places no premium upon ordering its materials in one way rather than in some other. Pesiqta deRab Kahana's authorship, by contrast, follows the fixed preference of setting the intersecting-verse/base-verse form first, followed by the exegetical form. That authorship makes use of the intersecting-verse/base-verse form — which I therefore called the propositional form — to expose its syllogism, then the exegetical form to repeat or prove it.

As to cogent discourse in the two Pesiqtas: the Pisqa' in Pesiqta deRab Kahana commonly makes a single point, fully spelled out and carefully instantiated, which will be generated to begin with by that intersection. The Pisqa' in the later Pesiqta by contrast works through a fixed theme, but more often than not delivers miscellaneous messages concerning that theme, and, in any event, through its several components does not ordinarily argue in favor of (or against) a single important proposition. It follows that the Pisqa' of Pesiqta deRab Kahana proves remarkably cogent in its mode of discourse, repeatedly saying one thing through diverse media. The Pisqa' in the later Pesiqta tends to be propositionally diffuse, from the legal colloquy forward simply saying different things about one topic. The Pisqa' of Pesiqta Rabbati may fall into the category of a collage, with its cogent message made up of discrete yet mutually illuminating parts, or it may appear to be little more than a scrapbook on a single topic. But it rarely, if ever, exhibits that syllogistic integrity that won my admiration for the authorship of Pesiqta deRab Kahana. The Pisqa' of the earlier Pesiqta, by contrast, ordinarily presents a proposition worked out in a well-composed syllogism.

What of the matter of topic? Were we to rely on the repertoire of the base-verses of either of the two Pesiqtas, we should not gain access to the program of the document. While, in Leviticus Rabbah, by reference to the meeting of the contents of a given chapter of Leviticus with the proposition important to the framer of a Parashah of Leviticus Rabbah, we can always explain the reason for the selection of the base verse, in the two Pesiqtas internal evidence never suffices to account for that same matter. The identification of the occasion associated with that base verse is the one fact not presented by the document itself. We have to appeal to the prior and external fact that a given passage serves as the synagogue lection on a given occasion to explain why a verse of said passage has been selected. Pesiqta deRab Kahana follows the synagogal lections from early spring through fall, in the Western calendar, from late February or early March through late September or early October, approximately half of the solar year, 27 weeks, and somewhat more than half of the lunar year. On the very surface, the basic building block is the theme of a given lectionary Sabbath — that is, a Sabbath distinguished by a particular lection — and not the theme dictated by a given passage of Scripture, let alone the exposition of the language or proposition of such a scriptural verse. The topical program of the document may be defined very simply: expositions of themes dictated by special Sabbaths or festivals and their lections. What of the program of Pesiqta Rabbati?

Pesiqta Rabbati goes over precisely the same liturgical calendar in pretty much the same way. That is why I classify Pesiqta Rabbati as a secondary and imitative compilation, one which goes over the ground of the earlier Pesiqta at each point in its topical program, item by item. The imitative character of the later Pesiqta is proven by a simple fact. The authorship of Pesiqta Rabbati has simply recapitulated the liturgical program of the authorship of the earlier Pesiqta, providing (mainly) new compositions for the same occasions, whole or in part, that are covered by Pesiqta deRab Kahana. We should therefore not find surprising that in matters of rhetorical or formal composition (but not logical cogency) the authorship of Pesiqta Rabbati has learned so much as they have from their predecessors.

The upshot of form-analysis and topical inquiry into the processes of laying out formalized material may be stated very simply. The formal repertoire of the two documents is pretty much the same. A single taxonomic system of formal classification serves them both, though requiring augmentation to be sure. The policy of arranging formalized materials in a consistent order is cogent, if not completely consistent, between the two. So, viewed as a the outcome of a literary and formal policy dictating rules of how things would be formulated and ordered, the plan of Pesiqta deRab Kahana and that of Pesiqta Rabbati are if not one, then at least closely related. Formally and redactionally they fall into the same literary genus. In terms of topic they are pretty much identical. Where they differ, it is at the level of the logical cogency of the Pisqa'ot of which each is made up.

X. COMPARATIVE MIDRASH [2]: THE TWO PESIQTAS SIDE BY SIDE

Now that we know how the two Pesiqtas compare with one another, we ask we wonder whether without external signals, we should have been able to pick out a Pisqa' primary to Pesiqta Rabbati and differentiate it from a Pisqa' shared by Pesiqta Rabbati with Pesiqta deRab Kahana. In terms of rhetoric (in the sense of large scale forms of syntactic conglomeration and aggregation) and logical cogency, we find no difficulty in identifying a Pisqa' shared by Pesiqta deRab Kahana and Pesiqta Rabbati apart from one particular to Pesiqta Rabbati. We may furthermore demonstrate that such a shared Pisqa' is primary to the earlier of the two Pesiqtas, in that it exhibits traits characteristic of other Pisqa'ot in the earlier Pesiqta and absent in those distinctive to the later Pesiqta. In terms of topic, we should not know why a given Pisqa' makes its appearance in one document rather than the other.

The authorship of the later Pesiqta has made a number of choices. It has imitated the earlier Pesiqta by compiling materials that illuminate the liturgical lections. It has adopted the earlier Pesiqta's formal repertoire, while augmenting it with a form found elsewhere, the legal colloquy. Most strikingly — and I think the mark of the imitator and not the original intellect — the authorship of the later Pesiqta has not replicated the remarkably cogent mode of logical discourse of the earlier one. While the earlier authorship managed in many and diverse ways to say one thing concerning a given topic, the later compositors collected a great many diverse and essentially unrelated thoughts about one topic. The difference is between an authorship that has a very specific message which it wishes to register with great force and urgency, and one that plans only to collect and arrange important materials: the creative thinker as against the heir and successor, the formative mind as against the traditional one. The one substantial rhetorical innovation yielded by the comparison of the two Pesiqtas is the legal colloquy (which, of course, was in circulation prior to the composition of Pesiqta Rabbati in any event). And the use of that rhetorical advance over the earlier Pesiqta proves random and not pointed, in that, in our sample, the point made in the legal colloquy ordinarily did not intersect with the points made in the exegetical passages. The may our master teach us-pericopes simply introduced a topic but imposed upon the treatment of that topic no paramount agenda.

Once more, formal innovation makes a profoundly conservative and traditional frame of mind. Seen in context, Pesiqta deRab Kahana stands forth as an act of supreme imagination and fresh insight. For its authorship selected a new text — one drawn from liturgical circumstances and occasions, rather than words alone — and through that new text managed to speak as cogently and as coherently as did the authorship of Leviticus Rabbah, the closest associates of Pesiqta deRab Kahana's authorities. By contrast, compared to the authorship of the earlier Pesiqta, the later one has botched the opportunity of a fresh rhetorical conceit by treating it not as the occasion for linking law to theology, let alone by showing how, in deed, people act out the convictions of the Torah, but by merely making one miscellaneous point on a theme in a new way, another in an old: imitation in the mark of creative and imaginative rhetorical innovation. I find it difficult to suppress my admiration for the authorship of Pesiqta deRab Kahana, and, guided by its preferences in aesthetics, to express disappointment with the work of the later authorship.

XI. LEVITICUS RABBAH, PESIQTA DERAB KAHANA, AND PESIQTA RABBATI: THE THREE KINDRED COMPILATIONS AND THE DOCUMENTARY READING OF THE RABBINIC CANON

In historical sequence, Leviticus Rabbah, Pesiqta deRab Kahana, and Pesiqta Rabbati reached closure in that order. The three compilations therefore intersect, in that the first of the two documents share five Pisqa'ot, and, as we have noted, the second of the two share four as well. Comparison of Midrash-compilations therefore requires us to ask how the three intersecting documents relate to one another.

The answer is now clear. Leviticus Rabbah's rhetorical and logical program is taken up but revised by the authorship of Pesiqta deRab Kahana, just as, in a different way, the authorship of Pesiqta Rabbati has taken up and — whether through reworking or imitating what it has received — made its own the rhetorical and logical program of Pesiqta deRab Kahana. Pisqa'ot of Pesiqta deRab Kahana that are shared with Leviticus Rabbah conform to the rhetorical plan of that document and therefore are primary to Leviticus Rabbah and secondary to Pesiqta deRab Kahana. The reason that the authorship of the latter document has made use of these materials requires explanation as part of the larger syllogistic program of Pesiqta deRab Kahana. Pisqa'ot shared between Pesiqta deRab Kahana and Pesiqta Rabbati turn out to exhibit traits otherwise characteristic of Pisqa'ot of Pesiqta deRab Kahana and not commonly present in Pisqa'ot unique to Pesiqta Rabbati. If each of the three compilations — Leviticus Rabbah, Pesiqta deRab Kahana, and Pesiqta Rabbati — follows its own distinctive rhetorical and logical program of formulation, all three of them pursue a topical program that, at its foundations, appears to be single and uniform. Defining the program that is common to the three documents and shared by many others is a difficult task, well beyond the limits of the comparative study of Midrash-compilations undertaken here. For it is not a problem of exegesis of Scripture, but, in the most profound sense, of the exegesis of exegesis.

For the case of Pesiqta deRab Kahana and Pesiqta Rabbati, the differences we have noted between the one and the other prove beyond doubt that each editorship or authorship has made and carried out definitive choices. These choices involved indicative traits of rhetorical form and logical cogency of discourse. Since we can fairly easily distinguish one document from the other, and both documents from their closest antecedent, Leviticus Rabbah, it follows that both fall into the category of texts, not scrapbooks. But, as we have also noticed, while Pesiqta deRab Kahana exhibits remarkably coherent discourse, in which a single implicit premise comes to diverse expression, Pesiqta Rabbati does not. It is in some Pisqa'ot not so much a propositional statement as — at best — a collage, with discrete items linked to a common and shared canvas of a single theme. And, within our sample, the compilation may also present us with Pisqa'ot that are little more than assemblages of material on a common theme. Accordingly, we have found within the Rabbinic canon examples not only of well composed texts — into which category I assign both Leviticus Rabbah and also Pesiqta deRab Kahana (not to mention, for quite distinct reasons, Sifré to Numbers), but also compilations that fall somewhere between the classifications of collage and scrapbook. And that interesting literary fact underlines the as yet unresolved theological problem of the canon.

It is how these sharply defined and diverse compilations come together, as they assuredly do, to form a single, vast and cogent statement: a single implicit syllogism, everywhere uniform beneath the uneven surfaces of the discrete and diverse writings. Like the magma that courses upward from the earth's deepest bowels, so that massive, simple syllogism erupts and overwhelms the surfaces — but only irregularly and unpredictably. When we discern the regularity and predict where it will or will not come to expression, we shall have penetrated far more deeply into the heart and soul of the Judaism of the dual Torah than — in these exercises of mine at any rate — the comparative study of Midrash has permitted.

PART THREE

SHOWING THAT SHARED TRA-
DITIONS, PRIOR TO AND
AUTONOMOUS OF
THE TWO TALMUDS DO NOT
LINK THE BAVLI TO THE
YERUSHALMI

4.

DO THE YERUSHALMI AND THE BAVLI POINT TOWARD AN AUTONOMOUS TRADITION?

I. A NULL-HYPOTHESIS: THE YERUSHALMI AND THE BAVLI DRAW ON COMMON SOURCES OTHER THAN THE MISHNAH, THE TOSEFTA, AND COUNTERPART CANONICAL DOCUMENTS

Precisely what Goldberg-Schaefer-Becker and others of their view conceive in the terms, "autonomous tradition" and similar language is unclear. They can contemplate a corpus of traditions outside of documentary lines that form a miscellany, in which case they will want to formulate a theory of how such "traditions" were formulated and transmitted and drawn upon by the compilations now in our hands. They may conceive a corpus of traditions that did not surface in particular documents but that formed a coherent body of statements on their own. In that case they will want to tell us the indicative traits of these "autonomous traditions," independent of extant documents but themselves constituting a collection. These and comparable obscurities make difficult an *Auseinandersetzung* between proponents of the documentary hypothesis and critics of that hypothesis. The latter are clearer in their negative judgment than in their constructive alternative to the hypothesis they propose to refute. So we are left to do their work for them: to construct, and test, a contrary view of matters.

For that purpose, we turn to the two Talmuds in search of a source that is prior to the documents and autonomous of them: what evidence do we have in the two Talmuds for the existence of such a source, and what traits do we impute to it In fact, I undertake a quite routine and necessary exercise, the construction and testing of a null-hypothesis. Let me explain.

To deal with the claim that autonomous traditions come to the surface in two or more documents, I now frame matters in terms of a null-hypothesis. I do so in the setting of the two documents that are the most likely of all canonical writings to draw upon a common core of autonomous, non-documentary, and (plausibly) pre-documentary formulations: autonomous traditions of law — if such existed.[3] That hypothetical exercise of disproving the documentary hypothesis begins with the question, What kind of evidence should we find to disprove the documentary hypothesis of the Rabbinic

---

[3] I hasten to add, I do not deal with the designated baraita-corpus, e.g., compositions in one or another of the Talmuds that bear a mark of Tannaite origin. These represent a separate set of problems, awaiting formulation and solution. But they clearly do not represent what Goldberg-Schaefer-Becker mean by "autonomous traditions," even though they are not redacted in a finished document comparable to the Mishnah or the Tosefta or Genesis Rabbah. From Michael Higger's time forward, I know of no systematic critical reading of the baraita-corpus; I do not even know how one would define those finished sayings as a corpus, or of what it would consist. Clearly, the documentary reading of the Rabbinic canon pertains to how framers of a complete document utilize received materials for their own distinctive purpose; that reading would subsume the baraita-corpus, so it seems to me at first glance. But it is a problem for investigation in its own terms: what, precisely, do we mean by Tannaite sayings, beyond the limits of the Mishnah and the Tosefta and the Talmuds' designated items (TNY' and related markings).

canon? The exercise proceeds to answer the question by examining pertinent data. Let me explain.

The documentary hypothesis in the reading of the Rabbinic canon, as its name implies, deems critical the respective documents' indicative traits of rhetoric (form), topic (propositional program) and logic of coherent discourse. Each canonical compilation exhibits a distinctive combination of those traits. Every one of them brings to bear upon their compositions and composites an indicative documentary program and perspective. So we can describe and on objective, factual grounds readily differentiate even kindred compilations such as Genesis Rabbah and Leviticus Rabbah, or Leviticus Rabbah and Pesiqta deRab Kahana, or Pesiqta deRab Kahana and Pesiqta Rabbati. On that basis, with a fair degree of success (if not invariably), we can also assign to a determinate documentary setting, e.g., Genesis Rabbah and not the Mishnah, Song of Songs Rabbah and not Lamentations Rabbati, an otherwise-unmarked composition. That probability points toward the work of document-making as a task of composition, not only compilation. It further forms a powerful demonstration that documentary lines matter, that occurrences of the same story in two or more documents represent an anomaly, not a definitive trait of the canon, and that autonomous traditions, which do exist, defy the prevailing literary conventions of Rabbinic Judaism in its formative age. But that same probability does not always hold. And the facts now established serve only partially to validate the documentary hypothesis.

There is another set of facts to be taken up, such as those raised by Arnold M. Goldberg and his disciple Peter Schaefer and his disciple Hans-Jürgen Becker. What about traditions that generate writing in more than a single document, that are not particular to any one document? These circulating compositions and composites are autonomous of any one document. It should follow that we indeed are able to identify fixed wording, and more important, determinate conceptions or propositions that animate systematic expositions of two or more documents. Would these not represent an autonomous tradition, which would call into question the basic determinacy of documentary boundaries that I have defined?

Now that form-analysis has made a positive case for a documentary reading of the Rabbinic writings, accordingly we turn to such a null-hypothesis. What evidence would form a prima facie case in favor of the presence, in the Rabbinic canonical writings, of a tradition essentially autonomous of documentary boundaries? Such evidence if proportionate would call into question the primacy of documentary discourse. It would permit us not only to form a hypothesis on the character of writing for other-than-documentary purposes, such as we shall take up at the end of this book. It would also alert us to the presence, in primary canonical documents, of compositions and composites that by definition cannot have responded to the programs of those who compiled the respective documents. I refer to that autonomous tradition of which people speak. In that way we should address facts sustaining an alternate theory to the primacy of documentary discourse. That is the one I have set forth, that documents form coherent statements in accord with a particular program of indicative traits of rhetoric, topic, and logic of coherent discourse.

Where to turn? An obvious corpus of distinct but interrelated documents presents itself. The two Talmuds serving the Mishnah and Tosefta in Talmud form a natural starting point for the shaping of a null-hypothesis. That is because they share a common task, exegesis of the law of the Mishnah, the Tosefta, and the *baraita*-corpus, to which both Talmuds have access. If there is a an autonomous tradition, separate from the documents in which it survives, we should find marks of its presence in the two Talmuds. There, naturally, we should expect to identify the outlines of an autonomous tradition, prior to both completed documents.

The claim of the two Talmuds is irresistible. Those documents address the same legal texts. They preserve traditions in the name of the same authorities. And they go over the same problems of legal exegesis and theory. There, if anywhere, an autonomous, prior tradition should assert itself. Not only so, but in the two Talmuds we are able to distinguish a shared received text (the Mishnah, the Tosefta) from a shared tradition of an autonomous, other-than-documentary, point of origin. That is because there is a reliable control-mechanism. That is, we have in hand the documents on which they draw in common, the Mishnah and the Tosefta, as well as their own designation of sayings of the circulating baraita-corpus.

So these form a control, allowing us — if such is present — to identify a common source attested to, drawn upon, by both documents, *but not itself constituting a document.* We go in search of the common source not given documentary formalization in the way in which the Mishnah and the Tosefta constitute documents. That shared source — we might call it, the *Quelle* — would constitute evidence of the presence of that autonomous tradition such as people posit. Indeed, if we are able to identify a common, non-documentary source, the two Talmuds form a sufficiently sizable corpus to afford the possibility of not only identifying but describing such a source in some detail. For the Goldberg-Schaefer-Becker school and its Israeli and American adherents face an as-yet unattended to task: to offer an account of the Rabbinic tradition, its history and formulation, that explains the data now in our hands, and that does so in a more plausible manner than the thesis that proclaims the primacy of documentary discourse. So far, none of the critics has done even a small part of the descriptive work that is required to render the criticism compelling.

II. A COMMON SOURCE UTILIZED BY BOTH TALMUDS

Where and how do the Bavli and Yerushalmi meet in prior writings? At some, very few passages, as in the following instance, the two Talmuds say the same thing in the same way. We may say that, at such points, the two Talmuds, quite independent of one another, draw on common sources.[4] Here is one such case, at the two Talmuds serving Mishnah-tractate Makkot 1:10:

[I.A] [Trial before a] Sanhedrin applies both in the Land and abroad [M. 1:8E],	II.1A. Trial before] a Sanhedrin applies both in the land and abroad:
[B] as it is written, "And these things shall be for a statute and ordinance to you throughout your generations in all your dwellings" (Num. 35:29).	B. *What is the source of this rule?*
	C. *It is in line with that which our rabbis have taught on Tannaite authority:*
[C] And why does Scripture say, "You shall appoint judges and officers in all your towns [which the Lord your God gives you]" (Deut. 16:18) In the towns of the Land of Israel.	D. "And these things shall be for a statute of judgment to you throughout your generations in all your dwellings" (Num. 35:29) —
	E. we learn from that statement that the Sanhedrin operates both in the land and abroad.
	F. If that is so, then why does

[4] That the Bavli does not carry forward and stand in a traditional relationship to the Yerushalmi is an established fact, which I have no reason to challenge. But if it should be shown that the Bavli is dependent upon the Yerushalmi in its treatment of those tractates commented upon by both Talmuds, then the argument concerning a common source, and the entire null-hypothesis, will require complete revision.

[D] The meaning is that in the towns of Israel they set up judges in every town, but abroad they do so only by districts. [E] It was taught: R. Dosetai b. R. Yannai says, "It is a religious requirement for each tribe to judge its own tribe, as it is said, 'You shall appoint *judges* and officers in all your towns which the Lord your God gives you, according to your tribes' " (Deut. 16:18).	Scripture state, "Judges and offices you shall make for yourself in all your gates that the Lord God gives you tribe by tribe" (Dt. 16:18) [meaning only in the tribal land, in the land of Israel]? G. "In your own gates you set up courts in every district and every town, but outside of the land of Israel you set up courts in every district but not in every town."

Here is a fine example of how both Talmuds say the same thing in the same way and for the same purpose. If this were a common phenomenon, then comparison would prove much more productive. But my outline of the two Talmuds and comparative outline has shown otherwise.[5]

---

[5]I refer the reader to the following outlines of the two Talmuds, respectively, and comparative outlines of the two of them together:

The Talmud of Babylonia. A Complete Outline. Atlanta, 1995-6: Scholars Press for *USF Academic Commentary Series.*

    I.A.   *Tractate Berakhot and the Division of Appointed Times. Berakhot, Shabbat, and Erubin.*
    I.B   *Tractate Berakhot and the Division of Appointed Times. Pesahim through Hagigah.*
    II.A.   *The Division of Women. Yebamot through Ketubot*
    II.B.   *The Division of Women. Nedarim through Qiddushin*
    III.A   *The Division of Damages. Baba Qamma through Baba Batra*
    III.B   *The Division of Damages. Sanhedrin through Horayot*
    IV.A   *The Division of Holy Things and Tractate Niddah. Zebahim through Hullin*

IV.B   *The Division of Holy Things and Tractate Niddah. Bekhorot through Niddah*

The Talmud of The Land of Israel. An Outline of the Second, Third, and Fourth Divisions. Atlanta, 1995-6: Scholars Press for USF Academic Commentary Series.

I.A   *Tractate Berakhot and the Division of Appointed Times. Berakhot and Shabbat*
I.B   *Tractate Berakhot and the Division of Appointed Times. Erubin, Yoma, and Besah*
I.C   *Tractate Berakhot and the Division of Appointed Times. Pesahim and Sukkah*
I.D   *Tractate Berakhot and the Division of Appointed Times. Taanit, Megillah, Rosh Hashanah, Hagigah, and Moed Qatan*
II.A.   *The Division of Women. Yebamot to Nedarim*
II.B.   *The Division of Women. Nazir to Sotah*
III.A   *The Division of Damages and Tractate Niddah. Baba Qamma, Baba Mesia, Baba Batra, Horayot, and Niddah*
III.B   *The Division of Damages and Tractate Niddah. Sanhedrin, Makkot, Shebuot, and Abodah Zarah*

The Two Talmuds Compared. Atlanta, 1995-6: Scholars Press for USF Academic Commentary Series.

I.A   *Tractate Berakhot and the Division of Appointed Times in the Talmud of the Land of Israel and the Talmud of Babylonia. Yerushalmi Tractate Berakhot*
I.B   *Tractate Berakhot and the Division of Appointed Times in the Talmud of the Land of Israel and the Talmud of Babylonia. Tractate Shabbat.*
I.C   *Tractate Berakhot and the Division of Appointed Times in the Talmud of the Land of Israel and the Talmud of Babylonia. Tractate Erubin*
I.D   *Tractate Berakhot and the Division of Appointed Times in the Talmud of the Land of Israel and the Talmud of Babylonia. Tractates Yoma and Sukkah*

And it should also be said: Goldberg-Schaefer-Becker and their circle have yet to do their homework. It is easier to emote abstractions than to confront the concrete data and explain them in one way, rather than in some other. My citations of Schaefer's critique of the documentary hypothesis, presented in Appendix Two, sustain this judgment that abstraction and rhetoric have replaced sustained, detailed scholarship. Collecting the variant readings without a systematic engagement with them such as Schaefer and his helpers have carried out also does not suffice. Comparing the variant wordings of a handful of stories that occur in more than a single document proves nothing consequential, as Becker's

---

I.E   *Tractate Berakhot and the Division of Appointed Times in the Talmud of the Land of Israel and the Talmud of Babylonia. Tractate Pesahim*

I.F   *Tractate Berakhot and the Division of Appointed Times in the Talmud of the Land of Israel and the Talmud of Babylonia. Tractates Besah, Taanit, and Megillah*

I.G   *Tractate Berakhot and the Division of Appointed Times in the Talmud of the Land of Israel and the Talmud of Babylonia. Tractates Rosh Hashanah, Hagigah, and Moed Qatan*

II.A   *The Division of Women in the Talmud of the Land of Israel and the Talmud of Babylonia. Tractates Yebamot and Ketubot.*

II.B   *The Division of Women in the Talmud of the Land of Israel and the Talmud of Babylonia. Tractates Nedarim, Nazir, and Sotah.*

II.C   *The Division of Women in the Talmud of the Land of Israel and the Talmud of Babylonia. Tractates Qiddushin and Gittin.*

III.A   *The Division of Damages and Tractate Niddah in the Talmud of the Land of Israel and the Talmud of Babylonia. Tractates Baba Qamma and Baba Mesia*

III.B   *The Division of Damages and Tractate Niddah in the Talmud of the Land of Israel and the Talmud of Babylonia. Baba Batra and Niddah.*

III.C   *The Division of Damages and Tractate Niddah. Sanhedrin and Makkot.*

III.D   *The Division of Damages and Tractate Niddah. Shebuot, Abodah Zarah, and Horayot.*

Habilitationsschrift demonstrates. He is stronger on paraphrasing his data than on interpreting them.

Neither scholar has examined in detail evidence such as what is before us, which can support their hypothesis of an autonomous tradition, external to all documents. The case before us shows that some sort of common, ante-documentary corpus can have circulated. It remains to prove that such a body of writing (or of oral traditions) did circulate — and to describe, analyze, and interpret its components and their construction. But those who hold a view contrary to mine have not yet undertaken to offer such detailed proof.

Granted, the Talmuds intersect in Scripture, the Mishnah, the Tosefta, Sifra, the two Sifrés, and other already-redacted documents. But when they meet, is it for a stable union or a brief and casual encounter? And, we ask further about their meeting in sayings that circulated one by one, and not in the fully-redacted setting of a composition, a composite, a whole document. That work has been done for kindred writings, the synoptic Gospels, as everybody knows. Can it be done for the Yerushalmi and the Bavli? My answer is in the next stage of the argument.

III. DO THE BAVLI AND YERUSHALMI DRAW ON (A) "Q"? AND DOES A TOPICAL PROTOCOL DEFINE THE TALMUDS' MISHNAH-EXEGESIS?

Gospels' scholarship has (in the opinion of some scholars) shown that collections of sayings attributed to Jesus circulated independent of the Gospels and were utilized by the Evangelists themselves, specifically, Mark, Matthew and Luke. This is called "Q," or Quelle, "source." Specifically, is there then the Rabbinic counterpart to the alleged "Q," that is to say, a source of sayings, collected and set forth, upon which the Bavli and Yerushalmi draw, each for its own purposes or for shared purposes (it would make no difference for our problem)? And, if there is such a "Q," is the collection dominant and definitive, so that we can show how both Talmuds meet at a starting point other than known writings such as the Mishnah, Tosefta, and baraita-corpus?[6] If that is so, then how shall I able to claim that the Bavli stands entirely on its own, never meeting the Yerushalmi at a third-party meeting point, never drawing upon "autonomous traditions"? That forms the logical next question in this development of a null-hypothesis: proof of a non-documentary, extra-documentary corpus of traditions, drawn upon by documents but unaffected by their indicative traits and program.

It is a demonstrable fact that, here and there, the Bavli cites the same saying in the same wording that the Yerushalmi presents in its composition on a given Mishnah-pericope. That is in three aspects.

First, it is the simple fact that, occasionally, sayings not found in any prior document are shared in the same or nearly the same wording by the Yerushalmi and the Bavli. That on the face of it is not surprising. Stories in both Talmuds speak of constant communications among the authorities of each country's Jewish polity. That the Bavli had access to sayings assigned to the authorities prominent in the Land of Israel and critical to the Yerushalmi is shown on virtually every other page of the document, where Simeon b. Laqish or Yohanan or their colleagues are cited. It follows that the stories about circulating sayings are matched by the data themselves, which show the Babylonians' utilizing sayings in the names of the other country's sages. *But whether or not collections*

---

[6]Once more with the stipulation that the baraita-corpus can be identified and defined. If not, not.

of such sayings existed, as a counterpart to "Q," and, if they did, what such collections looked like, is a separate question.

For a saying to occur in the Rabbinic "Q," I should want it to be cited in both Talmuds and in the same context or for the same purpose. If a saying imputed to a Yerushalmi figure occurs only in the Bavli, e.g., in a dispute involving Rab and Samuel, Simeon b. Laqish and Yohanan, that may show that the Babylonians had access to sayings from the Land of Israel (if we take the names at face value), but it does not show that a common corpus of sayings circulated in both countries. Indeed, it shows the exact opposite. If a saying assigned to a Yerushalmi sage occurs in both the Yerushalmi and the Bavli but not in the same context, e.g., "R. Simeon b. Laqish says, 'It is unfit,'" that is inconsequential, because indeterminate.

But if, in the same setting, e.g., of Mishnah-exegesis or analysis of legal principle or premise, the same saying occurs in the same way in both documents (but in no other, prior or contemporary document, not in, e.g., the Mishnah, Tosefta, or Sifra or the two Sifrés), and if that saying is so worded as to be particular to the issue or distinctive to the context, then we may propose a theory. It is that that saying derives from a circulating collection of sayings of Yerushalmi sages (or Babylonian ones, for that matter); and then there was a "Q."

I state very simply that, in the sample of the Bavli I examined in *The Bavli's Unique Voice*,[7] there are too few such

---

[7]*The Bavli's Unique Voice. A Systematic Comparison of the Talmud of Babylonia and the Talmud of the Land of Israel.* Volume One. *Bavli and Yerushalmi Qiddushin Chapter One Compared and Contrasted.* Atlanta, 1993: Scholars Press for South Florida Studies in the History of Judaism.

The Bavli's Unique Voice. A Systematic Comparison of the Talmud of Babylonia and the Talmud of the Land of Israel. Volume Two. *Yerushalmi's, Bavli's,* sayings, to suggest that the framers of the Bavli drew to any extent on a corpus of set sayings in the formation of their compositions. If there was such a "Q," the part of it the existence of which we can demonstrate through hard evidence was both trivial and lacking in all influence. In the sample I have examined, I have never found a case in which that shared saying, from a hypothetical "Q," influenced the au-

---

and Other Canonical Documents' Treatment of the Program of Mishnah-Tractate Sukkah Chapters One, Two, and Four Compared and Contrasted. A Reprise and Revision of The Bavli and its Sources. Atlanta, 1993: Scholars Press for South Florida Studies in the History of Judaism.

The Bavli's Unique Voice. A Systematic Comparison of the Talmud of Babylonia and the Talmud of the Land of Israel. Volume Three. *Bavli and Yerushalmi to Selected Mishnah-Chapters in the Division of Moed. Erubin Chapter One, and Moed Qatan Chapter Three.* Atlanta, 1993: Scholars Press for South Florida Studies in the History of Judaism.

The Bavli's Unique Voice. A Systematic Comparison of the Talmud of Babylonia and the Talmud of the Land of Israel. Volume Four. *Bavli and Yerushalmi to Selected Mishnah-Chapters in the Division of Nashim. Gittin Chapter Five and Nedarim Chapter One. And Niddah Chapter One.* Atlanta, 1993: Scholars Press for South Florida Studies in the History of Judaism.

The Bavli's Unique Voice. A Systematic Comparison of the Talmud of Babylonia and the Talmud of the Land of Israel. Volume Five. *Bavli and Yerushalmi to Selected Mishnah-Chapters in the Division of Neziqin. Baba Mesia Chapter One and Makkot Chapters One and Two.* Atlanta, 1993: Scholars Press for South Florida Studies in the History of Judaism.

The Bavli's Unique Voice. A Systematic Comparison of the Talmud of Babylonia and the Talmud of the Land of Israel. Volume Six. *Bavli and Yerushalmi to a Miscellany of Mishnah-Chapters. Gittin Chapter One, Qiddushin Chapter Two, and Hagigah Chapter Three.* Atlanta, 1993: Scholars Press for South Florida Studies in the History of Judaism.

The Bavli's Unique Voice. Volume Seven. *What Is Unique about the Bavli in Context? An Answer Based on Inductive Description, Analysis, and Comparison.* Atlanta, 1993: Scholars Press for South Florida Studies in the History of Judaism.

authors of the two Talmuds' compositions to say the same thing in the same way. To the contrary, shared sayings were used in different ways, with the consequence that, if there was a "Q," it made no difference to the authors of the Bavli's compositions as they contemplated their exegetical or hermeneutical program. If there was a "Q," what would it have looked like? Here is a candidate for consideration:

M. NIDDAH 1:1: Here neither set of authors does more than give a reprise of received materials. But if I had to specify the character of the received materials, I should have to say that, as to wording, they do not appear the same in both Talmuds; it is the gist that can be shown to play a role in both Talmuds' compositions, not the wording — so surely no "Q' by any definition that pertains. I underline what I take to be the candidate for "Q."

[I.A] Samuel said, "This teaching [of A] applies only to a virgin and an old lady. But as to a pregnant woman and a nursing mother, they assign to her the entire period of her pregnancy or the entire period of her nursing [respectively, for the blood ceases, and what does flow is inconsequential, so there is no retroactive contamination at all]."	VIII.1A. **And of what case did they speak when they said, "Sufficient for her is her time"? In the case of the first appearance of a drop of blood. But in the case of the second appearance of such a drop of blood, she conveys uncleanness to whatever she touched during the preceding twenty-four hours.**
[B] Rab and R. Yohanan — both of them say, <u>"All the same are the virgin, the old lady, the pregnant woman, and the nursing mother [= B]."</u>	B. Said Rab, <u>"The statement **[But in the case of the second appearance of such a drop of blood, she conveys uncleanness to whatever she touched during the preceding twenty-four hours]** applies to all the listed cases."</u>
[C] Said R. Zeira, "The opinion of Rab and R. Yohanan accords with the position of R. Haninah, and all of them differ from the position of Samuel."	C. And Samuel said, "It refers only to the virgin and the old lady,

[D] For R. Eleazar said in the name of R. Haninah, "On one occasion Rabbi gave instruction in accord with the lenient rulings of R. Meir and in accord with the lenient rulings of R. Yosé."

[E] What was the nature of the case?

[F] [If] the fetus was noticeable, and then [the woman] produced a drop of blood —

[G] R. Meir says, "She is subject to the rule of the sufficiency of her time [of actually discovering the blood]."

[H] R. Yosé says, "She imparts uncleanness retroactively for twenty-four hours."

[I] [If] she produced many drops of blood, then missed three periods, and afterward produced a drop of blood,

[J] R. Meir says, "She imparts uncleanness retroactively for twenty-four hours."

[K] R. Yosé says, "She is subject to the rule of the sufficiency of her time [of actually discovering blood]."

[L] Now if you say that they assign to her the entire period of her pregnancy or the entire period of her nursing, what need do I have for the lenient ruling of R. Yosé? The teaching of R. Meir [in such a case] produces a still more lenient ruling than does that of R. Yosé. [For so far as Meir is concerned, if we read his view in the light of Samuel's opinion (A), the nursing mother and the pregnant

but as to the pregnant woman and the nursing mother, throughout all the days of pregnancy or through all the days of nursing, it is sufficient for them to reckon uncleanness not retroactively but only from the time of observing a flow."

D. And so said R. Simeon b. Laqish, "The statement **[But in the case of the second appearance of such a drop of blood, she conveys uncleanness to whatever she touched during the preceding twenty-four hours]** applies to all the listed cases."

E. And R. Yohanan said, "It refers only to the virgin and the old lady, but as to the pregnant woman and the nursing mother, throughout all the days of pregnancy or through all the days of nursing, throughout all the days of pregnancy or through all the days of nursing, it is sufficient for them to reckon uncleanness not retroactively but only from the time of observing a flow."

F. *The dispute follows the lines of a dispute among Tannaite versions:*

G. "A pregnant woman or a nursing mother who were **[11A]** bleeding profusely — throughout all the days of pregnancy or through all the days of nursing, it is sufficient for them to reckon uncleanness not retroactively but only from the time of observing a flow," the words of R. Meir.

H. R. Yosé and R. Judah and R.

woman enjoy the stated leniency throughout the period of nursing or pregnancy. The issue, then, is that Meir deems this drop of blood (I) as a second one. Yosé regards the cessation of the period as consequential.] [M] Said R. Mana before R. Yosé, "Or perhaps we should assign [Rabbi's ruling] to the case of the milk [dealt with above, in which Meir and Yosé dispute about whether the woman who hands over her son to a wet-nurse retains the stated leniency. At issue then is whether the matter depends upon the status of the woman's milk or on the status of the child]." [N] He said to him, "The matter was explicitly stated in regard to the present issue."	Simeon say, "The ruling that sufficient for them is the time of their actually seeing a drop of blood applies only to the first appearance of a drop of blood, but the second imparts uncleanness for the preceding twenty-four hours or from one examination to the prior examination."

I see no material differences as to the gist of the law, between the two Talmuds' representation of the matter. But this kind of intersection has proven very, very rare in my sample. So all we can conclude is that we have a fine example of what the two Talmuds would have looked like, had the Bavli's authors satisfied themselves a reprise constructed by reference not to the Yerushalmi itself but to some sort of handbook of sayings. "Q" here would then have consisted of something that yielded the underlined wording in the respective documents, that is to say, that would have permitted the Bavli's composition's author to word matters as he did. If this were our sole evidence, then we should have to posit a "Q" consisting of paraphrases and allusions, the gist of what was said, not the wording; but then the analogy collapses, that is not what "Q" consists of.

Second, some items that appear to attest to a "Q" of sayings, not the gist, show the opposite, for what appears to be a shared saying may turn out, on closer examination, to be two distinct sayings, one for each Talmud. Hence, even where a saying appears to originate in the Rabbinic counterpart to "Q," in fact it shows the opposite: not a well-crafted source-book of sayings, but a rather slovenly process of tradition, operating so that handing on whatever was shared was botched. Let me give a single example of such a phenomenon, one in which (as a matter of fact) the Yerushalmi's version in fact is superior to the Bavli's.

M. M.Q. 3:4: We have a somewhat odd situation at Y. 3:4III and B. 3:4 I.2. As it stands, the latter is incomprehensible, and it clearly presupposes the former. Then there is no discussion, at B.'s version, of Rab's views:

[III.A] Someone lost his *Tefillin* on the intermediate days of a festival. He came to R. Hananel [who was a scribe and who would prepare a new set for him]. He sent him to R. Abba bar Nathan. He said to him, "Give him your *Tefillin* [phylacteries] and go, write a new set for yourself." [B] Said to him Rab, "[It is permitted to] go and write them for him [without practicing deception]." [C] The Mishnah stands at variance with the view of Rab: A *man may write out Tefillin and mezuzahs for his own use* [M. 3: 4G]. [D] Lo, for someone else he may	I.2 A. *Rab instructed R. Hananel, and some say, Rabbah bar bar Hanna instructed R. Hananel,* "The decided law is this: He may write them out and sell them in the ordinary way if it is to make his living."

not do so. [E] Interpret the passage to speak of not doing so merely by writing them out and leaving them [for future sale].	

As we have it, B.'s version is strange and out of context; read as a continuation of B. 3:4 I.1, the statement does not intersect with Y.'s case at all; but then how explain the reference to Hananel?! So, in all, here is a case in which a fragment of a formulation has been inserted, and without the Yerushalmi, the fragment is not to be interpreted. Yet a second look calls that judgment into question. In fact, Rab's instructions to Hananel in B. have to do with writing Tefillin and selling them on the intermediate days of the festival if it is to make a living; Y.'s formulation does not introduce that consideration at all. And the reason that the consideration of making a living is introduced at B. 3:4 I.2 is Yosé's reference to it at I.1D! So, in fact, while somewhere in the dim past of both Talmuds' compositions may lie a statement of Rab to Hananel (or: Rabbah bar bar Hanna!), the use of the same by each depends entirely on considerations particular to each Talmud respectively. Here is no instance in which making sense of the Bavli requires that we resort to the Yerushalmi or to "Q"; to the contrary, all we have to do is back up one line to make sense of the Bavli's formulation entirely in the Bavli's own terms.

Where then is our "Q" to link the two Talmuds, that is, the second to the first? It is only in the corpus of compositions bearing the mark of Tannaite standing, that is, marked by TNY, TNY', and the like, the baraita-corpus, to which I made reference above. There was a corpus of sayings assigned to Tannaim, but not encompassed by the Tosefta. It did circulate in both countries. No one doubt that a baraita-corpus circulated, but no one has yet succeeded in systematically giving us an account of the matter. The great exercise of Michael Higger not withstanding, the work awaits.

Here is one of the few well-constructed examples of how it was used in each place. We deal with the two Talmuds to **M. B.M. 1:1**:

[V.A] It was taught: **Two who were laying hold of a document [bond] —** [B] *This* one says, "It is mine, and I lost it!" [C] And that one says, "It was in my possession, and 1 already paid you for it!" — [D] "Let the document be confirmed through the signatures of the witnesses which it bears," the words of Rabbi. [E] And (Rabban Simeon b.) Gamaliel says, "Let them divide it the money] between them" (T. B.M. 1:15]. [F] R. Eleazar said, "All follows the circumstance of which of the claimants holds the part on which the witnesses have signed their name." [G] Said R. Hisda, "If you accept this view, you accord with the position of R. Simeon [b. Gamaliel]. [But Rabbi will want the witnesses to confirm the bond in court.]"	5.A. We have learned on Tannaite authority: B. "Two were holding on to a bond — C. "the lender says, 'It's mine and fell from me and I found it.' E. "The borrower says, 'It's yours, but I paid it off' — F. "let the bond be confirmed by its signatories [verifying their signatures]," the words of Rabbi. G. Rabban Simeon b. Gamaliel says, "Let them divide it up." H. If it came into the possession of a judge, he may never again produce it. I. R. Yosé says, "Lo, it remains subject to the presumption pertaining to it [that it is valid, and the creditor may demand return of the document and collect on the strength of it]." 6.A. [Analyzing the passage just now cited,] a master has said, "'let the bond be confirmed by its signatories [verifying their signatures]'" — *and may the lender ben col-*

lect on the strength of the bond the whole
of the debt confirmed therein?! Does not
the master concur with our Mishnah-
paragraph: **Two lay hold of a
cloak?**

B. *Said Raba said R. Nahman, "In a
case in which the document is confirmed
[in court, with the witnesses verifying
their signatures and the judges the en-
dorsement,] all parties concur that the
two litigants are to divide the contested
sum. Where they differ is in a case in
which the document is not confirmed in
court.*

C. *"Rabbi takes the view that if the
debtor concedes that he has written a
bond, nonetheless it is necessary to confirm the signatories, and, if it is confirmed in court, then the contested sum is
divided, and if it is not confirmed in
court, there is no division at all. What
is his reasoning? It is a mere shard [if
the document is not confirmed in court,
and has no value whatever]. For, under
these conditions, by what testimony is
the bond validated anyhow? It is by the
testimony of the borrower — who also
maintains that he has paid!*

D. *"And Rabban Simeon b. Gama-
liel takes the view that in the case of one
who concedes in the case of a bond that
he has written it, it is not necessary to
confirm the document, and   even
though it is not confirmed, the litigants
divide the contested sum."* [Daiches:
Even if the bill is not endorsed,
the borrower cannot plead that he
has paid the debt when the lender
produces the document. The validity of the docuament does not
depend on the plea of the bor-

	rower to that extent. Hence they divide the amount.]

As it happens, the Tosefta presents the shared materials; but since the Tosefta-passage is identical in both Talmuds, we have fair reason to classify what is shared as a counterpart to "Q."

But our interest is in a null-hypothesis. So what if we should appeal to "Q" in this form and passage with the specific plan of demonstrating the dependence of the Bavli on a prior tradition, other than the Mishnah (now add: or its equivalent[s], the Tosefta, collections of finished sayings, whether marked as Tannaite or not)? That is what is at stake in the issue of "Q"! But then, alas, the evidence of "Q" proves precisely the opposite. Let me state the matter with emphasis, since it is a critical result for our null hypothesis:

The Bavli does not stand in a traditional relationship to this version of "Q," but utilizes the materials of "Q" to its own ends. It is free-standing and autocephalous, not dependent on either Q or (all the more so) the Yerushalmi's theory of what Q means.

No autonomous tradition here! What about the Yerushalmi? The Yerushalmi (F) explains the positions taken in the Tosefta-passage and their implications (G). The Bavli draws the passage into relationship to our Mishnah-rule and proposes that it conforms to the premise of that rule (6.A). Then we proceed to isolate the situation concerning which Rabbi and Simeon b. Gamaliel his father disagree, 6.B-C. As is clear from 6.C, this speculative reading draws us far afield. Now at issue is the status of the bond. So how do the Talmuds compare? The first Talmud analyzes evidence, the second investigates premises; the first remains wholly within the limits of its case, the second vastly transcends them; and the first wants to know the rule, the second asks about the principle and its implications for other cases. The one Talmud provides an exegesis and amplification of the Mishnah, the other, a theoretical study of the law in all its magnificent abstraction — transforming the Mishnah into testimony to a deeper reality altogether: to the law behind the laws.[8]

Do the Bavli and Yerushalmi draw on (a) "Q"? At some points, they do draw on finished, and available materials. It is very common that these finished materials occur also in the Tosefta, which is hardly surprising, but, occasionally, the finished materials are not located in any other document.[9]

---

[8]I make reference to my *The Law Behind the Laws. The Bavli's Essential Discourse*. Atlanta, 1992: Scholars Press for South Florida Studies in the History of Judaism, even though the results of that probe proved somewhat limited.

[9]When, in his *Tannaitic Parallels to the Gospels* (Philadelphia, 1953), Morton Smith pointed out the "parallel of parallelism" between the relationship of the Mishnah and the Tosefta to "Q," he was wrong. There is no parallel between the Mishnah's and the Tosefta's relationships (which are varied) and the relationship of "Q" to Mark, Matthew, and Luke (in any of the variations that have been posited in those relationships). The correct parallel, as shown here, is the relationships of the two Talmuds to the Tosefta; but then the parallel proves inconsequential and trivial, as I have now shown. For there to be a consequential parallel between the relationships of the two Talmuds to the Tosefta or comparable compositions, we should have to have a much more complex interplay between the respective Talmuds' authors and the materials that are shared and so derive from their counterpart to "Q." I do not think any Gospels' scholar would find a parallel of parallelism between the fact that both Talmuds cite a sizable, completed pericope, each using it for its clearly distinctive purpose, and the fact that two or more Gospels cite a saying, often reworking the very wording of that saying in accord with their respective purposes. No "Q" here! In retrospect, *Tannaitic Parallels* proves a collection of unsystematic aperçus, not all of them simply wrong or based on a misunderstanding of the data, but most of them misguided and ignorant. As Smith used to say of others, you just have to check him point by point. By that, Smith meant, you can rely on nothing this poor fellow tells you, and that, alas, has now to be said of one of Smith's two important contributions to learn-

So there can have been a "Q." But if there was a Quelle, it is not like a "Q" of the size and importance of the one that in the opinion of New Testament scholars of a certain school is attested by Matthew and Mark and used by Luke.

But if there was a shared corpus of sayings besides those in available documents, what difference does that fact make for the description of the Bavli? None. The Bavli emerges, all the more so, as a free-standing document, written by its compositions' writers and its composites' compilers, for whatever purpose suited them. They used traditions, whether deriving from Scripture or the Mishnah or the Tosefta or other compilations bearing the sign of Tannaite status; this they did for their own purposes, in their own way, for the presentation of their own statement. They used traditions, they were not traditional.

What about sayings that float from document to document, of which Becker makes so much? Let us conclude this inquiry with an examination of a story that certainly is shared, pretty much verbatim, in the two Talmuds. Here is an unambiguous piece of evidence on what difference access to something one might wish to call a "Q" (in this context, a shared corpus of stories) made to the two Talmuds. A look at the Yerushalmi's secondary development draws attention to the fact that, like the Bavli, the Yerushalmi introduces the

---

ing. In its day, Tannaitic Parallels proved stimulating and suggestive, and when I wrote my *Aphrahat and Judaism. The Christian Jewish Argument in Fourth Century Iran.* Leiden, 1971: Brill, I found it instructive in defining the problem of parallels. But as learning proceeded, it became clear that Smith did not know what he was talking about, but did some fine guessing, in a situation in which no one else was doing anything. The other, *Palestinian Parties...*, has had its critics, who appear unpersuaded by the merit of Smith's ideas. As to the Clement fragment, here Smith really did leave a lasting legacy: a famous forgery, so Quentin Quesnell proved in *Catholic Biblical Quarterly* 1976.

story of Simeon the righteous, and the versions of the story differ at some interesting details. Here is a case in which the two Talmuds use the same item, serving **M NED 1:1**. Here we find an occasion on which a story from some sort of prior source (if there was such a thing) has been drawn for use by the framers of both documents' composition. Let us see how they contrast:

[D] The Mishnah passage before us accords with the view of R. Judah. It has been taught in the name of R. Judah:

[E] "The pious men of old used to want to bring a sin offering. But the space on the altar was not sufficient for the bringing in their behalf of offerings in expiation of inadvertent sins. So they would offer Nazirite vows as freewill offerings, so that they might bring a sin offering."

[F] Rabban Simeon b. Gamaliel says, "They were sinners, for they would take a vow as a Nazir, as it is said 'And he shall make atonement for him, because he sinned against the soul'" (Num. 6: 11) [T. Ned. 1: 1H-P].

[G] This sin, to which reference is made, against his soul, is that he has kept himself from drinking wine.

[H] Now this view of R. Simeon [b. Gamaliel] accords with the view of Simeon the Righteous. For it has been taught:

[I] Said Simeon the Righteous, "In my entire life I ate the guilt offering of a Nazir only one time. Once a man came to me from the south, and I saw him, that he had beautiful eyes and a lovely face, and curly hair. I said to him, 'My son, why did you destroy that lovely hair of yours?'

E. *Well, that solves the problem in regard to a freewill-offering in the classification of ordinary sacrifices, but what about the freewill-offering presented in the context of the Nazirite vow?* [Freedman: since the possibility of violating one of the laws of the Nazirite may also form a stumbling block].

F. *The operative theory is that of Simeon the Righteous, for it has been taught on Tannaite authority:*

G. Said Simeon the Righteous, "Only once in my lifetime have I eaten a guilt-offering presented by a Nazirite who had become unclean. Once a Nazirite came to me from the south, and I saw that he had beautiful eyes, a handsome face, and thick curly locks. I said to him, 'My son, how come you vowed to destroy this lovely hair of yours [in a Nazirite's hair-offering]?"

H. "He said to me, 'I was a shepherd in my village. I came to draw water from a well, saw my reflection in the water, and my evil impulse rushed upon me and tried to drive me out of this world [by making me sin, with pride]. I said to it, "Evil one! You oughtn't to have taken pride in something that does not belong to you, something that is going to turn into dust, worms, and corruption. Lo, I take upon myself the obligation to shave you off for the sake of Heaven."'

[J] "He said to me, 'Rabbi, I was a shepherd in my town, and I came to draw water from the river. I looked at my reflection, and my evil impulse grew proud within me and besought thereby to remove me from the world. I said to it, 'Evil one, Have you a right to be jealous of a thing which really is not yours, of something which is destined to turn into dust, worms, and maggots? Lo, it is incumbent on me to shave you off for the sake of Heaven' [and that constituted the vow of a Nazir].

[K] "I kissed him on his head, saying to him, 'My son, may people like you become many, who do the will of the Omnipresent. Through you is fulfilled this Scripture, 'When either man or a woman makes a special vow, the vow of a Nazirite, to separate himself to the Lord'" (Num. 6: 2) [T. Naz. 4: 7].

[L] R. Mana raised the question: "Why do I have to interpret the matter [of M. 1:1 H] in accord with Simeon the Righteous? It accords even with R. Simeon."

[M] Simeon the Righteous did not eat the fat of a sin offering in his entire life, nor did he consume the blood of a sin offering in his entire life.

[N] Simeon the Righteous maintained that people take vows out of ill temper.

I. "Forthwith I got up and kissed him on the head, saying, 'My son, may there be many Nazirites of such pure motive as you in Israel. You are the person to whom Scripture referred when it said, "When ei there a man or a woman shall separate themselves to vow a vow of a Nazirite, to separate themselves to the Lord" (Num. 6:2)'" [T. Naz. 4:7].

J. *Objected R. Mani, "And what differentiates the guilt-offering of an unclean Nazirite, that he never ate meat from one? It is because it is presented on account of sin. But then he should not have eaten meat from any guilt-offering, since all of them are presented on account of sin!"*

K. *Said to him R. Jonah, "This is the operative consideration:* It is when people are in a state of discombobulation that they take Nazirite vows, but then, when they contract uncleanness, and [having to start all over again] the days of their Nazirite vows become many, that they regret their vows, in which case, they turn out to bring unconsecrated beasts [animals they have consecrated to carry out a vow that is in fact null, hence, unconsecrated animals] to the Temple courtyard."

L. *Well, if that's the case, then the same consideration applies also to a Nazirite who has not contracted uncleanness!*

[O] Since they take vows out of ill temper, in the end it will come to nothing.

[P] Since in the end it comes to nothing, the offerings brought by a Nazir, when slaughtered in the Temple courtyard, are equivalent to unconsecrated offerings slaughtered in the Temple courtyard. But this particular one took his vow in a serene spirit, when what he said and what he was thinking were one and the same thing.

M. *A Nazirite who has not contracted uncleanness is not subject to the same consideration, because he has made a careful estimate of himself that he can take the vow [and carry it out].*

There we have it at last, a story occurring in both Talmuds. Does the Bavli's composition draw closer to the Yerushalmi's at a point at which both Talmuds' authors address a single, sustained story in common? A comparison of the utilization of the story by each set of writers gives us a simple and absolutely final answer to that question: no.[10]

For the Yerushalmi, the issue is the sin of the Nazirite, which is defined at IX.G, and the story of Simeon the Righteous is introduced in that context. L objects, and then M-P go their own way. The Bavli wants to know why a vow to present a freewill offering is not reprehensible, and the answer is drawn from the case of Hillel; but this requires us to

---

[10]It is fair to observe that Goldberg, Schaefer, Becker, and others pay remarkably little attention to the substance of the stories and sayings that they collate in various versions, and when it comes to the Halakhic sources, they show considerable reticence indeed. But without attention to what a story says, how are they to evaluate diverse readings of a particular detail? For a systematic account of the costs of not paying attention to the details of the Halakhic texts but merely collating manuscript variants and the like, see my *The Place of the Tosefta in the Halakhah of Formative Judaism. What Alberdina Houtman Didn't Notice.* Atlanta, 1998: Scholars Press for South Florida Studies in the History of Judaism.

ask about the free will offering in the context of the Nazirite vow, and that brings us to the story of the Nazirite vow, which may be taken on account of a totally pure motive, as in the story at hand. J-M then complete the matter. So, in general, the context is the same, but, in detail, it is not. What is important to the Bavli is the matter of the motive of the Nazirite, so the Bavli's version of Simeon's blessing refers to that fact, while the Yerushalmi's version simply praises the man for overcoming the sin of pride. There is quite a difference in that detail — the difference between (from the perspective of the Bavli) using the story and not using it. To close on the main point: when the two Talmuds use the same story, the Bavli's authors have no hesitation in inserting into the story a point that concerns them; the story is made relevant to the context. The Bavli wants to show that one who takes a Nazirite vow is a sinner; it says so in so many words at B. II.5:

> Said Abbayye, "Simeon the Righteous, R. Simeon, and R. Eleazar Haqqappar – all of them concur that the Nazirite is a sinner. *Simeon the Righteous and R. Simeon as we have just now said...*"

Does the Yerushalmi concur on that point? Of course it does — and it says so in so many words. But that is not in the context of an analytical argument aiming at a coherent presentation of the proposition with which we began: "Since they take vows out of ill temper, in the end it will come to nothing. Since in the end it comes to nothing, the offerings brought by a Nazir, when slaughtered in the Temple courtyard, are equivalent to unconsecrated offerings slaughtered in the Temple courtyard. But this particular one took his vow in a serene spirit, when what he said and what he was thinking were one and the same thing.".

If, then, there was a "Q," what difference does it make? The answer is, none at all. The incoherence of the Yerushalmi is not the point; rather, the power of the Bavli's author to hold the whole together in a continuous argument becomes all the more impressive, when contrasted with the Yerushalmi's somewhat disjointed presentation of exactly the same materials. The Bavli's framers did not hesitate to shape the story to their purpose, and why not? they impose their determinative purpose on everything else they do. To repeat what scarcely requires articulation: theirs is a unique voice, they speak for themselves — and they make everyone else, through all times, also speak in behalf of their program and make a contribution to their statement.

IV.   DOES A TOPICAL PROTOCOL DEFINE THE TALMUDS' MISHNAH-EXEGESIS?

What about autonomous traditions not given verbal formulation in the strict manner of the Mishnah and the Tosefta. The next question in the null hypothesis addresses the possibility that, while no considerable corpus of writing joins the two Talmuds other than Scripture, the Mishnah, and the Tosefta, there may have been a protocol of topics or problems associated with a given Mishnah- or Tosefta-pericope. Such a protocol would have told the exegetes of that pericope, or the compilers of compositions deemed pertinent to that pericope, what subject they should treat (over and above the subject of the pericope); or what problem they should investigate (over and above the problem explicit in the pericope). Obviously, every Mishnah-pericope treated differently in the two Talmuds gives evidence that there was no such protocol of topics or problems. But more specific evidence can be adduced, where the Mishnah-pericope does not demand attention to a topic, but both Talmuds address said topic. It is at **MISHNAH MOED QATAN 3:5-6**, where the absence of a protocol of problems, over and above those of Scripture, emerges:

[XXXIX.A] For they have said, "The Sabbath counts in the days of mourning, but does not interrupt the period of mourning, while the festivals interrupt the period of mourning, and do not count in the days of mourning" [M. 3: 5C].

[B] "[The festivals do not count,]" R. Simon in the name of R. Yohanan [explained], "Because one is permitted on them to have sexual relations."

[C] R. Jeremiah dealt with R. Judah b. R. Simon, saying to him, "Do all the disciples of R. Yohanan report this tradition? Not one person has ever heard this tradition from him, except for your father!"

[D] Said to him R. Jacob, "If it was said, it was said only by those who say, 'Thus and so is the matter' [without knowing what they are talking about]!

[E] "For R. Joshua b. Levi said, 'Lo, [on the festival] it is forbidden [for a mourner] to have sexual relations.'"

[F] For R. Simon said in the name of R. Joshua b. Levi, "Have they not said, 'A mourning does not apply on a festival, but people observe mourning discretely'?"

[G] What is the context for this

II.1A. For they have said, "The Sabbath counts [in the days of mourning] but does not interrupt [the period of mourning], [while] the festivals interrupt [the period of mourning] and do not count [in the days of mourning]":

B. *Judeans and Galilaeans –*

C. *These say,* [23B] "Mourning pertains to the Sabbath."

D. *And those say,* "Mourning does not pertain to the Sabbath."

E. *The one who says,* "Mourning pertains to the Sabbath," *cites the Mishnah's statement,* **The Sabbath counts [in the days of mourning].**

F. *The one who says,* "Mourning does not pertain to the Sabbath," *cites the Mishnah's statement,* **but does not interrupt [the period of mourning].** *Now if you take the view that mourning applies to the Sabbath, if mourning were observed, would there be any question of its interrupting the counting of the days of mourning?*

G. *Well, as a matter of fact, the same passage does say* **The Sabbath counts [in the days of mourning]***!*

H. *The inclusion of that phrase is on account of what is coming, namely,* **[while] the festivals interrupt [the period of mourning] and do not count [in the days of** discretion? It has to do with sexual relations [which are not to be performed on the festival by a mourner].

[H] [Reverting to the discussion broken off at B:] They objected, "Lo, in the case of the festival, lo, the mourner is prohibited from having sexual relations, and yet it does not count [toward the days of mourning]. Also in regard to the Sabbath, since a mourner is forbidden to have sexual relations, the Sabbath should not count [among the days of mourning, and yet it does, so the reason proposed at B is not likely]."

[I] Said R. Ba, "It is possible that seven days can pass without a festival, but it is not possible that seven days can pass without a Sabbath[, and if the Sabbath does not suspend the rites of mourning, there will be eight days of mourning, and not seven] ."

mourning], *so the Tannaite formulation to balance matters also stated,* **The Sabbath counts [in the days of mourning].**

I. *And as to the position of him who says,* "Mourning pertains to the Sabbath," *does the passage not say,* **but does not interrupt [the period of mourning]?**

J. *That is because the framer of the passage wishes to include,* **the festivals interrupt [the period of mourning],** *so for the sake of balance he stated as well,* **The Sabbath...does not interrupt [the period of mourning]**

II.2A. *May we say that at issue is what is under debate among the Tannaite authorities in the following:*

B. As to one whose deceased [actually] lies before him, he eats in a different room. If he does not have another room, he eats in the room of his fellow. If he has no access to the room of his fellow, he makes a partition and eats [separate from the corpse]. If he has nothing with which to make a partition, he.

turns his face away and eats.

C. He does not recline and eat, he does not eat meat, he does not drink wine, he does not say a blessing before the meal, he does not serve to form a quorum, and people do not say a blessing for him or include him in a quorum.

D. He is exempt from the requirement to recite the Shema and from the Prayer and from the requirement of wearing phylacter-

ies and from all of the religious
duties that are listed in the Torah.

E. But on the Sabbath he does recline and eat, he does eat meat, he
does drink wine, he does say a blessing before the meal, he does serve to
form a quorum and people do say
a blessing for him and include
him in a quorum. And he is liable
to carry out all of the religious duties that are listed in the Torah.

F. Rabban Simeon b. Gamaliel
says, "Since he is liable for these
[religious duties], he is liable to
carry out all of them."

G. And [in connection with the
dispute just now recorded], R.
Yohanan said, "*What is at issue between [Simeon and the anonymous au-
thority]? At issue is the matter of
having sexual relations.* [Simeon
maintains that the mourner on the
Sabbath has the religious obligation to have sexual relations with
his wife, and the anonymous
authority does not include that
requirement, since during the
mourning period it does not apply.]"

H. Is now this what is at stake
between them, namely, one
authority [Simeon b. Gamaliel]
maintains, "Mourning pertains to
the Sabbath," and the other takes
the view, "Mourning does not
pertain to the Sabbath"?

I. *What compels that conclusion?
Perhaps the initial Tannaite authority
takes the view that he does there only
because of the simple consideration that*

> the deceased is lying there awaiting bur-
> ial, but in the present case, in which the
> deceased is not lying there awaiting bur-
> ial, he would not take the position that
> he does. And, further, perhaps Rabban
> Simeon b. Gamaliel takes the position
> that he does in that case because, at that
> point [prior to burial] the restrictions of
> mourning do not pertain, but, here,
> where the restrictions of mourning do
> pertain, he would concur [that the
> mourning does pertain to the Sabbath].
> II.3A. [24A] R. Yohanan asked
> Samuel, "Does mourning pertain
> to the Sabbath or does mourning
> not pertain to the Sabbath?"
> B. He said to him, "Mourning
> does not pertain to the Sabbath."

Now what is interesting is not that the passages do not intersect. It is that the Bavli introduces here the case of one's deceased's actually lying there in the room, and links that case
with the present dispute. But the Yerushalmi treats that situation in a completely different context, namely, at Y. 3:5 VI.
What makes that evidence probative is simple. *The passage
where the Yerushalmi treats the cited question serves not our Mishnah-
pericope but, rather, M. Ber. 3:1!*

Since it has nothing to do with the Mishnah-passage
to which, in the Bavli, the topic is tied, here is no argument
from silence. It is, rather, decisive evidence that no topical
protocol told sages in both the land of Israel and Babylonia
where and how to address a given theme that was not in the
Mishnah but somehow deemed connected to it. Where the

framers of the Yerushalmi thought a given subject, not introduced by the Mishnah but held relevant to it, should be addressed, the authors of the compositions and composites of
the Bavli had no such notion, and, it goes without saying, vice
versa.

This brings us back to the issue of a Rabbinic "Q,"
and here again, an analogy may clarify for New Testament
scholars what is at stake here. It is clear that for the authors
of the four Gospels, a shared protocol, not spelled out, dictated the subjects that should be treated and the order in
which they should occur. That is to say, if we propose to talk
about Jesus Christ, we are going to discuss, e.g., the Passion,
and, moreover, the Passion is going to appear at the end of
the narrative. That protocol governs in all four Gospels,
without regard to the character of the Passion Narrative, on
the one side, or the program of sayings and stories to be utilized in the articulation of the various Gospels, respectively,
on the other: a fine example of a governing topical protocol.

If such a protocol were in play here, then, when dis-
cussing a given Mishnah-paragraph, compilers of both Talmuds will have introduced the same themes, not mentioned
in the Mishnah (whether in the paragraph at hand or in some
other paragraph) but held in common to belong to the clarification of that Mishnah-paragraph. But where a topic not introduced in a given Mishnah-paragraph is treated by both
Talmuds, the framers of one Talmud will deal with that topic
in one place, those of the other, in a different place; nothing
tells them both to treat the same topic in the same context.
That is so when it comes to matters of lore; where we have
the same story, it will not always serve the same purpose; and
it is true when it comes to matters of law.

V. DOES A SHARED PROGRAM OF QUESTIONS DICTATE THE SHAPE OF THE TALMUDS' MISHNAH-EXEGESIS?

We should not think that the results of inquiry run along parallel lines, even while the modes of thought differ. That is not the case — nor should it be the case if, as is generally agreed, the two Talmuds derive from separate universes of thought. Still, it is somewhat jarring to notice that in reading the same Mishnah-paragraph, the Rabbinic sages in the one country see one point that demands attention, those in the other, another point, and neither, the same point. I take this fact to mean that no agreed-upon agenda of questions guided sages in both countries in the reading of the Mishnah-statements; each brought its problems and interests, made its observations, drew its distinctions. So the differences are not only in modes of thought and argument, but in the very reading of the Mishnah itself. That hardly sustains the proposition of a shared corpus of autonomous traditions, guiding both parties in the reading of the shared document, the Mishnah-Tosefta.

Here is a striking case in which what seems important to the one side is of no consequence to the other, and vice versa, at **M. GIT. 5:1**:

[X.A] And the marriage contract of a woman is collected from property of the poorest quality [M. 5: 1C] .

[B] Said R. Jeremiah, "This has been taught only in respect to the payment of the *maneh* [or] the two hundred zuz [as the case may be to a widow or a virgin at the time of marriage]. But as to a marriage settlement, in addition of a thousand *denars,* this is collected from real estate of middling quality."

[C] And R. Yosé says, "Even the marriage settlement of a thousand *denars is* collected only from real estate of the poorest quality."

[D] And this dispute is along the same lines as another dispute.

[E] ["So long as she is in her husband's house, she collects her marriage contract within twenty-five years for in that period she may do favors for friends and neighbors to the value of her marriage contract," the words of R. Meir]. [And sages say,] "So long as she is in her husband's house, she collects her marriage contract at any time. So long as she is in her father's house, she collects her marriage contract within twenty-five years" [M. Ket. 12:4].

[F] R. Simeon said R. Joshua b. Levi [maintained], "This dispute deals only with the base value of a marriage settlement, a maneh or two hundred 2UZ, [as the case may be].

[G] "But if her marriage settlement

III.1A. And [they pay] the marriage contract of a woman out of the poorest quality [real estate]:

B. *Said Mar Zutra b. R. Nahman, "We impose this rule only where collection is from the estate, but if it is from the husband himself, it is collected from real property of middling quality."*

C. *Well, why single out the woman's marriage settlement in the context of exacting payment for the woman's marriage settlement? The same rule applies to all payments made by an estate, as we have learned in the Mishnah:* **They exact payment from the property of an estate ["orphans"] only from the poorest quality [real estate]**? *Isn't it the case, therefore, that the rule pertains even to payment by the husband himself?*

D. *In point of fact, the rule pertains only to collection of the marriage contract from the estate, and it was necessary to specify that that is so even in the case of the marriage settlement of a woman. For it might have entered your mind to suppose that, on account of making the whole prospect of marriage appealing to her, rabbis have imposed a lenient ruling in her case. So we are informed that that is not the case.*

E. *Said Raba, "Come and take note:* **R. Meir says, 'Also: The marriage contract of a woman do [they pay] out of middling quality [real estate].'** *Now from whom is the collection made? If we should say, from the orphans, doesn't R. Meir concur with that which we have learned in the Mishnah,* **They exact payment from the property of an estate ["orphans"] only from the poorest quality [real estate]**? *So isn't* was a thousand denars, she collects what is owing to her on [the rest of] her marriage settlement at any time, without limit."

[H] R. Abbahu in the name of R. Yohanan proposed: "And even if the marriage settlement is a thousand denars, she collects it only over a period of twenty-five years."

[I] [46d] And that which R. Yosé said accords with the view of R. Yohanan, and that which R. Jeremiah said accords with the opinion of R. Joshua b. Levi.

[J] Now we have learned there: **He who writes over as a gift all of his property to his children, but wrote to his wife a piece of land of any size at all — she has lost the right to collect any further on her marriage settlement [M. Pe. 3:9].**

[K] Rab said, "This rule applies in a case in which he transferred ownership through her [to the children]."

[L] And Samuel said, "It applies to a case in which he makes the division in her presence [so that she has every right to cavil and refrains from doing so]."

[M] R. Yosé bar Haninah said, "This is one of the lenient rulings applicable to the marriage settlement which they have taught here."

[N] And Bar Qappara taught, "This is one of the lenient rulings which they have taught with regard to the damage settlement."

[O] Said R. Ba, "The reasoning of R. Yosé b. Haninah [= C, H, I] is this: It is not the end of the matter

it from the husband himself? Then it must follow that rabbis take the view that, even in the case of the husband himself, it is collected from land of the poorest quality!"

F. *Not at all. In point of fact, it involves collection from an estate, but the case of collecting the marriage settlement of a woman is exceptional, on account of making the whole prospect of marriage appealing to her, rabbis have imposed a lenient ruling in her case.*

G. *Said Abbayye, "Come and take note:* **Damages — they pay compensation for them out of the highest quality [real estate], and [they pay] a debt out of middling quality [real estate], and [they pay] the marriage contract of a woman out of the poorest quality [real estate].** *Now from whom is the collection made? Should we say that it is from an estate? Then why make reference in particular to collecting a woman's marriage settlement, since all classifications of collections from an estate are in the same category, so is it not from the husband himself?"*

H. Said R. Aha bar Jacob, "Here with what situation do we deal? It is a case in which a man served as surety for compensation for damages due to be paid by his son or for his son's debt or for his daughter-in-law's marriage settlement. *Each item then is subject to its own rule Compensation for damages and payment of debts, which ordinarily are paid in the lifetime of the responsible party, are paid in this case as if in the lifetime of the responsible party; the* that if her marriage-settlement was a maneh or two hundred zuz [that the stated rule applies]. But even if her marriage settlement was worth a thousand denars, it still is one of the lenient rulings involving the marriage settlement which they have taught here."

woman's marriage settlement is usually paid after the death of the responsible party, therefore by whom? By the estate, and that is paid in this case, as if it were after the death of the responsible party."

I. *But why not derive the rule from the simple fact that someone who is surety for payment of a marriage settlement is not responsible to pay it?*

J. *We refer her to a go-between.*

K. *Well, that poses no problem to the position of him who has said, "A go-between even though the borrower has no property [when the debt is contracted] is responsible [if he gets property later on and the debt is not paid], but what can you say to the one who holds the position that if at the time of the loan the borrower has property, he is responsible, but if the borrower at that point has no property, he is not responsible* [Simon: since no one would guarantee a loan where it is known that the debtor has no means wherewith to repay; a guarantee in such a case cannot therefore be taken seriously]*?*

L. *If you wish, I may say, in this case we assume the son had property, but it was later on blighted; and if you wish, I may say, in respect to a son, a man under all circumstances will obligate himself.*

When it comes to comparing types of discourse, I see fixed differences between the Bavli and the Yerushalmi. When we address the exegesis of the same Mishnah-paragraph, I see no basis on which to formulate a rule governing differences in exegesis: this party says what it says, and that party says what it says, and there is no predicting which will say what or why.

In the present instance, the Yerushalmi maintains that the base-payment in the marriage contract is collected from property of poorest quality; all else is from property of middling quality. The Bavli maintains, the rule that the payment of the marriage contract — the whole of the contract, not only the base-sum of 200 zuz — is paid out of poorest quality land only if it is payable by the husband's estate (e.g., after he has died). But if he pays the sum himself, he pays out of real estate of middling quality. So the Yerushalmi distinguishes that for which money is paid out, one category being paid out of real estate of one classification, another out of another; the Bavli distinguishes the source or circumstance of the payment: the husband's estate, in which case we invoke the welfare of his surviving family alongside the welfare of his widow, as against the husband himself, in which case the husband pays property of decent quality.

Why the Bavli should invoke what seems to me humanitarian or family considerations, while the Yerushalmi makes its distinction on another basis altogether, namely, the provocation for the payment, I cannot say, and I doubt that there is any foundation in a fixed rationality to dictate the one position over the other in a variety of situations. Here is an instance at which there is a difference, but it is not a fixed difference governed by an a priori principle, one that states in general terms the bases for positions in particular cases, e.g., for considerations that derive from exegesis of language, social policy, or whatever.

The same, to-me, random difference between what one set of exegetes of the Mishnah will identify as an operative consideration and what the other set will find occurs in the treatment of M. 5:2. Here the Yerushalmi asks, what is good for the estate, e.g., a case in which a bond involves usury, a case in which there is maintenance to be paid to the widow; in such cases, we want to pay off the debt as soon as we can. The Bavli has a different exegetical program altogether, namely, the formulation of secondary, theoretical problems, at **M. GIT. 5:2:**

[I.A] R. Yohanan in the name of R. Yannai, "They exact payment from the property of an estate only in the case of a bond in which usury is eating up the estate."

[B] And there are those who say, "Also in the case of paying off the marriage settlement of a wife."

[C] Said R. Immi, "It is because the estate has to supply maintenance [to the widow, and it is better to pay off the estate in marriage contract instead]."

[D] Said R. Matteniah, "Who takes account of the charge against the estate represented by the widow's maintenance? It is R. Simeon.

[E] "For R. Simeon said, '[The widow's enjoying maintenance from the estate] depends on [whether or not the marriage contract] has been collected. [If she has gotten some payment, she no longer may charge her maintenance to the estate.]' "

[F] And what is [the reason of rabbis (A, as against B), who do not concur that the widow must be prevented from eating up the resources of the estate]?

[G] It is on account of preserving her attractiveness, so that people should want to marry her.

[H] And there are those who say, "Also for payment of what the deceased has stolen or for damages he has caused."

[I] Said R. Yosé b. R. Bun, "Also we too have learned in the Mishnah both of these:

V.1 A. **They exact payment from the property of an estate ["orphans"] only from the poorest quality [real estate]:**

B. *R. Ahadeboi bar Ammi raised this question: "As to* **the orphans** *of which they have spoken, does this mean minors, or does it include even adults? Did rabbis make this particular enactment only for minor orphans, but not for adults? Or perhaps, since it never entered the mind of the creditor that the debtor would die and leave his property to his estate, there is no consideration in play here of locking the door in the face of borrowers, with the result that the rule pertains also to adult orphans?"*

C. *Come and take note of what Abbayye the Elder set forth as a Tannaite ruling:* "[The rule that payment claimed from orphans on the father's debt requires the claimant to take an oath refers] to adult [heirs], and it is hardly required to say that it covers minors as well."

D. *But maybe that pertains to the oath, since, in relationship to the affairs of the father, even an adult heir is in the position of a minor, but as to the consideration of payment from land of the poorest quality, that would not be the case.*

E. *And the decided law is,* **[50B]** [the rule refers] to adult [heirs], and it is hardly required to say that it covers minors as well — both with regard to an oath and with regard to payment from land of the poorest quality.

[J] "As to theft, from the following: If it is a matter for which the deceased bore responsibility should the object be lost, the heir is liable to pay compensation [M. B.B. 10:1].

[K] "As to damages from the following: **They exact payment from the property of an estate only from the poorest quality [real estate] [M. 5:2C].**

[L] "Thus does the Mishnah teach: They do collect from the property of an estate for *damages* only from the poorest quality [real estate]."

VI.1A. **They do not exact payment from mortgaged property in a case in which there also is unencumbered property, even if it is of the poorest quality:**

B. R. *Ahadeboi bar Ammi raised this question: "What is the rule in respect to a gift? This is a provision that rabbis have enacted on account of the loss that may accrue to purchasers [Simon: who bought land from a man after he had contracted a debt to a third party], and that would not apply to a gift, where there is no consideration of loss to purchasers of the land, or do we maintain that the same rule pertains even in the case of a gift, for, if the donor had not gotten some sort of benefit, he would never have given the land to him, and therefore the loss of the donee is the same as the loss of the purchaser?"*

What is interesting is not that the two Talmuds do not intersect in reading the same Mishnah-paragraph; it is the unpredictable character of the difference, which is in no way fixed. Here, whatever the inherited repertoire of comments on the passage at hand, e.g., formulations of pertinent problems in Sifra or Sifré or by a Tannaite saying or by a major Amoraic authority's opinion (Yohanan/Yannai, for instance), Bavli's framers simply pursue their own interest, which is in the set of theoretical questions of Ahadeboi. Now his really is a narrowly-focused exegetical question, namely, the definition of the language of the Mishnah, so V.1. At VI.1, his is still an exegetical question generated by the Mishnah-rule, now one involving a secondary issue, one that the Mishnah does not address but does provoke.

So what we learn is that, where there are fixed differences, these occur in the formation of compositions and composites that stand autonomous of Mishnah-exegesis (though obviously pertinent to that task); and in the formation of that kind of writing, the fixed differences govern modes of thought, inquiry, evidence, and argument, not matters of (mere) proposition. The two Talmuds may say the same thing, but differ on how they reach their shared conclusion; or they may say different things about the same thing, and the differences on how these different conclusions are reached will be fixed and constant throughout. The probability of common access to a shared "autonomous tradition" of exegesis of the Mishnah, whether in so many words or in the gist of matters, is remote.

VI. DOES A COMMON EXEGETICAL PROGRAM DICTATE THE TALMUDS' READING OF THE SAME TOSEFTA-PERICOPE

So much for Mishnah-exegesis, what about the Tosefta? We have already noted that the Talmuds go over the same passage of Tosefta. But where they do, it is most common for a single difference to characterize their respective treatments. At the point that the Yerushalmi completes its presentation, it falls silent. But the Bavli finds a great deal of work to do. So, it is clear, the two Talmuds are not joined by a common exegetical program for the Tosefta, any more than a single hermeneutic, or a single protocol, tells them how to read a given Mishnah-paragraph. Once more, the claim that "autonomous traditions" stand behind and generate the two Talmuds' reading of a passage in common finds little support in the texts to which that claim allegedly makes reference.

For **M. MAKKOT 2:8**, Bavli, at I.1, begins its work: "how come...."? at the very point at which the Yerushalmi concludes its labors. And a full talmud follows. It would be pointless to set up a long right hand column of citation, against a blank left hand column; but that does show the difference. We do have a more routine intersection:

[III.A] It was taught: R. Eliezer b. Jacob says, "Refuge . . . ,' 'Refuge. . . ,' is stated [two times] at the crossroads,
[B] "so that the manslaughterer may see that which is written and know in which direction to go."
[C] Said R. Abun, "There was a sign shaped like a hand, showing them the way."

[II.1A. **And [direct] roads [were prepared] from one to the other, as it is said, "And you shall prepare the way and divide the borders of your land"** (Dt. 19:3):
B. *It has been taught on Tannaite authority:*
C. **R. Eliezer b. Jacob says, [10B] "They write signs, saying, 'Refuge, refuge,' at the cross roads, so that the manslayer may see and go into exile to the cities of refuge"** [T. Mak. 3:5A-B].
B. *Said R. Kahana, 'What verse of Scripture makes that point?* 'You shall prepare for yourself the way' (Dt. 19:3) — you make preparation for the proper road."

I see no material differences of consequence between these Talmuds. And, what is fascinating, note what follows:

[IV.A] Said R. Phineas: " 'Good and upright [is the Lord; therefore he instructs sinners in the way]' (Ps. 25:8).

[B] "Why is he good? Because he is upright.

[C] "And why is he upright? Because he is good.

[D] " 'Therefore he instructs sinners in the way — that is, he teaches them the way to repentance."

[E] They asked wisdom, "As to a sinner, what is his punishment?"

[F] She said to them, "Evil pursues the evil" (Prov. 13:21).

[G] They asked prophecy, "As to a sinner, what is his punishment?"

[H] She said to them, "The soul that sins shall die" (Ez. 18:20).

[I] They asked the Holy One, blessed be he, "As to a sinner, what is his punishment?"

[J] He said to them, "Let the sinner repent, and his sin will be forgiven for him."

[K] This is in line with the following verse of Scripture: "Therefore he instructs sinners in the way" (Ps. 25:8).

[L] "He shows the sinners the way to repentance."

2.A.R. *Hama bar Hanina opened his course on the subject with this verse of Scripture:* "'Good and upright is the Lord, therefore he instructs sinners in the way' (Ps. 25:8). If he instructs sinners, all the more so the righteous!"

B. R. *Simeon b. Laqish opened his course on the subject with this verse of Scripture:* "'And if a man not lie in wait, but God cause it to come to hand, then I will appoint you a place where he may flee' (Ex. 21:13). 'As says the proverb of the ancients, out of the wicked comes forth wickedness, but my hand shall not be upon you' (1 Sam. 24:13-14). Of whom does the former verse of Scripture speak? Of two people who killed someone, one did it inadvertently, the other did it deliberately. Against this one are not witnesses, and against that one are know witnesses. So the Holy One, blessed be he, arranges for them to chance upon the same inn. The one who killed deliberately seats himself under a ladder, and the one who killed inadvertently comes down the ladder and falls on him and kills him. The one who killed deliberately then is killed, and the one who killed inadvertently goes into exile."

3.A. Said Rabbah bar R. Huna said R. Huna, and some say, said R. Huna said R. Eleazar, "From the Torah, the Prophets, and the Holy Writings, it is shown that on the way on which a person wants to go — in that way is he led.

B. ""From the Torah: 'And God said to Balaam, You shall not go with them' (Num. 22:12), and then: 'if the men came to call you, rise up and go with them' (Num. 22:20);

C. "the Prophets: 'I am the Lord your God who teaches you for your profit, who leads you by the way that you should go' (Is. 48:17);

D. "and the Holy Writings: 'If he is of the scorners, he will be allowed to speak scorn, and if he is of the meek, he will show forth grace' (Prov. 3:34)."

Here is a case in which the same verse of Scripture is cited in the same context, and yet the two Talmuds take separate paths. Phineas's treatment, in Y., makes a point that has nothing to do with our legal context at all. By contrast, Simeon b. Laqish's statement shows how, even though someone is not penalized by a court, still, Heaven arranges a just recompense. B.'s No. 3, moreover, shares its generative form with Y. — and yet makes a totally different point. B. wants us to know that Heaven makes it possible for someone to achieve his goals, even though these are sinful. Y. makes a different point, which is, the sinner may repent and be forgiven. Do the two Talmuds address the same problem? They most certainly do, the condition of the one who sins by inadvertence. The Bavli's position, beautifully expounded, is that, in the end, one is punished for what seems inadvertent, if Heaven determines it was deliberate; and the Yerushalmi's frames make their own point, which is not that people do what they really want to do, but rather, God forgives sinners who repent.

We close with yet another example of how, addressing the same statements, drawing upon the same sources, the two authorships manage utterly to bypass one another's concerns:

[I.A] [As to the rights of possession accruing to the Levites in the cities of refuge,] it was taught: R. Judah says, "They were given [to the Levites] for division [as their permanent possession in the Land]."

[B] R. Yosé says, "They were given for dwelling [but not as a permanent possession and inheritance]."

[C] The view of R. Yosé [at Y. M.S. 5:5] is in accord with the opinion of R. Meir, and that of R. Judah is consistent with what he has already- said [at M. 2:7A].

[D] For we have learned, **"They pay Levites a rental, "** the words of R. Judah. R. Meir says, **"They do not pay them a rental. "**

I.1 A. **["They pay Levites a rental," the words of R. Judah. R. Meir says, "They did not pay them a rental:"]** Said R. Kahana, "The dispute concerns the six principal cities of refuge. *For one master maintains,* 'and the cities shall be for you for refuge' (Num. 35:6) means, 'for the purpose of refuge and no other purpose,' *and the other master takes the view that* 'to you' *means,* 'yours for all your needs.' But in regard to the other forty-two cities, they concur that the manslayers who settle there do pay rent.."

B. Said to him Raba, "Well, there is no doubt whatsoever that 'to you' *means,* 'yours for all your needs.'"

C. Rather, said Raba, "At issue is the status of the other forty-two cities. *One master takes the view that* 'and to them you shall add forty-two cities' (Num. 35:12) *means, they shall be in the status of the others as to affording shelter [and so the same rules apply]. The other master maintains that the language,* 'and to them you shall add forty-two cities' (Num. 35:12) *means,* 'yours for all your needs.' *Just as the others are* 'yours for all your needs,' *so these are,* 'yours for all your needs.'" *But in respect to the six principal cities, both parties concur that* they did not pay the Levites rent."

The Yerushalmi's interest focuses upon the relationships among Mishnah-rules; the Bavli wants to know how a dispute flows from contrary readings of Scripture. That difference is not a consistent one; the Yerushalmi will ask about scriptural bases for the Mishnah's rules or disputes, and the Bavli takes a keen interest in harmonizing discrete Mishnah-rules, indeed, in uncovering the premises that are shared among superficially-unrelated rules to permit a study in harmonization of conflict.

VII. DO THE YERUSHALMI AND THE BAVLI FORM DISTINCT EXPRESSIONS OF A SINGLE TRADITION? THE NULL-HYPOTHESIS REVISITED

No. There is no substantial, shared tradition, either in fully-spelled out statements in so many words, or in the gist of ideas, or in topical conventions, or in intellectual characteristics.

And no, the null-hypothesis has failed. A survey of pertinent cases turns up no data to support it.

What we have seen is that there is no autonomous tradition, e.g., of Mishnah-exegesis, Tosefta-exegesis, of Halakhic exegesis in more general terms, that circulates outside of the two Talmuds and leaves evidence of its presence within them. The Bavli presents an utterly autonomous statement, speaking in its own behalf and in its own way about its own interests. The shared traits are formal: documents cited by one set of writers and by another. The differentiating characteristics are substantive: what is to be done with the shared formed statements taken from prior writings. The framers of the Bavli in no way found guidance in the processes by which the Yerushalmi's compositions and composites took shape, in the dim past of the document such as is delineated in Chapter Five, or, it goes without saying, in the results of those processes as well. The Talmuds differ not in general only, but in detail; not in how they make their statements or in what they say but, at a more profound level, in their very generative layers, in the intellectual morphology characteristic of each. Evidence for an autonomous tradition will have to derive from some other source than the two Talmuds.

Now that the Midrash-compilations and the two Talmuds have failed to supply weighty evidence for the existence of autonomous traditions, let us ask the question of proportions. It is clear that stories and sayings do circulate across documentary boundaries. It is also clear that, when we go in search of them, we do not find evidence of their presence and impact. So it is time to ask how sizable a proportion of the several documents the autonomous traditions comprise to begin with.

PART FOUR

TOWARD A GENERAL THEORY OF THE FORMATION OF THE RABBINIC TRADITION

5.

THE PRIOR RABBINIC TRADITION: THE THREE STAGES IN THE FORMATION OF CANONICAL DOCUMENTS

I.   A THEORY OF THE FORMATION OF THE RABBINIC DOCUMENTS: ACCOUNTING FOR DIFFERENT KINDS OF WRITING

We have at present no theory of the formation of the various documents of the Rabbinic literature that derives from an inductive sifting of the evidence. Nor do we have even a theory as to the correct method for the framing of a hypothesis for testing against the evidence. I propose to lay out the main outlines of such a theory. Writings that peregrinate by definition do not carry out the rhetorical, logical, and topical program of a particular document. So we can always discern what the framers of a given document or the editors of materials used therein have contributed to accommodate an alien composition to their context. In framing a theory to accommodate the facts that documents are autonomous but also connected through such shared materials, therefore, we must account for the formative history of not only the documents in hand but also the completed pieces of writing that move from here to there.

It is easy to demonstrate that the compilers of the documents utilized, whole and complete and unchanged, ready-made compositions and composites, small and large. These extra-documentary compositions and composites are of two kinds, first, those that occur in more than one document, second, those that appear in only one document but do not conform to the indicative traits of said document. How we account for writings that do not respond to, or realize, documentary programs requires attention. Just as the critics have to frame their literary theory of the formation of the documents, the proponents of the documentary hypothesis have to account for the formation of autonomous traditions, compositions and composites that circulate from one compilation to another for example.

There can be no begging of the question. As a matter of simple fact, all documents in the canon of Rabbinic Judaism receive from prior writings, starting with Scripture, materials for further use. At issue are not citations from determinate documents, e.g., the Mishnah of Scripture, the Tosefta of Scripture and the Mishnah. These are routine and support the documentary hypothesis by showing the intratextuality of the Rabbinic canonical documents. In later Rabbinic writings we find compositions that occur, also, in earlier Rabbinic writings, but that do not exhibit traits particular to those earlier writings, e.g., distinctive qualities that mark Scripture or the Mishnah or Genesis Rabbah. These completed compositions are handed on from generation to generation, never taking on the distinctive traits of any particular document; they form a distinct tradition, from Scripture or the Mishnah or the Tosefta or Sifra or other writings that exhibit highly distinctive traits of their own.

II. THE THREE STAGES IN THE LITERARY HISTORY OF THE RABBINIC CANONICAL DOCUMENTS AND HOW WE DISCERN THEM

My theory on the literary history of the Rabbinic canon posits three stages in the formation of writing. These stages are delineated not from discrete saying to massive composite but from the whole to the parts, the largest to the smallest unit (and we never reach the discrete saying). I start with the given, the irreducible facticity of the document as a whole, final, complete, and (but for wordings or readings here and there, which may massively vary) done.[11]

1. THE LATEST STAGE IN THE LITERARY HISTORY OF THE RABBINIC DOCUMENTS: WRITINGS THAT CONFORM TO THE PARTICULAR DOCUMENT'S INDICATIVE TRAITS:

Moving from the latest to the earliest, one stage is marked by the definition of a document, its topical program, its rhetorical medium, its logical message. The document as

---

[11]I concur with Schaefer that for some Rabbinic documents we have no solid textual tradition at all. But for most Rabbinic documents, we have a very solid, because repetitive, structural, e.g., formal, tradition, defined by fixed traits of rhetoric, logic, and topic, and these permit us to speak of the Bavli as distinct, e.g., from Pesiqta deRab Kahana of the Mishnah. Chapter One has demonstrated that fact. The wording of the Bavli or other writings is fluid in detail, but the forms are fixed and never vary from their defined traits. That is why we may start from the largest units, the whole, then the parts into which the whole may be divided, then the parts of the parts (but, in my experience, not much further). These largest aggregates of data do yield fixed traits, which permit us to speak of the Bavli. An examination of the first of Schaefer's and his colleagues' compilations of Yerushalmi variants leaves no doubt that we may well speak of *the Yerushalmi* (for the tractates under discussion), even though, at any given point, we may have a variety of readings of sentences and even paragraphs. Analysis of the formal traits of large aggregates of materials therefore validates the view that, for the Rabbinic writings of antiquity, we may indeed speak of documents that can be defined at a determinate moment and treated as statements at a given point in time.

we know it in its basic structure and main lines therefore comes at the end. It follows that writings that clearly serve the program of that document and carry it the purposes of its authorship were made up in connection with the formation of *that* document.

2. AN INTERMEDIATE EARLIER STAGE IN THE LITERARY HISTORY OF THE RABBINIC DOCUMENTS: WRITINGS THAT CAN HAVE SERVED REDACTORS OF DOCUMENTS BUT THAT DID NOT SERVE THE REDACTORS OF THE PARTICULAR DOCUMENTS THAT WE NOW HAVE

Another, and I think, prior stage is marked by the preparation of writings that do not serve the needs of a particular document now in our hands, but can have carried out the purposes of an authorship working on a document of a *type* we now have. The existing documents then form a model for defining other kinds of writings worked out to meet the program of a documentary authorship. We have no systematic exegetical document serving, e.g., the book of Job. But we do have composites that are put together as systematic exegeses of verses in the book of Job. These point to work undertaken for redactors of a Rabbinic document of a type that we now have, but on a problem, e.g., a book of Scripture, not treated by a systematic document. The Bavli has numerous topical anthologies that attest to work of redaction and composition for compilations comparable to Genesis Rabbah or Song of Songs Rabbah. But these never reached the volume and systematic realization of the documents we do have.

3. A STILL EARLIER STAGE IN THE LITERARY HISTORY OF THE RABBINIC DOCUMENTS: WRITINGS

Autonomous of a Particular Document's Indicative Traits. The Peripatetic Composition:

The third class of writing is comprised by compositions that in no way serve the needs or plans of any document we now have, and that, furthermore, also cannot find a place in any document of a type that we now have. These writings very commonly prove peripatetic, traveling from one writing to another, equally at home in, or alien to, the program of the documents in which they end up. These writings therefore were carried out without regard to a documentary program of any kind exemplified by the canonical books of Rabbinic Judaism. They form what I conceive to be the earliest in the three stages of the writing of the units of completed thought that in the aggregate form the canonical literature of Rabbinic Judaism of late antiquity.

4. Classes of Writing, Stages of Formation:

As a matter of fact, therefore, a given canonical document of Rabbinic Judaism draws upon three classes of materials, and these were framed in temporal order. Last comes the final class, the one that the redactors themselves defined and wrote; prior is the penultimate class that can have served other redactors but did not serve these in particular; and earliest of all in the order of composition (at least, from the perspective of the ultimate redaction of the documents we now have) is the writing that circulated autonomously and served no redactional purpose we can now identify within the canonical documents.

III. The Correct Starting Point

Where to start, the whole or the smallest whole unit of discourse? The answer derives from how we think the documents begin, in bits and pieces or with a comprehensive plan. In beginning the inquiry with the traits of documents seen whole, as we did in parts One through Three, I reject the assumption that the building block of documents is the smallest whole unit of thought, the lemma. Nor can we proceed in the premise that a lemma traverses the boundaries of various documents and is unaffected by the journey.[12] The opposite premise is that we start our work with the traits of documents as a whole, rather than with the traits of the lemmas of which documents are (supposedly) composed. In a variety of books[13] I have set forth the documentary hypothesis for the analysis of the Rabbinic literature of late antiquity. But how shall we proceed, if we take as our point of entry the character and conditions of the document, seen whole? And what are the results of doing so?

Having demonstrated beyond any doubt that a Rabbinic text is a document, that is to say, a well-crafted text and not merely a compilation of this and that, and further specified in acute detail precisely the aesthetic, formal, and logical program followed by each of those texts, accordingly, I am able to move to the logical next step. That is to show that in the background of the documents that we have is writing that

---

[12]As a matter of fact, the identification of the lemma as the primary unit of inquiry rests upon the premise that the person to whom a saying is assigned really said that saying. That premise is untenable. But for the sake of argument, I bypass that still more fundamental flaw in the methodology at hand.

[13]Particularly *From Tradition to Imitation. The Plan and Program of Pesiqta deRab Kahana and Pesiqta Rabbati, Canon and Connection: Intertextuality in Judaism, Midrash as Literature: The Primacy of Documentary Discourse*, and *The Bavli and its Sources: The Question of Tradition in the Case of Tractate Sukkah*, as well as *The Talmud of the Land of Israel. 35. Introduction. Taxonomy*, and *Judaism. The Classic Statement. The Evidence of the Bavli*,

is *not* shaped by documentary requirements, writing that is not shaped by the documentary requirements of the compilations we now have, and also writing that is entirely formed within the rules of the documents that now present that writing. These then are the three kinds of writing that form, also, the three stages in the formation of the classics of Judaism.

IV. REDACTION AND WRITING. THE EXTREME CASE OF THE MISHNAH

My example of a document that is written down essentially in its penultimate and ultimate stages, that is, *a document that takes shape within the redactional process and principally there*, is, of course, the Mishnah. In that writing, the patterns of language, e.g., syntactic structures, of the apodosis and protasis of the Mishnah's smallest whole units of discourse are framed in formal, mnemonic patterns. They follow a few simple rules. These rules, once known, apply nearly everywhere and form stunning evidence for the document's cogency. They permit anyone to reconstruct, out of a few key phrases, an entire cognitive unit, and even complete intermediate units of discourse. Working downward from the surface, therefore, anyone can penetrate into the deeper layers of meaning of the Mishnah. Then and at the same time, while discovering the principle behind the cases, one can easily memorize the whole by mastering the recurrent rhetorical pattern dictating the expression of the cogent set of cases. For it is easy to note the shift from one rhetorical pattern to another and to follow the repeated cases, articulated in the new pattern downward to its logical substrate. So syllogistic propositions, in the Mishnah's authors' hands, come to full expression not only in *what* people wish to state but also in *how* they choose to say it. The limits of rhetoric define the arena of topical articulation. Now to state my main point in heavy emphasis: *the Mishnah's formal traits of rhetoric indicate that the document has been formulated all at once, and not in an incremental, linear process extending into a remote (mythic) past, (e.g., to Sinai).*

These traits, common to a series of distinct cognitive units, are redactional, because they are imposed at that point at which someone intended to join together discrete (finished) units on a given theme. The varieties of traits particular to the discrete units and the diversity of authorities cited therein, including masters of two or three or even four strata from the turn of the first century to the end of the second, make it highly improbable that the several units were formulated in a common pattern and then preserved, until, later on, still further units, on the same theme and in the same pattern, were worked out and added. The entire indifference, moreover, to historical order of authorities and concentration on the logical unfolding of a given theme or problem without reference to the sequence of authorities, confirm the supposition that the work of formulation and that of redaction go forward together.

The principal framework of formulation and formalization in the Mishnah is the intermediate division rather than the cognitive unit. The least-formalized formulary pattern, the simple declarative sentence, turns out to yield many examples of acute formalization, in which a single distinctive pattern is imposed upon two or more (very commonly, groups of three or groups of five) cognitive units. While an intermediate division of a tractate may be composed of several such conglomerates of cognitive units, it is rare indeed for cognitive units formally to stand wholly by themselves. Normally, cognitive units share formal or formulary traits with others to which they are juxtaposed and the theme of which they share. It follows that the principal unit of formulary formalization is the intermediate division and not the cognitive unit. And what that means for our inquiry, is simple: we can tell when it is that the ultimate or penultimate redactors of a document do the writing. Now let us see that vast collection of writings that exhibit precisely the opposite trait: a literature in which, while doing some writing of their own, the redactors collected and arranged available materials.

V. WHEN THE DOCUMENT DOES NOT DEFINE THE LITERARY PROTOCOL: STORIES TOLD BUT NOT COMPILED AND THE AUTONOMOUS TRADITION

Now to the other extreme, the autonomous tradition. Can I point to a kind of writing that in no way defines a document now in our hands or even a type of document we can now imagine, that is, one that in its particulars we do not have but that conforms in its definitive traits to those that we do have? Indeed I can, and it is the writing of stories about sages and other exemplary figures. To show what might have been, I point to the simple fact that the final organizers of the Bavli, the Talmud of Babylonia had in hand a tripartite corpus of inherited materials awaiting composition into a final, closed document.

First, the first type of material, in various states and stages of completion, addressed the Mishnah or took up the principles of laws that the Mishnah had originally brought to articulation. These the framers of the Bavli organized in accord with the order of those Mishnah-tractates that they selected for sustained attention.

Second, they had in hand received materials, again in various conditions, pertinent to Scripture, both as Scripture related to the Mishnah and also as Scripture laid forth its own narratives. These they set forth as Scripture-commentary. In this way, the penultimate and ultimate redactors of the Bavli laid out a systematic presentation of the two Torahs, the oral, represented by the Mishnah, and the written, represented by Scripture.

And, third, the framers of the Bavli also had in hand materials focused on sages. These in the received form, attested in the Bavli's pages, were framed around twin biographical principles, either as strings of stories about great sages of the past or as collections of sayings and comments drawn together solely because the same name stands behind all the collected sayings. These can easily have been composed into biographies. In the context of Christianity and of Judaism, it is appropriate to call the biography of a holy man or woman, meant to convey the divine message, a gospel.[14] This is writing that is utterly outside of the documentary framework in which it is now preserved; nearly all narratives in the Rabbinic literature, not only the biographical ones, indeed prove remote from any documentary program exhibited by the canonical documents in which they now occur.

The Bavli as a whole lays itself out as a commentary to the Mishnah. So the framers wished us to think that whatever they wanted to tell us would take the form of Mishnah commentary. But a second glance indicates that the Bavli is made up of enormous composites, themselves closed prior to

---

[14]I use the word "gospel" with a small G as equivalent to "didactic life of a holy man, portraying the faith." Obviously, the Christian usage, with a capital G, must maintain that there can be a Gospel only about Jesus Christ. Claims of uniqueness are, of course, not subject to public discourse. In the present context, I could as well have referred to lives of saints, since Judaism of the dual Torah produced neither a gospel about a central figure nor lives of saints. Given the centrality of Moses "our rabbi," for example, we should have anticipated a "Gospel of Moses" parallel to the Gospels of Jesus Christ, and, lacking that, at least a "life of Aqiba," scholar, saint, martyr, parallel to the lives of various saints. We also have no autobiographies of any kind, beyond some "I"-stories, which themselves seem to me uncommon.

inclusion in the Bavli. Some of these composites — around 35% to 40% of Bavli's, if my sample is indicative[15] — were selected and arranged along lines dictated by a logic other than that deriving from the requirements of Mishnah commentary. The components of the canon of Rabbinic Judaism prior to the Bavli had encompassed amplifications of the Mishnah, in the Tosefta and in the Yerushalmi, as well as the same for Scripture, in such documents as Sifra to Leviticus, Sifré to Numbers, another Sifré, to Deuteronomy, Genesis Rabbah, Leviticus Rabbah, and the like.

But there was no entire document, now extant, organized around the life and teachings of a particular sage. Even The Fathers According to Rabbi Nathan, which contains a good sample of stories about sages, is not so organized as to yield a life of a sage, or even a systematic biography of any kind. Where events in the lives of sages do occur, they are thematic and not biographical in organization, e.g., stories about the origins, as to Torah-study, of diverse sages; death-scenes of various sages. The sage as such, whether Aqiba or Yohanan ben Zakkai or Eliezer b. Hyrcanus, never in that document defines the appropriate organizing principle for sequences of stories or sayings. And there is no other in which the sage forms an organizing category for any material purpose.[16]

---

[15]I compared Bavli and Yerushalmi tractates Sukkah, Sanhedrin, and Sotah, showing the proportion of what I call Scripture-units of thought to Mishnah-units of thought. See my *Judaism. The Classic Statement. The Evidence of the Bavli* (Chicago, 1986: University of Chicago Press). I cannot find anything relevant to the problem before us in that book, which stands on its own. That is why I have not summarized the results here.

[16]The occasion, in the history of Judaism, at which biography defines a generative category of literature, therefore also of thought, will therefore prove noteworthy. The model of biography surely existed from the formation of the Pentateuch, with its lines of structure, from Exodus through Deuteronomy, set forth around the biography of Moses, birth, call, career,

Accordingly, the decision that the framers of the Bavli reached was to adopt the two redactional principles inherited from the antecedent century or so and to reject the one already rejected by their predecessors, even while honoring it. [1] They organized the Bavli around the Mishnah. But [2] they adapted and included vast tracts of antecedent materials organized as scriptural commentary. These they inserted whole and complete, not at all in response to the Mishnah's program. But, finally, [3] while making provision for small-scale compositions built upon biographical principles, preserving both strings of sayings from a given master (and often a given tradent of a given master) as well as tales about authorities of the preceding half millennium, they *never* created redactional compositions, of a sizable order, that focused upon given authorities. But sufficient materials certainly lay at hand to allow doing so.

We have now seen that some writings carry out a redactional purpose. The Mishnah was our prime example. Some writings ignore all redactional considerations we can identify. The stories about sages in the Fathers According to Rabbi Nathan for instance show us kinds of writing that are wholly out of phase with the program of the document that collects and compiles them. We may therefore turn to Midrash-compilations and find the traits of writing that clearly are imposed by the requirements of compilation. We further identify writings that clearly respond to a redactional program, but not the program of any compilation we now

---

death. And other biographies did flourish prior to the Judaism of the dual Torah. Not only so, but the wall of the Dura synagogue highlights not the holy people so much as saints, such as Aaron and Moses. Accordingly, we must regard as noteworthy and requiring explanation the omission of biography from the literary genres of the canon of the Judaism of the dual Torah. One obvious shift is marked by Hasidism, with its special interest in stories about saints and in compiling those stories.

have in hand. There is little speculation about the identification of such writings. They will conform to the redactional patterns we discern in the known-compilations, but presuppose a collection other than one now known to us. Finally, we turn to pieces of writing that respond to no redactional program known to us or susceptible to invention in accord with the principles of defining compilation known to us.

VI. PERICOPES FRAMED FOR THE PURPOSES OF THE PARTICULAR DOCUMENT IN WHICH THEY OCCUR

My analytical taxonomy of the writings now collected in various Midrash-compilations point to not only three stages in the formation of the classics of Judaism. It also suggests that writing went on both outside of the framework of the editing of documents, and also within the limits of the formation and framing of documents. Writing of the former kind — outside documentary lines — then constituted a kind of literary work to which redactional planning proved irrelevant. But the second and the third kinds of writing responds to redactional considerations. So in the end we shall wish to distinguish between writing intended for the making of books — compositions of the first three kinds listed just now — and writing not response to the requirements of the making of compilations.

The distinctions upon which these analytical taxonomies rest are objective and in no way subjective, since they depend upon the fixed and factual relationship between a piece of writing and a larger redactional context.

[1] We know the requirements of redactors of the several documents of the Rabbinic canon, because I have already shown what they are in the case of a large variety of documents. When, therefore, we judge a piece of writing to serve the program of the document in which that writing oc-

curs, it is not because of a personal impulse or a private and incommunicable insight, but because the traits of that writing self-evidently respond to the documentary program of the book in which the writing is located.

[2] When, further, we conclude that a piece of writing belongs in some other document than the one in which it is found, that too forms a factual judgment.

My example is a very simple one: writing that can serve only as a component of a commentary on a given scriptural book has been made up for the book in which it appears (or one very like it, if one wants to quibble). My example may derive from any of the ten Midrash-compilations of late antiquity. Here is one among innumerable possibilities.

SIFRÉ TO NUMBERS I:VII.1

A. "[The Lord said to Moses, 'Command the people of Israel that they put out of the camp every leper and every one having a discharge, and every one that is unclean through contact with the dead.] You shall put out both male and female, putting them outside the camp, that they may not defile their camp, in the midst of which I dwell'" (Gen. 5:1-4)

B. I know, on the basis of the stated verse, that the law applies only to male and female [persons who are suffering from the specified forms of cultic uncleanness]. How do I know that the law pertains also to one lacking clearly defined sexual traits or to one possessed of the sexual traits of both genders?

C. Scripture states, "...putting *them* outside the camp." [This is taken to constitute an encompassing formulation, extending beyond the male and female of the prior clause.]

D. I know, on the basis of the stated verse, that the law applies only to those who can be sent forth. How do I know that the law pertains also to those who cannot be sent forth?

E. Scripture states, "...putting them outside the camp." [This is taken to constitute an encompassing formulation, as before.]

F. I know on the basis of the stated verse that the law applies only to persons. How do I know that the law pertains also to utensils?

G. Scripture states, "...putting *them* outside the camp." [This is taken to constitute an encompassing formulation.]

I:VII.2. A. [Dealing with the same question as at 1.F,] R. Aqiba says, "'You shall put out both male and female, putting them outside the camp.' Both persons and utensils are implied."

B. R. Ishmael says, "You may construct a logical argument, as follows:

C. "Since man is subject to uncleanness on account of *Negaim* ["plagues"], and clothing [thus: utensils] are subject to uncleanness on the same count, just as man is subject to being sent forth [ostracism], likewise utensils are subject to being sent forth."

D. No, such an argument is not valid [and hence exegesis of the actual language of Scripture, as at A, is the sole correct route]. If you have stated the rule in the case of man, who imparts uncleanness when he exerts pressure on an object used for either sitting or lying, and, on which account, he is subject to ostracism, will you say the same rule of utensils, which do not impart uncleanness when they exert pressure on an object used for sitting and lying? [Clearly there is a difference between the uncleanness brought about by a human being from that brought about by an inanimate object, and therefore the rule that applies to the one will not necessarily apply to the other. Logic by itself will not suffice, and, it must follow, the proof of a verse of Scripture alone will suffice to prove the point.]

E. [No, that objection is not valid, because we can show that the same rule does apply to both an inanimate object and to man, namely] lo, there is the case of the stone affected with a *Nega'*, which will prove the point. For it does not impart uncleanness when it exerts pressure on an object used for sitting or lying, but it does require ostracism [being sent forth from the camp, a rule that Scripture itself makes explicit].

F. Therefore do not find it surprising that utensils, even though they in general do not impart uncleanness when they exert pressure on an object used for sitting or lying, are to be sent forth from the camp." [Ishmael's logical proof stands.]

I:VII.3 A. R. Yosé the Galilean says, "'You shall put out both male and female, putting them outside the camp, that they may not defile their camp, in the midst of which I dwell.'

B. "What marks as singular male and female is that they can be turned into a generative source of uncleanness [when they die and are corpses], and, it follows, they are to be sent forth from the camp when they become unclean [even while alive], so anything which can become a generative source of uncleanness will be subject to being sent forth from the camp.

C. "What is excluded is a piece of cloth less than three by three fingerbreadths, which in the entire Torah is never subject to becoming a generative source of uncleanness."

I:VII.4 A. R. Isaac says, "Lo, Scripture states, '[And every person that eats what dies of itself or what is to torn by beasts, whether he is a native or a sojourner, shall wash his clothes and bathe himself in water and be unclean until the evening; they he shall be clean.] But if he does not wash them or bathe his flesh, he shall bear his iniquity' (Lev. 17:15-16).

B. "It is on account of failure to wash one's body that Scripture has imposed the penalty of extirpation.

C. "You maintain that it is on account of failure to wash one's body that Scripture has imposed the penalty of extirpation. But perhaps Scripture has imposed a penalty of extirpation only on account of the failure to launder one's garments.

D. "Thus you may construct the argument to the contrary [*su eipas*]: if in the case of one who has become unclean on account of corpse-uncleanness, which is a severe source of uncleanness, Scripture has not imposed a penalty merely because of failure to launder

one's garments, as to one who eats meat of a beast that
has died of itself, which is a minor source of uncleanness, it is a matter of reason that Scripture should not
impose a penalty on the account of having failed to
launder the garments."

Why do I maintain that the composition can serve
only the document in which it occurs? The reason is that we
read the verse in a narrow framework: what rule do we derive
from the *actual* language at hand. No. 1 answers the question
on the basis of an exegesis of the verse. No. 2 then provides
an alternative proof. Aqiba provides yet another reading of
the language at hand. Ishmael goes over the possibility of a
logical demonstration. I find it difficult to see how Yosé's
pericope fits in. It does not seem to me to address the problem at hand. He wants to deal with a separate issue entirely,
as specified at C. No. 4 pursues yet another independent
question. So Nos. 3, 4 look to be parachuted down. On what
basis? No. 3 deals with our base verse. But No. 4 does not.
Then what guided the compositors to introduce Nos. 1, 2, 3,
and 4? Nos. 1, 2 deal with the exegesis of the limited rule at
hand: how do I know to what classifications of persons and
objects ostracism applies? No. 1 Answers to questions, first,
the classifications, then the basis for the rule. No. 2 introduces the second question: on what basis do we make our
rule? The answer, as is clear, is Scripture, not unaided reason.
Now at that point the issue of utensils emerges. So Yosé the
Galilean's interest in the rule governing a utensil — a piece of
cloth — leads to the intrusion of his item. And the same
theme — the rule governing utensils, garments — accounts
for the introduction of I:VII.4 as well. In sum, the redactional
principle is looks to be clear: treat the verse, then the theme
generated by the verse. Then this piece of writing can have
been formed only for the purpose of a commentary to the

book of Numbers: Sifré to Numbers is the only one we have.
QED

VII. PERICOPES FRAMED FOR THE PURPOSES OF A PARTICULAR DOCUMENT BUT NOT OF A TYPE WE NOW POSSESS

A piece of writing that serves nowhere we now know
may nonetheless conform to the rules of writing that we can
readily imagine and describe in theory. For instance, a propositional composition, that runs through a wide variety of texts
to make a point autonomous of all of the texts that are invoked, clearly is intended for a propositional document, one
that (like the Mishnah) makes points autonomous of a given
prior writing, e.g., a biblical book, but that makes points that
for one reason or another cohere quite nicely on their own.
Authors of propositional compilations self-evidently can
imagine that kind of redaction. We have their writings, but
not the books that they intended to be made up of those writings. In all instances, the reason that we can readily imagine a
compilation for that will have dictated the indicative traits of
a piece of writing will prove self-evident: we have compilations of such a type, if not specific compilations called for by
a given composition. A single example suffices. It derives
from Sifra.

If the canon of Judaism included a major treatise or
compilation on applied logic and practical reason, then a
principal tractate, or set of tractates, would be devoted to
proving that reason by itself cannot produce reliable results.
And in that treatise would be a vast and various collection of
sustained discussions, which spread themselves across Sifra
and Sifré to Numbers and Sifré to Deuteronomy, the
Yerushalmi and the Bavli, as well as other collections. Here is
a sample of how that polemic has imposed itself on the am-

plification of Lev. 1:2 and transformed treatment of that verse from an exegesis to an example of an overriding proposition. It goes without saying that where we have this type of proof of the priority of Scripture over logic, or of the necessity of Scripture in the defining of generative taxa, the discussion serves a purpose that transcends the case, and on that basis I maintain the proposition proposed here. It is that there were types of collections that we can readily imagine but that were not made up. In this case, it is, as is clear, a treatise on applied logic, and the general proposition of that treatise is that reliable taxonomy derives only from Scripture.

SIFRA PARASHAT VAYYIQRA DIBURA DENEDABAH PARASHAH 2=III.I.1.

A. "Speak to the Israelite people [and say to them, 'When any [Hebrew: Adam] of you presents an offering of cattle to the Lord, he shall choose his offering from the herd or from the flock. If his offering is a burnt offering from the herd, he shall offer a male without blemish; he shall offer it at the door of the tent of meeting, that he may be accepted before the Lord;] he shall lay [his hand upon the head of the burnt offering, and it shall be accepted for him to make atonement for him]'" (Lev. 1:2):

B. "He shall lay his hand:" Israelites lay on hands, gentiles do not lay on hands.

C. [But is it necessary to prove that proposition on the basis of the cited verse? Is it not to be proven merely by an argument of a logical order, which is now presented?] Now which measure [covering the applicability of a rite] is more abundant, the measure of wavings or the measure of laying on of hands?

D. The measure of waving [the beast] is greater than the measure of laying on of hands.

E. For waving [the sacrifice] is done to both something that is animate and something that is not animate, while the laying on of hands applies only to something that is animate.

F. If gentiles are excluded from the rite of waving the sacrifice, which applies to a variety of sacrifices, should they not be excluded from the rite of laying on of hands, which pertains to fewer sacrifices? [Accordingly, I prove on the basis of reason the rule that is derived at A-B from the verse of Scripture.]

G. [I shall now show that the premise of the foregoing argument is false:] [You have constructed your argument] from the angle that yields waving as more common and laying on of hands as less common.

H. But take the other angle, which yields laying on of hands as the more common and waving as the less common.

I. For the laying on of hands applies to all partners in the ownership of a beast [each one of whom is required to lay hands on the beast before it is slaughtered in behalf of the partnership in ownership of the beast as a whole],

J. but the waving of a sacrifice is not a requirement that applies to all partners in the ownership of a beast.

K. Now if I eliminate [gentiles' laying on of hands] in the case of the waving of a beast, which is a requirement applying to fewer cases, should I eliminate them from the requirement of laying on of hands, which applies to a larger number of cases?

L. Lo, since a rule pertains to the waving of the sacrifice that does not apply to the laying on of hands, and a rule pertains to the laying on of hands that does not apply to the waving of the sacrifice, it is necessary for Scripture to make the statement that it does, specifically:

M. "He shall lay his hand:" Israelites lay on hands, gentiles do not lay on hands.

The basic premise is that when two comparable actions differ, then the more commonly performed one imposes its rule upon further actions, the rule governing which is unknown. If then we show that action A is more commonly performed than action B, other actions of the same classification will follow the rule governing A, not the rule governing B. Then the correct route to overturn such an argument is to show that each of the actions, the rule governing which is known, differs from the other in such a way that neither the one nor the other can be shown to be the more commonly performed. Then the rule governing the further actions is not to be derived from the one governing the two known actions. The powerful instrument of analytical and comparative reasoning proves that diverse traits pertain to the two stages of the rite of sacrifice, the waving, the laying on of hands, which means that a rule pertaining to the one does not necessarily apply to the other. On account of that difference we must evoke the specific ruling of Scripture. The polemic in favor of Scripture, uniting all of the components into a single coherent argument, then insists that there really is no such thing as a genus at all, and Scripture's rules and regulations serve a long list of items, each of them *sui generis,* for discovering rules by the logic of analogy and contrast is simply not possible.

VIII. PERICOPES FRAMED FOR A PURPOSE NOT PARTICULAR TO. OR REALIZED IN. A TYPE OF DOCUMENT NOW IN OUR HANDS

Some writings stand autonomous of any redactional program we have in an existing compilation or of any we can even imagine on the foundations of said writings. Compositions of this kind, as a matter of hypothesis, are to be assigned to a stage in the formation of classics prior to the framing of all available documents. For, as a matter of fact, all of our now extant writings adhere to a single program of conglomeration and agglutination, and all are served by composites of one sort, rather than some other. Hence we may suppose that at some point prior to the decision to make writings in the model that we now have but in some other model people also made up completed units of thought to serve these other kinds of writings. These persist, now, in documents that they do not serve at all well. And we can fairly easily identify the kinds of documents that they can and should have served quite nicely indeed. These then are the three stages of literary formation in the making of the classics of Judaism.

Of the relative temporal or ordinal position of writings that stand autonomous of any redactional program we have in an existing compilation or of any we can even imagine on the foundations of said writings we can say nothing. These writings prove episodic; they are commonly singletons. They serve equally well everywhere, because they demand no traits of form and redaction in order to endow them with sense and meaning. Why not? Because they are essentially free-standing and episodic, not referential and allusive. They are stories that contain their own point and do not invoke, in the making of that point, a given verse of Scripture. They are sayings that are utterly ad hoc. A variety of materials fall into this — from a redactional perspective — unassigned, and unassignable, type of writing. They do not belong in books at all. By that I mean, whoever made up these pieces of writing did not imagine that what he was forming required a setting beyond the limits of his own piece of writing; the story is not only complete in itself but could stand entirely on its own; the saying spoke for itself and required no nurturing context; the proposition and its associated proofs in no way was meant to draw nourishment from roots penetrating nutriments outside of its own literary limits.

Where we have utterly hermetic writing, able to define its own limits and sustain its point without regard to anything outside itself, we know that here we are in the presence of authorships that had no larger redactional plan in mind, no intent on the making of books out of their little pieces of writing. We may note that, among the "unimaginable" compilations is not a collection of parables, since parables rarely[17] stand free and never are inserted for their own sake. Whenever in the Rabbinic canon we find a parable, it is meant to serve the purpose of an authorship engaged in making its own point; and the point of a parable is rarely, if ever, left unarticulated. Normally it is put into words, but occasionally the point is made simply by redactional setting.

It must follow that, in this canon, the parable cannot have constituted the generative or agglutinative principle of a large-scale compilation. It further follows, so it seems to me, that the parable always takes shape within the framework of a work of composition for the purpose of either a large-scale exposition or, more commonly still, of compilation of a set of expositions into what we should now call the chapter of a book; that is to say, parables link to purposes that transcend the tale that they tell (or even the point that the tale makes). Let me now give one example of what I classify as a free-standing piece of writing, one with no place for itself in accord with the purposes of compilers either of documents we now have in hand or of documents we can readily envisage or imagine. My example again derive from Sifra, although, as a matter of fact, every document of the canon yields illustrative materials for all three types of writing.

The issue of the relationship between the Mishnah and Scripture deeply engaged a variety of writers and compilers of documents. Time and again we have evidence of an interest in the scriptural sources of laws, or of greater consequence in the priority of Scripture in taxonomic inquiry. We can show large-scale compositions that will readily have served treatises on these matters. But if I had to point to a

---

[17]I should prefer to say "never," but it is easier to say what is in the Rabbinic literature than what is not there.

single type of writing that is quite commonplace in the compilations we do have, but *wholly* outside of the repertoire of
redactional possibilities we have or can imagine, it must be a
sustained piece of writing on the relationship of the Mishnah
to Scripture. Such a treatise can have been enormous, not
only because, in theory, every line of the Mishnah required attention. It is also because, in practice, a variety of documents,
particularly Sifra, the two Sifrés, and the Talmuds, contain
writing of a single kind, meant to amplify the Mishnah by appeal to Scripture (but never to amplify Scripture by appeal to
the Mishnah!).

It is perfectly clear that no one imagined compiling a
commentary to the Mishnah that would consist principally of
proofs, of a sustained and well-crafted sort, that the Mishnah
in general depends upon Scripture (even though specific and
sustained proofs that the principles of taxonomy derive from
Scripture are, as I said, susceptible of compilation in such
treatises). How do we know that fact? It is because, when
people did compile writings in the form of sustained commentaries to the Mishnah, that is to say, the two Talmuds,
they did not focus principally upon the scriptural exegesis of
the Mishnah; that formed only one interest, and, while an important one, it did not predominate; it certainly did not define
the plan and program of the whole; and it certainly did not
form a center of redactional labor. It was simply one item on
a list of items that would be brought into relationship, where
appropriate, with sentences of the Mishnah. And even then, it
always was the intersection at the level of sentences, not sustained discourses, let alone with the Mishnah viewed whole
and complete.

And yet — and yet if we look into compilations we
do have, we find sizable sets of materials that can have been
joined together with the Mishnah, paragraph by paragraph, in
such a way that Scripture might have been shaped into a

commentary to the Mishnah. Let me now give a sustained example of what might have emerged, but never did emerge, in the canonical compilations of Judaism. I draw my case from Sifra, but equivalent materials in other Midrash-compilations as well as in the two Talmuds in fact are abundant. In bold face type are direct citations of Mishnah-passages. I skip Nos. 2-12, because these are not germane to this part of my argument.

SIFRA PARASHAT BEHUQOTAI PARASHAH 3

CCLXX:I.1 A. ["The Lord said to Moses, Say to the people of Israel, When a man makes a special vow of persons to the Lord at your Valuation, then your Valuation of a male from twenty years old up to sixty years old shall be fifty shekels of silver according to the shekel of the sanctuary. If the person is a female, your Valuation shall be thirty shekels. If the person is from five years old up to twenty years old, your Valuation shall be for a male twenty shekels and for a female ten shekels. If the person is from a month old up to five years old, your Valuation shall be for a male five shekels of silver and for a female your Valuation shall be three shekels of silver. And if the person is sixty years old and upward, then your Valuation for a male shall be fifteen shekels and for a female ten shekels. And if a man is too poor to pay your Valuation, then he shall bring the person before the priest, and the priest shall value him; according to the ability of him who vowed the priest shall value him" (Lev. 27:1-8).]

B. **"Israelites take vows of Valuation, but gentiles do not take vows of Valuation [M. Ar. 1:2B].**

C. "Might one suppose they are not subject to vows of Valuation?

D. "Scripture says, 'a man,'" the words of R. Meir.

E. Said R. Meir, "After one verse of Scripture makes an inclusionary statement, another makes an exclusionary statement.

F. "On what account do I say that gentiles are subject to vows of Valuation but may not take vows of Valuation?

G. **"It is because greater is the applicability of the rule of subject to the pledge of Valuation by others than the applicability of making the pledge of Valuation of others [T. Ar. 1:1A].**

H. **"For lo, a deaf-mute, idiot, and minor may be subjected to vows of Valuation, but they are not able to take vows of Valuation [M. Ar. 1:1F]."**

I. R. Judah says, **"Israelites are subject to vows of Valuation, but gentiles are not subject to vows of Valuation [M. Ar. 1:2C].**

J. "Might one suppose that they may not take vows of Valuation of third parties?

K. "Scripture says, 'a man.'"

L. Said R. Judah, "After one verse of Scripture makes an inclusionary statement, another makes an exclusionary statement.

M. "On what account do I say that gentiles are not subject to vows of Valuation but may take vows of Valuation?

N. **"It is because greater is the applicability of the rule of pledging the Valuation of others than the applicability of being subject to the pledge of Valuation by others [T. Ar. 1:1C].**

O. **"For a person of doubtful sexual traits and a person who exhibits traits of both sexes pledge the Valuation of others but are not subjected to the pledge of Valuation to be paid by others" [M. Ar. 1:1D].**

13. A. And how do we know that the sixtieth year is treated as part of the period prior to that year?

B. Scripture says, "from twenty years old up to sixty years old" —

C. **this teaches that the sixtieth year is treated as part of the period prior to that year.**

D. I know only that that is the rule governing the status of the sixtieth year. How do I know the rule as to assigning the fifth year, the twentieth year?

E. It is a matter of logic:

F. Liability is incurred when one is in the sixtieth year, the fifth year, and the twentieth year.

G. Just as the sixtieth year is treated as part of the period prior to that year,

H. so the fifth and the twentieth years are treated as part of the period prior to that year.

I. But if you treat the sixtieth year as part of the prior period, imposing a more stringent law [the Valuation requiring a higher fee before than after sixty],

J. shall we treat the fifth year and the twentieth year as part of the period prior to that year, so imposing a more lenient law in such cases [the Valuation being less expensive]?

K. Accordingly, Scripture is required to settle the question when it refers repeatedly to "year,"

L. thus establishing a single classification for all such cases:

M. just as the sixtieth year is treated as part of the prior period, so the fifth and the twentieth years are treated as part of the prior period.

N. And that is the rule, whether it produces a more lenient or a more stringent ruling [M. Ar. 4:4M-Q, with somewhat different wording].

14. A. R. Eliezer says, "How do we know that a month and a day after a month are treated as part of the sixtieth year?

B. "Scripture says, 'up....:'

C. "Here we find reference to 'up...,' and elsewhere we find the same. Just as 'up' used elsewhere means that a month and a day after the month [are included in the prior span of time], so the meaning is the same when used here. [M. Ar. 4:4R: R. Eleazar says, "The foregoing applies so long as they are a month and a day more than the years which are prescribed."]

15.   A.   I know only that this rule applies after sixty. How do I know that the same rule applies after five or twenty?

B.   It is a matter of logic:

C.   One is liability to pay a pledge of Valuation if the person to be evaluated is old than sixty, and one is liable if such a one is older than five or older than twenty.

D.   Just as, if one is older than sixty by a month and a day, , the person is as though he were sixty years of age, so if the one is after five years or twenty years by a month and a day, lo, these are deemed to be the equivalent of five or twenty years of age.

16.   A.   "And if a man is too poor to pay your Valuation:"

B.   this means, if he is too impoverished to come up with your Valuation.

17.   A.   "then he shall bring the person before the priest:"

B.   this then excludes a dead person.

C.   I shall then exclude a corpse but not a dying person?

D.   Scripture says, "Scripture says, "then he shall bring the person before the priest, and the priest shall value him" —

E.   one who is subject to being brought is subject to being evaluated, and one who is not subject to being brought before the priest [such as a dying man] also is not subject to the pledge of Valuation.

18.   A.   Might one suppose that even if someone said, "The Valuation of Mr. So-and-so is incumbent on me," and he died, the man should be exempt?

B.   Scripture says, "and the priest shall value him."

C.   That is so even if he is dead.

19.   A.   "and the priest shall value him:"

B.   This means that one pays only in accord with the conditions prevailing at the time of the Valuation.

20.   A.   "according to the ability of him who vowed the priest shall value him:"

B. It is in accord with the means of the one who takes the vow, not the one concerning whom the vow is taken,

C. whether that is a man, woman or child.

D. In this connection sages have said:

E. The estimate of ability to pay is made in accord with the status of the one who vows;

F. and the estimate of the years of age is made in accord with the status of the one whose Valuation is vowed.

G. And when this is according to the Valuations spelled out in the Torah, it is in accord with the status, as to age and sex, of the one whose Valuation is pledged.

H. And the Valuation is paid in accordance with the rate prescribed at the time of the pledge of Valuation [M. Ar. 4:1A-D].

21. A. "the priest shall value him:"

B. This serves as the generative analogy covering all cases of Valuations, indicating that the priest should be in charge.

The program of the Mishnah and the Tosefta predominates throughout, e.g., Nos. 1, 12, 13, 14-15. The second methodical inquiry characteristic of our authorship, involving exclusion and inclusion, accounts for pretty much the rest of this well-crafted discussion. Now we see a coherent and cogent discussion of a topic in accord with a program applicable to all topics, that trait of our document which so won our admiration. Thus Nos. 2-11, 17-20, involve inclusion, exclusion, or extension by analogy. I should offer this excellent composition as an example of the best our authorship has to give us, and a very impressive intellectual gift at that. The point throughout is simple. We know how the compilers of canonical writings produced treatments of the Mishnah. The one thing that they did not do was to create a scriptural commentary to the Mishnah. That is not the only type of writing lacking all correspondence to documents we have or can imagine, but it is a striking example.

IX.   THE THREE STAGES OF LITERARY FORMATION

Now to return to my starting point, namely, those sizable selections of materials that circulated from one document to another, the autonomous compositions and composites. I labeled these writings as a still-earlier stage than those compositions and composites that exhibit documentary traits but do not fit into the framework of any document now in our hands. Let me explain why I tend to think they were formed earlier than the writings particular to documents.[18]

The documentary hypothesis affects our reading of the itinerant compositions, for it identifies what writings are extra-documentary and non-documentary and imposes upon the hermeneutics and history of these writings a set of distinctive considerations. The reason is that these writings serve the purposes not of compilers (or authors or authorships) of distinct compilations, but the interests of a another type of authorship entirely: one that thought making up stories (whether or not for collections) itself an important activity; or making up exercises on Mishnah-Scripture relationships; or other such writings as lie beyond the imagination of the com-

---

[18]I am probably the only person who thinks it necessary even to raise this question; those who believe the inerrancy of attributions also know as fact that attributed statements are prior to unattributed ones (unless they decide, for whatever reason, that unattributed ones are prior to attributed ones); but as to cogent compositions, those who identify the discrete saying as the building block of all composition also "know" that all compositions are prior to the composites of which they form a part and do not find it necessary to ask the question I answer here, and only then with considerable reluctance.

pilers of the score of documents that comprise the canon. When writings work well for two or more documents therefore they must be assumed to have a literary history different from those that serve only one writing or one type of writing, and, also, demand a different hermeneutic.

My "three stages" in ordinal sequence correspond, as a matter of fact, to a taxic structure, that is, three types of writing. The first — and last in assumed temporal order — is writing carried out in the context of the making, or compilation, of a classic that is extant. That writing responds to the redactional program and plan of the authorship of a classic. The second, penultimate in order, is writing that can appears in a given document but better serves a document other than the one in which it (singularly) occurs. This kind of writing seems to me not to fall within the same period of redaction as the first. For while it is a type of writing under the identical conditions, it also is writing that presupposes redactional programs in no way in play in the ultimate, and definitive, period of the formation of the canon: when people did things this way, and not in some other. That is why I think it is a kind of writing that was done prior to the period in which people limited their redactional work and associated labor of composition to the program that yielded the books we now have.

The upshot is simple: whether the classification of writing be given a temporal or merely taxonomic valence, the issue is the same: have these writers done their work with documentary considerations in mind? I believe I have shown that they have not. Then where did they expect their work to makes its way? Anywhere it might, because, so they assumed, fitting in no where in particular, it found a suitable locus everywhere it turned up. But I think temporal, not merely taxonomic, considerations pertain.

The third kind of writing seems to me to originate in a period prior to the other two. It is carried on in a manner independent of all redactional considerations such as are known to us. Then it should derive from a time when redactional considerations played no paramount role in the making of compositions. A brief essay, rather than a sustained composition, was then the dominant mode of writing. My hypothesis is that people can have written both long and short compositions — compositions and composites, in my language — at one and the same time. But writing that does not presuppose a secondary labor of redaction, e.g., in a composite, probably originated when authors or authorships did not anticipate any fate for their writing beyond their labor of composition itself. An example of this kind of writing is the story about Simeon the Righteous that appears in both Talmuds, as we shall see. Since no one collected stories of holy men into biographies or gospels, it follows, whoever made up and wrote down that story (or gave it fixed form for oral formulation and transmission in the medium of memory) cannot have had in mind a story that would form part of a biography; then it was a story without a further redactional destination.

Along these same lines of argument, this writing may or may not travel from one document to another. What that means is that the author or authorship does not imagine a future for his writing. What fits anywhere is composed to go nowhere in particular. Accordingly, what matters is not whether a writing fits one document or another, but whether, as the author or authorship has composed a piece of writing, that writing meets the requirements of any document we now have or can even imagine. If it does not, then we deal with a literary period in which the main kind of writing was ad hoc and episodic, not sustained and documentary.

Now extra- and non-documentary kinds of writing seem to me to derive from either q[1] a period prior to the work of the making of Midrash-compilations and the two Talmuds alike; or

[2] a labor of composition not subject to the rules and considerations that operated in the work of the making of Midrash-compilations and the two Talmuds.

As a matter of hypothesis, I should guess that non-documentary writing comes prior to making any kind of documents of consequence, and extra-documentary writing comes prior to the period in which the specificities of the documents we now have were defined. That is to say, writing that can fit anywhere or nowhere is prior to writing that can fit somewhere but does not fit anywhere now accessible to us, and both kinds of writing are prior to the kind that fits only in what documents in which it is now located.

And given the documentary propositions and theses that we can locate in all of our compilations, we can only assume that the non-documentary writings enjoyed, and were assumed to enjoy, ecumenical acceptance. That means, very simply, when we wish to know the consensus of the entire textual (or canonical) community[19] — I mean simply the people, anywhere and any time, responsible for everything we now have — we turn not to the distinctive perspective of documents, but the (apparently universally acceptable) perspective of the extra-documentary compositions. That is the point at which we should look for the propositions everywhere accepted but no where advanced in a distinctive way, the "Judaism beyond the texts" — or behind them.

Do I place a priority, in the framing of a hypothesis, over taxonomy or temporal order? Indeed I do. I am inclined to suppose that non-documentary compositions took shape not only separated from, but in time before, the documentary

---

[19]I prefer Brian Stock's "textual community," see his *Implications of Literacy* (Princeton, 1986: Princeton University Press).

ones did. My reason for thinking so is worth rehearsing, even though it is not yet compelling. The kinds of non-documentary writing I have identified in general focus on matters of very general interest. These matters may be assembled into two very large rubrics: virtue, on the one side, reason, on the other. Stories about sages fall into the former category; all of them set forth in concrete form the right living that sages exemplify.

Essays on right thinking, the role of reason, the taxonomic priority of Scripture, the power of analogy, the exemplary character of cases and precedents in the expression of general and encompassing rules — all of these intellectually coercive writings set forth rules of thought as universally applicable, in their way, as are the rules of conduct contained in stories about sages, in theirs. A great labor of generalization is contained in both kinds of non-documentary and extra-documentary writing. And the results of that labor are then given concrete expression in the documentary writings in hand; for these, after all, do say in the setting of specific passages or problems precisely what, in a highly general way, emerges from the writing that moves hither and yon, never with a home, always finding a suitable resting place.

Now, admittedly, that rather general characterization of the non-documentary writing is subject to considerable qualification and clarification. But it does provide a reason to assign temporal priority, not solely taxonomic distinction, to the non-documentary compositions. We can have had commentaries of a sustained and systematic sort on Chronicles, on the one side, treatises on virtue, on the second, gospels, on the third — to complete the triangle. But we do not have these kinds of books.

In conclusion, let me confess that I wish our sages had made treatises on right action and right thought, in their own idiom to be sure, because I think these treatises will have shaped the intellect of generations to come in a more effective way than the discrete writings, submerged in collections and composites of other sorts altogether, have been able to do. Compositions on correct behavior made later on filled the gap left open by the redactional decisions made in the period under study; I do not know why no one assembled a Midrash on right action in the way in which, in Leviticus Rabbah and Genesis Rabbah, treatises on the rules of society and the rules of history were compiled.

And still more do I miss those intellectually remarkable treatises on right thought that our sages can have produced out of the rich resources in hand: the art of generalization, the craft of comparison and contrast, for example. In this regard the Mishnah, with its union of (some) Aristotelian modes of thought and (some) neo-Platonic propositions forms the model, if a lonely one, for what can have been achieved, even in the odd and unphilosophical idiom of our sages.[20] The compositions needed for both kinds of treatises — and, as a matter of fact, many, many of them — are fully in hand. But no one made the compilations of them.

The books we do have not only preserve the evidences of the possibility of commentaries and biographies. More than that, they also bring to rich expression the messages that such books will have set forth. And most important, they also express in fresh and unanticipated contexts those virtues and values that commentaries and biographies ("gospels") meant to bring to realization, and they do so in accord with the modes of thought that sophisticated reflection on right thinking has exemplified in its way as well. So when people when about the work of making documents,

---

[20]This is fully explained in my *Philosophical Mishnah* (Atlanta, 1989: Scholars Press for Brown Judaic Studies) I-IV, and in my *Judaism as Philosophy. The Method and Message of the Mishnah*. Columbia, 1991: University of South Carolina Press..

they did something fresh with something familiar. They made cogent compositions, documents, texts enjoying integrity and autonomy. But they did so in such a way as to form of their distinct documents a coherent body of writing, of books, a canon, of documents, a system. And this they did in such a way as to say, in distinctive and specific ways, things that, in former times, people had expressed in general and broadly-applicable ways.

For the documentary reading of the Rabbinic canon I have now spelled out the evidence and the literary theory generated by that evidence. Clearly, to advance a different reading of the same writings it will not do merely to assemble variant readings of a given story or diverse manuscript evidence for a given Rabbinic document. A large-scale theory, not merely some abstract ruminations, alone will serve. The evidence demands attention, and not merely bits and pieces of evidence, exemplary of we know not what, such as Becker collects, let alone the confusions put forth as arguments, such as Schaefer emits, in the works treated in the following appendices. I can account for different kinds of writing and for the traits of the canonical books. Can exponents of a different view of matters spell out that view and show us how they address the same evidence that sustains the documentary reading? Time will tell.

APPENDIX A

POINTLESS PARALLELS AND SUPERFICIAL FRAMING OF ISSUES:

HANS-JUERGEN BECKER, *DIE GROSSEN RABBINISCHEN SAMMELWERKE PALAESTINAS. ZUR LITERARISCHEN GENESE VON TALMUD YERUSHALMI UND MIDRASH BERESHIT RABBA*

Hans-Juergen Becker, newly-appointed Professor of New Testament and Ancient Judaism at Goettingen, here[21] presents his dissertation (*Habilitationsschrift*), devoted to relationships between Genesis Rabba and the Talmud of the Land of Israel. Specifically, he compares the wording of passages that occur in both documents, not the documents as a whole, which are essentially autonomous of one another, except at a handful of intersecting passages such as he considers. But the comparison is, to say the least, selective and superficial. In fact Becker takes exactly four points at which comparable compositions occur in both documents: [1] narratives of Creation at Y. Hag. 2:1 and Gen. R. 1-12; [2] Halakhic texts in Genesis Rabbah with parallels in Yerushalmi,

---

[21] *Die grossen rabbinischen Sammelwerke Palaestinas. Zur literarischen Genese von Talmud Yerushalmi und Midrash Bereshit Rabba* Tuebingen, 1999: J. C. B. Mohr (Paul Siebeck). 218 pp.

Yerushalmi, [3] Genesis Rabbah parallels in the Babot-tractates of Yerushalmi, and [4] the narratives of the death of R. Samuel bar R. Isaac. At each point he identifies "parallels," undertakes analysis of components of those parallels ("einzelanalysen"), and attempts then to draw some conclusions.

These conclusions of his, alas, are uniformly indeterminate, e.g., "In Bezug auf die Schoepfungs-Aggadot insgesamt ist festzuhalten, dass unsere Textvergleiche nicht zu der einen Quelle gefuehrt haben, aus der alle diese Traditionen fliessen, sondern zu mehreren verschiedenen Quellen, von denen widerum verschiedene Fassungen existierten" (p. 60). Given the deplorable condition of MS evidence and text traditions, what other conclusion can have been anticipated? So too, "...ein wichtiges Ergebnis unserer Einzelanalysen festgehalten werden, dass eine dirkete Uebertragung der untersuchten Texte aus dem Y in der BerR oder umgekehrt in allen Faellen ausgeschlossen ist" (p. 101) — I wonder who thought otherwise? On the relationships of Gen. R. parallels to the Babas: "die jeweiligen Versionen sind nicht direkt voneinander abhaengig; die verwendeten Traditionen lagen Y und BerR bereits in verschiedenen Fassungen vor...," and so forth (p. 132). And finally, on the diverse readings of the story of R. Samuel's death, "Die unvollstaendige Textevidenz, die einen direkten Vergleich zwischen Vorlage(n) unter Bearbeitung ausschliesst, tragt aber ihr Teil dazu bei, die redaktionskritische Arbeit auch an einzelnen Punkten dieser fluktuierenden Ueberlieferung beinahe unmoeglich zu machen" (p. 148). The upshot is, a great deal of industrious work of detail has produced some unsurprising conclusions about the indeterminacy of readings of compositions and composites shared among kindred documents. I do not think anyone who has worked on these documents over the past century will find that conclusion astonishing. The explanation of the project is equally puzzling: "Diese Arbeit behandelt rabbinische Texts als Texte" (p. 1), something I thought pretty commonplace. Who thinks otherwise? What exactly it means, in German, to deal with "rabbinic texts as texts" I cannot say, but in American English, it comes out as a banality. In the next Appendix, we shall encounter much murkier formulations than Becker's and find still more intractable problems of understanding what is in the mind of the German scholars.

Then to what end? Becker directs the entire project into a critique of my documentary reading of the Rabbinic classics. That is a matter that, his discussion and bibliography indicate, he grasps imperfectly, if at all. That is because his research is superficial, as seems to be the case in his sector of German scholarship on Judaism. The issue was originally raised in response to my *Judaism: The Evidence of the Mishnah* (1981), which does not appear even in the bibliography; the most systematic critique was that of Peter Schaefer, "Research into Rabbinic literature," *Journal of Jewish Studies* 1986, 37:139-152, which does appear in the bibliography. To this critique, which I deemed weighty, I replied in a variety of books and articles, for example, *Midrash as Literature: The Primacy of Documentary Discourse.* Lanham, 1987: University Press of America *Studies in Judaism* series, *Sifra in Perspective: The Documentary Comparison of the Midrashim of Ancient Judaism* Atlanta, 1988: Scholars Press for Brown Judaic Studies, and most notably, *The Documentary Foundation of Rabbinic Culture. Mopping Up after Debates with Gerald L. Bruns, S. J. D. Cohen, Arnold Maria Goldberg, Susan Handelman, Christine Hayes, James Kugel, Peter Schaefer, Eliezer Segal, E. P. Sanders, and Lawrence H. Schiffman.* Atlanta, 1995: Scholars Press for South Florida Studies in the History of Judaism. None of these nor their companions appears in Becker's bibliography! That is what I mean when I call his work superficial. But that bibliography does include a sizable proportion of items not cited in the text. That is a mark of politics, not scholarship: citing the right people, not listing the wrong ones. The upshot is infelicitous. Becker does not seem to understand what is alleged, and not alleged, in that documentary theory that he has written an entire dissertation to disprove but that he has to begin with not conscientiously researched. He has framed his entire inquiry to address an issue that he knows only in a superficial way, and understands not at all. The data that he assembles have no bearing on what is alleged — a considerable failure. Becker simply misses the mark.

But that his data have slight bearing on the documentary hypothesis in no way deprives the dissertation of considerable value in its own terms. Despite the indeterminacy of his diffuse results, his dissertation contains many useful observations about this and that. Anyone interested in the texts he addresses will find indispensable his presentation of the variants and other text problems.

APPENDIX B

But What If We Have No Documents? The Problem of Establishing the Text and the Solution of Form-Analysis:

The Debate with Arnold Goldberg and Peter Schaefer

From the beginnings of the formation of the Rabbinic literature at the closure of the Mishnah, the Rabbinic sages and their heirs and continuators recognized the fluid state of the textual tradition, both mnemonic and oral for the Mishnah, and in writing or in notes for other components of the canon. The pages of the Talmud present rich evidence of the variety of readings and versions that sages possessed, and some of the most adventurous — and successful — analytical-dialectical compositions propose to interpret textual variations by appeal to conflicting legal theories. A landmark study of the text of the Mishnah sits on the shelf of every active scholar of the field, Y. N. Epstein, *Mebo lenusah hammishnah* (1954). Not only so but the diversity of the readings finds its match in the paucity of manuscript evidence. And, finally, modern scholarship, under academic and theological auspices alike, has yet to produce critical texts for the various documents, or even reached a consensus on what we can mean by a critical text. It follows that admonitions to the scholarly world to take account of the parlous textual tradition for the

Rabbinic documents repeat the obvious.

Along with everybody else, I was taught to take account of variants, large and small. That is why, from the very beginning of the documentary method, I took account of the problem of determining that on which I was working, taking full account of the uncertainty of the text tradition for any given passage or even for documents as a whole. As I have made clear for the case of the Mishnah and each subsequent compilation, the method focused upon the characteristics that recur throughout a document. No conclusions or characterizations depend solely on the details that appear only here or there. Not episodic but fixed traits of form therefore dictated the analytical procedures: recurrent patterns in rhetoric, definitive and ubiquitous traits in the principles of logical coherence in holding together compositions in composites, composites in a whole and complete statement. At no point does the description of a document rest upon a specific reading or unique traits that occur in some one place. On the contrary, the very essence of the documentary method is to describe, analyze, and interpret the whole, and that means, traits that are uniform throughout. That focus on the permanent, the recurrent, and the characteristic and definitive takes full account of variations of detail.

Now, when we ask which text tradition, or which version, of a document we subject to documentary description, analysis, and interpretation, we therefore take up a question that by definition simply does not apply. For, as a matter of fact, every Rabbinic document we possess from the formative age, however diverse or fluid the text tradition on which we work, exhibits throughout its textual testimonies precisely those uniformities of rhetorical, topical, and logical traits that come under description in the documentary method. I cannot point to a single judgment of a documentary character set forth in any of my accounts that relies upon one reading, rather than another. Where we have critical editions, it goes without saying I translate and analyze those versions, e.g., Theodor-Albeck for Genesis Rabbah, Finkelstein for Sifra and Sifré to Deuteronomy; where we do not, I work on the standard printed edition and consult such variants as have been collected in that connection. Controlling for variables of text-transmission, I thus characterize the documents.

Two scholars, Arnold Maria Goldberg and his student, Peter Schaefer, have found themselves so impressed by the obstacles put forth by a fluid and sparse text tradition as to claim we have no documents at all, only variant readings. That nihilistic position then defines the task of learning as the assembly of variant readings and the publication, with virtually no critical judgment, of a mass of this and that. Work of a historical and cultural character simply loses its bearings, if we have no documents at all.

That rather odd position is taken by Arnold Maria Goldberg, "Der Diskurs im babylonischen Talmud. Anregungen für eine Diskursanalyse," in *Frankfurter Judaistische Beiträge* 1983, 11:1-45: "Once it has been written, every text is exclusively synchronic, all the textual units exist simultaneously, and the only diachronic relation consists in the reception of the text as a sequence of textual units whose 'first' and 'then' become 'beforehand' and 'afterwards' in the reception of the text...The synchronicity of a text is...the simultaneous juxtaposition of various units, independent of when the units originated."[22] This murky prose scarcely speaks for itself; it competes with Becker's emphatic and unintelligible statement at the beginning, "Diese Arbeit behandelt rabbinische Texts als Texte"!

But Schaefer helps us follow Goldberg's thought,

---

[22]Cited in Peter Schaefer, "Research into Rabbinic Literature," *Journal of Jewish Studies* 1986, 37:145.

when he proceeds, "This emphasis on a fundamental syn-chronicity of the texts of rabbinic literature is completely consistent with Goldberg's methodological approach. The text as it stands is exclusively synchronic and, since we cannot go back beyond this state, there remains only the classifying description of that which is there...A historical differentiation is deliberately excluded, because in effect the texts do not permit it. Whilst analysis of the forms and functions of a text makes its system of rules transparent, 'the comprehension of rabbinic texts through habituation and insight could be super-seded by a comprehension of the rules of this discourse as competence....'"[23]

Goldberg's dogmatic definition of matters notwith-standing, a sustained examination of the various documents leaves no doubt whatsoever that we can identify not only "beforehand" but "first," showing that the formation of composites out of fully-articulated compositions took place prior to the definition of a document's distinctive traits. Had Goldberg read my *The Formation of the Jewish Intellect. Making Connections and Drawing Conclusions in the Traditional System of Judaism*. Atlanta, 1988: Scholars Press for Brown Judaic Studies, he would have found ample grounds, based on the logics of coherent discourse alone, to reconsider his position. But Goldberg was not interested in Auseinandersetzungen with those who saw matters differently. Indeed, when I came to Frankfurt University to serve as Buber Professor, I discov-ered that Goldberg had instructed his students at Frankfurt University, in his dying breaths, that they were not to study with me, and only one of them did.

We cannot know how Goldberg will have dealt with the contrary viewpoint. But now data that prove the exact opposite of Goldberg's premised position emerge fully and

---

[23]*ibid., ad loc.*

completely, for the Talmud, in my *The Talmud of Babylonia. An Academic Commentary.* Atlanta, 1994-5: Scholars Press for *USF Academic Commentary Series,* and in its companion, *The Talmud of Babylonia. A Complete Outline.* Atlanta, 1994-1995: Scholars Press for *USF Academic Commentary Series.* Not only so, but I have devoted *Initial Phases,* cited above, to just this problem. Why Goldberg takes the position that he does I cannot say. The facts that are set forth in *Academic Commentary, Complete Outline,* and *Initial Phases,* indicate that Goldberg certainly cannot have known through his own, first-hand analysis, a great deal about the literary traits of the Rabbinic literature. He seems to have confused a kind of abstract philosophizing with the concrete acts of detailed learning that scholarship requires. That explains why he left no imposing legacy of scholarship to sustain his opinion, which is at once doctrinaire, ignorant, and eccentric. Goldberg's nihilism[24] has no continuators,[25] except for his student, Peter Schaefer, and I do not see much basis on which to contend with his obscure and solipsistic legacy. We shall deal with Schaefer's own, equally nihilistic, position in due course.

I do not share Goldberg's position, because I have shown, on the same basis of phenomenology on which he lays out his view, that the contrary is the fact. Having completed the work on the Talmud of Babylonia, I only now be-

---

[24]I do not think that his conversion from Judaism to another religion necessarily comes to expression in his dismissal of the Rabbinic corpus as a literature without a history, but given the historicistic world in which he lived, the upshot of his position was to remove Rabbinic Judaism from the realm of culture and civilization altogether. I find in his writing slight respect for Judaism and those who practice that religion.

[25]When in late April, 1991, just after Goldberg died, I came to Goldberg's University, the University of Frankfurt, as Martin Buber Visiting Professor of Judaic Studies, for the Summer Semester, I was saddened to find that had left as his legacy strict instructions to his students, not only not to study with me or but not even to meet me.

gin the equivalent academic commentary and complete outline for the Yerushalmi, with the plan of proceeding to the
score of Midrash-compilations, so I cannot say what I shall
find in continuing a uniform analysis. But the naked eye suggests that Goldberg's position will not find in the other
documents any support at all. The documents as we know
them certainly encompass not only materials that serve the
clearly-manifest program of the framers or compilers of the
documents, but also the self-evident interests of authors of
compositions and framers of composites who had other plans
than those realized in the documents as we have them.

But the question is, how do we identify components
of a composition, or of a composite, that took shape outside
of the documentary framework and prior to the definition of
the documentary traits of a given compilation? Unless we
take at face value the attributions of sayings to specific,
named authorities at determinate times and places, we must
work by paying close attention to the material traits of the
compositions and composites. That requires, as I said, moving from the end-product backward and inward — and in no
other way. Two intellectually lazy ways have led nowhere,
Goldberg's denial that it is a question, and the Israelis' insistence that attributions eo ipse equal facts. Finding no promise
in such labor-saving devices — settling questions by decree
— I have resorted to sifting the facts, and that is what I have
done and now do.

This brings us, finally, to the explicit statement of Peter Schaefer that we have no documents. This he states in the
following language, beginning with his critique of Goldberg
and pronouncement of a still more extreme position; I number those paragraphs that I shall discuss below.

> 1.   The question that arises here is obviously what is
> meant by 'texts.' What is the text 'once it has been writ-
> ten' — the Babylonian Talmud, the Midrash, a definite

Midrash, all Midrashim, or even the whole of rabbinic literature as a synchronic textual continuum whose inherent system of rules it is necessary to describe? Indeed, in such a description, neither the concrete text concerned, nor the form a particular textual tradition takes, needs to be important. Every text is as good — or rather as bad — as every other, the 'best" being presumably the one representing the latest redactional stage.

2.   But this is precisely where the problem begins. Goldberg himself must finally decide on one text, and, in doing so...must decide against or or several other texts. Whether he wants to or not, he inevitably faces historical questions. This problem can be elucidated by the second line of research within the 'literary' approach.

3.   This second line of research...is that of the interpretation immanent in the work. Complete literary works are analyzed as a whole, as literary systems so to speak, and are examined for their characteristic arguments...Neusner has ...sent to press such analyses...The plane on which this research approach moves...is the final redaction of the respective work...Two closely related problems arise from this.

4.   The approach inevitably disregards the manuscript traditions of the work in question. But especially in the case of rabbinic literature, this is essential. Thus, to give an example, both Vatican manuscripts of the Bereshit Rabba...represent texts which are quite different from that of the London manuscript...The variations are sometimes so great that the redactional identity of the work is debatable. Is it meaningful to speak of one work at all, or rather of various recensions of a work? But then how do these recensions relate to one another? Are they different versions of one and the same text...or are they autonomous to a certain extent, and is Bereshit Rabba' merely an ideal or a fictitious entity? What then constitutes the identity of the work 'Bereshit Rabbah'? Any preserved manuscript or the modern 'critical' edition by Theodor-Albeck...

5.   The problem becomes more acute when the ques-

tion of the boundaries of works is taken into consideration. To remain with the example of Bereshit Rabba, the problem of what relation Bereshit Rabba and the Yerushalmi bear to one another has been discussed since the time of Frankel...How are Bereshit Rabba and Yerushalmi related to one another...? Does Bereshit Rabba quote Yerushalmi, i.e., can we regard Bereshit Rabba and Yerushalmi at the time of the redaction of Bereshit Rabba as two clearly distinguishable works, one of which being completed? Did the redactor of Bereshit Rabbah therefore 'know' with what he was dealing and from what he was 'quoting'? With regard to the Yerushalmi, this conclusion is obviously unreasonable, for we immediately have to ask how the Yerushalmi of the Bereshit Rabba is related to the Yerushalmi existent today. The Yerushalmi cannot have been 'complete' at the time of the redaction of Bereshit Rabba since it is not identical to the one we use today.[26]

6.   A brief reference to Hekhalot literature will constitute a last example. This is without doubt the prototype of a literature where the boundaries between the works are fluid. Every 'work' in this literary genre that I have investigated more closely proves to be astonishingly unstable, falls into smaller and smaller editorial units, and cannot be precisely defined and delimited, either as it is or with reference to related literature. This finding is of course valid with regard to the works of Hekhalot literature to a varying degree, but can be generalized as a striking characteristic feature of the whole literary genre....[27]

7.   The questioning of the redactional identity of the individual works of rabbinic literature inevitably also disavows the research approach to the work at the level of the final redaction. The terms with which we usually work — text, "Urtext," recension, tradition, citation, redaction, final redaction, work — prove to be fragile

---

[26]Schaefer, pp, 146-147.
[27]*ibid., ad loc.*, p. 149.

and hasty definitions that must be subsequently questioned. What is a "text" in rabbinic literature? Are there texts that can be defined and clearly delimited, or are there only basically "open" texts which elude temporal and redactional fixation? Have there ever been "Urtexte" of certain works with a development that could be traced and described? How do different recension of a "text" relate to one another with respect to the redactional identity of the text? How should the individual tradition, the smallest literary unit, be assessed in relation to the macroform of the "work" in which it appears? What is the meaning of the presence of parts of one "work" in another more or less delimitable "work"? Is this then a quotation i work X from work Y?

8.   And finally what is redaction or final redaction? Are there several redactions of a "work" — in chronological order — but only one final redaction? What distinguishes redaction from final redaction? What lends authority to the redaction? Or is the final redaction merely the more or less incidental discontinuation of the manuscript tradition?[28]

I ask the reader to stipulate that this parody of academic prose is not my caricature but Schaefer's prose. Enough of Schaefer's presentation has now been quoted to permit a simple statement in response. The "text" loses its quotation-marks and becomes the text when we describe, analyze, and interpret recurrent formal properties that occur in one document, but not in some other, or, in the particular congeries at hand, not in any other. To state matters as required in the present context, we simply reverse the predicate and the subject, thus: a writing that exhibits definitive traits of rhetoric, logic, and topic, that occur in no other writing constitutes a text. And enough has been said in this chapter on the definition of the document and the explanation of the

---

[28]*ibid., ad loc.*, pp. 149-150

documentary method to make no further clarification necessary.

That simple definition permits us to respond to the long list of questions and to sort out the confusion that characterizes Schaefer's conception of matters. Let me systematically respond to Schaefer's unsystematic formulation of his position, which, as we see at the end, rests heavily on his observations of an odd and unrepresentative writing, which may or may not originate in the Rabbinic canon at all.

[1] I have now defined what is meant by "documents," and I shall stipulate that my "document" corresponds to Schaefer's "text." The rest of this paragraph is unintelligible to me.

[2] Goldberg's comments leave no doubt on his meaning; he denies all possibility of historical or cultural research.

[3] Schaefer's characterization of my description ("for their characteristic arguments" proves uncomprehending, though correct in its main point: I do focus on what in his terms is "the final redaction of the work," and, in my terms, the definitive congeries of traits distinctive to this complex of composites and no other.

[4] Here Schaefer spells out what he means by disregarding manuscript traditions, and he gives as his example the diverse versions of Genesis Rabbah.

But he would do well to address more directly the question of the occurrence of a single pericope in two or more documents. When we find such a case, are we able to identify the document to the definitive traits of which the pericope conforms? If we are, then we can safely describe the pericope within the framework of one document and not the other(s) in which it appears. His silence on this matter since he printed the paper at hand suggests that Schaefer appears quite oblivious to work that raised precisely the question he asks and answered it: *From Tradition to Imitation. The Plan and Program of Pesiqta deRab Kahana and Pesiqta Rabbati.* Atlanta, 1987: Scholars Press for Brown Judaic Studies. There I am able to show that pericopes common to both compilations conform to the definitive traits that characterize Pesiqta deRab Kahana and do not conform to those that characterize those pericopes of Pesiqta Rabbati that do not occur, also, in Pesiqta deRab Kahana.

[5] Schaefer's problem with "boundaries of works" suggests he cannot hold to a single subject. For the problem of the peripatetic pericope has nothing to do with that of the shared pericope. The entire range of questions he raises here reveals an underlying confusion, which can be overcome by detailed work, an examination of the specifics of matters; this Schaefer has never done for the matter at hand. But, at any rate, for reasons already stated, his questions have nothing to do with the documentary method.

[6] Schaefer here talks about that on which he is expert. His allegation about generalizing from the document he knows to those he has not worked on hardly demands serious consideration. He can be shown to be wrong in treating the one as in any way analogous, or even comparable, to the other.

[7] Here Schaefer confuses the pre-history of documents with the documents as we now know them. What I have said about the phenomenological inquiry into the pre-history of documents suffices to answer the questions that he raises. His questions are probably meant, in his mind, to form arguments in behalf of his fundamental proposition. In fact they are susceptible to clear answers; his labor-saving device of sending up obscure clouds of rhetorical questions accomplishes no good purpose. But for his instruction, let me take up his questions and address those that pertain to the documentary method.

[A] What is a "text" in rabbinic literature? A text in Rabbinic literature, as I said, is a writing that conforms to a distinctive set of definitive traits of rhetoric, topic, and logic.

[B] Are there texts that can be defined and clearly delimited, or are there only basically "open" texts which elude temporal and redactional fixation? The Rabbinic canon (with only a few exceptions) contains texts that can be defined and clearly delimited (from one another) by reference to the distinctive congeries of rhetoric, topic, and logic, characteristic of one but not the other, or, as I said, characteristic solely of the one. We can establish sequence and order among these documents, determining what is primary to a given document because it conforms to the unique, definitive traits of that document. What Schaefer means by "open" texts I cannot say, so I do not know the answer to his "or"-question, but what I do grasp suggests he is reworking Goldberg's position.

[C] Have there ever been "Urtexte" of certain works with a development that could be traced and described? The answer to this question remains to be investigated, text by text (in my language: document by document). I do not know the answer for most of the documents. The Mishnah, it is clear, proves uniform through all but two of its tractates, Eduyyot and Abot. All the others conform to the single program of formulary traits, logical characteristics, modes of exposition and argument.

That does not suggest within the Mishnah are not already-completed compositions, utilized without much change; the contrary can be demonstrated on formal grounds alone. Forming compositions by appeal to the name of a single authority, as in Mishnah-tractate Kelim, or by utilization of a single formulary pattern, as in Mishnah-tractate Arakhin and Megillah, or by illustration through diverse topics of a single abstract principle, — all these other-than-standard modes of composition and composite-making do occur. But these ready-made items take up a tiny proportion of the whole and do not suggest the characteristics of an Urtext that would have held together numerous compositions and even composites of such an order. We may then posit (and many have posited) the existence of documents like the Mishnah but in competition with it, formed on other rhetorical, logical, and even topical bases than the Mishnah. But these do not stand in historical relationship with the Mishnah, e.g., forming a continuous, incremental tradition from some remote starting point onward to the Mishnah as we know it.

[D] How do different recensions of a "text" relate to one another with respect to the redactional identity of the text? This repeats Schaefer's earlier question, e.g., concerning Yerushalmi and Genesis Rabbah.

[E] How should the individual tradition, the smallest literary unit, be assessed in relation to the macroform of the "work" in which it appears? The answer to this question is both clear and not yet fully investigated. It is obvious that we move from the whole to the parts, so the individual composition (Schaefer's "tradition," whatever he can mean by that word) finds its place within the framework of the document's definitive characteristics. But the investigation of the traits of compositions and composites that stand autonomous of the documents in which they occur has only just begin, and only with the continuation and completion of my Academic Commentary will the data have been collected that permit us to deal with this question document by document. For the Bavli we have a set of viable answers; for no other document do I claim to know the answer. For the Mishnah, as I said, I do not think that this is an urgent question, though it is a marginally relevant one.

[F] What is the meaning of the presence of parts of one "work" in another more or less delimitable "work"? Is this then a quotation i work X from work Y? The question of the composition or even composite that moves hither and yon is a variation of the question just now considered. My preliminary probe is in *The Peripatetic Saying: The Problem of the Thrice-Told Tale in Talmudic Literature.* Chico, 1985: Scholars Press for Brown Judaic Studies. Reprise and reworking of materials in *Development of a Legend; Rabbinic Traditions about the Pharisees before 70* I-III. Schaefer does not appear to know that work, which appeared before the article under discussion here — let alone Rabbinic Traditions, which appeared fifteen years before he gave his Oxford lecture on which the article is based.

[G] And finally what is redaction or final redaction? Are there several redactions of a "work" — in chronological order — but only one final redaction? What distinguishes redaction from final redaction? What lends authority to the redaction? Or is the final redaction merely the more or less incidental discontinuation of the manuscript tradition? These questions suggest only more confusion in Schaefer's mind, and since I cannot fathom what he wants to know, or why he frames matters as he does, I also cannot presume to respond. If Schaefer spelled out with patience and care precisely what he wishes to know, others could follow his line of thought, e.g., what he means by "authority...redaction?" When we look at the sentences, <u>And finally what is redaction or final redaction? What distinguishes redaction from final redaction?</u> we wonder, indeed, whether Schaefer is not simply saying the same thing over and over and over again.

All this suggests that, like his student, H.-J. Becker, Schaefer has only a superficial grasp of the issues under debate. My best sense is that Schaefer has not reflected very deeply on the premises and arguments of the work he wishes to criticize; if he had, he would have grasped the monumental irrelevance of his critique. The formulation of his thought suggests to me not so much confusion as disengagement; the wordiness conceals imprecision, for we naturally assumed that each sentence bears its own thought and are not disposed to conclude that he is simply repeating himself. But one judgment surely pertains: in the end, Schaefer simply has not understood that in taking account of precisely the considerations that he raises, I formulated the form-analytical problem in such a way address the issue of the definition of a text.

As I reflect his machine-gun bursts of questions and slowly examine each in turn, I find not so much a close engagement with issues as utter disengagement, an offhand contentiousness rather than a considered critique — in all, more silliness than sense. But Schaefer's inattention to how others have responded to precisely the problems he highlights finds its match in the case that comes next, which draws our attention to a failure even to grasp the sorts of data that yield the results of form-analysis. In the end, computer-work in collating variant readings, otherwise not commented-upon, does not constitute scholarship. It only prepares the way for scholarship. Schaefer has helped us all by supplying *Hilfsbücher*, handbooks of variant readings of the Yerushalmi tractates for which we must be grateful, both to him and to the computer-programmers who did the actual work.

BIBLIOGRAPHY

These are the titles of mine that contribute to the arguments of the present book.

The Talmud of the Land of Israel. A Preliminary Translation and Explanation. Chicago: The University of Chicago Press: 1983. XXXV. *Introduction. Taxonomy.*

The Integrity of Leviticus Rabbah. The Problem of the Autonomy of a Rabbinic Document. Chico, 1985: Scholars Press for Brown Judaic Studies.

Comparative Midrash: The Plan and Program of Genesis Rabbah and Leviticus Rabbah. Atlanta, 1986: Scholars Press for Brown Judaic Studies.

From Tradition to Imitation. The Plan and Program of Pesiqta deRab Kahana and Pesiqta Rabbati. Atlanta, 1987: Scholars Press for Brown Judaic Studies. [With a fresh translation of Pesiqta Rabbati *Pisqaot* 1-5, 15.]

Canon and Connection: Intertextuality in Judaism. Lanham, 1986: University Press of America. *Studies in Judaism* Series.

Midrash as Literature: The Primacy of Documentary Discourse. Lanham, 1987: University Press of America *Studies in Judaism* series.

The Bavli and its Sources: The Question of Tradition in the Case of Tractate Sukkah. Atlanta, 1987: Scholars Press for Brown Judaic Studies.

Sifré to Deuteronomy. An Introduction to the Rhetorical, Logical, and Topical Program. Atlanta, 1987: Scholars Press for Brown Judaic Studies.

Uniting the Dual Torah: Sifra and the Problem of the Mishnah. Cambridge and New York, 1989: Cambridge University Press.

Sifra in Perspective: The Documentary Comparison of the Midrashim of Ancient Judaism Atlanta, 1988: Scholars Press for Brown Judaic Studies.

Mekhilta Attributed to R. Ishmael. An Introduction to Judaism's First Scriptural

Encyclopaedia. Atlanta, 1988: Scholars Press for Brown Judaic Studies.

The Midrash Compilations of the Sixth and Seventh Centuries. An Introduction to the Rhetorical Logical, and Topical Program. I. *Lamentations Rabbah.* Atlanta, 1990: Scholars Press for Brown Judaic Studies

The Midrash Compilations of the Sixth and Seventh Centuries: An Introduction to the Rhetorical Logical, and Topical Program. II. *Esther Rabbah I.* Atlanta, 1990: Scholars Press for Brown Judaic Studies

The Midrash Compilations of the Sixth and Seventh Centuries: An Introduction to the Rhetorical Logical, and Topical Program. III. *Ruth Rabbah.* Atlanta, 1990: Scholars Press for Brown Judaic Studies

The Midrash Compilations of the Sixth and Seventh Centuries: An Introduction to the Rhetorical Logical, and Topical Program. IV. *Song of Songs Rabbah.* Atlanta, 1990: Scholars Press for Brown Judaic Studies

Making the Classics in Judaism: The Three Stages of Literary Formation. Atlanta, 1990: Scholars Press for Brown Judaic Studies.

The Canonical History of Ideas. The Place of the So-called Tannaite Midrashim,Mekhilta Attributed to R. Ishmael, Sifra, Sifré to Numbers, and Sifré to Deuteronomy. Atlanta, 1990: Scholars Press for South Florida Studies in the History of Judaism.

Tradition as Selectivity: Scripture, Mishnah, Tosefta, and Midrash in the Talmud of Babylonia. The Case of Tractate Arakhin. Atlanta, 1990: Scholars Press for South Florida Studies in the History of Judaism.

Language as Taxonomy. The Rules for Using Hebrew and Aramaic in the Babylonian Talmud. Atlanta, 1990: Scholars Press for South Florida Studies in the History of Judaism.

The Bavli That Might Have Been: The Tosefta's Theory of Mishnah-Commentary Compared with That of the Babylonian Talmud. Atlanta, 1990: Scholars Press for South Florida Studies in the History of Judaism.

The Rules of Composition of the Talmud of Babylonia. The Cogency of the Bavli's Composite. Atlanta, 1991: Scholars Press for South Florida Studisin the History of Judaism.

The Bavli's One Voice: Types and Forms of Analytical Discourse and their Fixed Order of Appearance. Atlanta, 1991: Scholars Press for South Florida Studies in the History of Judaism.

The Bavli's One Statement. The Metapropositional Program of Babylonian Talmud Tractate Zebahim Chapters One and Five. Atlanta, 1991: Scholars Press for South Florida Studies in the History of Judaism.

How the Bavli Shaped Rabbinic Discourse. Atlanta, 1991: Scholars Press for South Florida Studies in the History of Judaism.

The Bavli's Massive Miscellanies. The Problem of Agglutinative Discourse in the Talmud of Babylonia. Atlanta, 1992: Scholars Press for South Florida Studies in the History of Judaism.

Sources and Traditions. Types of Composition in the Talmud of Babylonia. Atlanta, 1992: Scholars Press for South Florida Studies in the History of Judaism.

The Law Behind the Laws. The Bavli's Essential Discourse. Atlanta, 1992: Scholars Press for South Florida Studies in the History of Judaism.

The Bavli's Primary Discourse. Mishnah Commentary, its Rhetorical Paradigms and their Theological Implications in the Talmud of Babylonia Tractate Moed Qatan. Atlanta, 1992: Scholars Press for South Florida Studies in the History of Judaism.

The Discourse of the Bavli: Language, Literature, and Symbolism. Five Recent Findings. Atlanta, 1991: Scholars Press for South Florida Studies in the History of Judaism.

How to Study the Bavli: The Languages, Literatures, and Lessons of the Talmud of Babylonia. Atlanta, 1992: Scholars Press for South Florida Studies in the History of Judaism.

Form-Analytical Comparison in Rabbinic Judaism. Structure and Form in The Fathers *and* The Fathers According to Rabbi Nathan. Atlanta, 1992:

Scholars Press for South Florida Studies in the History of Judaism.

The Bavli's Intellectual Character. The Generative Problematic in Bavli Baba Qamma Chapter One and Bavli Shabbat Chapter One. Atlanta, 1992: Scholars Press for South Florida Studies in the History of Judaism.

Decoding the Talmud's Exegetical Program: From Detail to Principle in the Bavli's Quest for Generalization. Tractate Shabbat. Atlanta, 1992: Scholars Press for South Florida Studies in the History of Judaism.

The Principal Parts of the Bavli's Discourse: A Final Taxonomy. Mishnah-Commentary, Sources, Traditions, and Agglutinative Miscellanies. Atlanta, 1992: Scholars Press for South Florida Studies in the History of Judaism.

The Bavli's Unique Voice. A Systematic Comparison of the Talmud of Babylonia and the Talmud of the Land of Israel. Volume One. *Bavli and Yerushalmi Qiddushin Chapter One Compared and Contrasted.* Atlanta, 1993: Scholars Press for South Florida Studies in the History of Judaism.

The Bavli's Unique Voice. A Systematic Comparison of the Talmud of Babylonia and the Talmud of the Land of Israel. Volume Two. *Yerushalmi's, Bavli's, and Other Canonical Documents' Treatment of the Program of Mishnah-Tractate Sukkah Chapters One, Two, and Four Compared and Contrasted. A Reprise and Revision of* The Bavli and its Sources. Atlanta, 1993: Scholars Press for South Florida Studies in the History of Judaism.

The Bavli's Unique Voice. A Systematic Comparison of the Talmud of Babylonia and the Talmud of the Land of Israel. Volume Three. *Bavli and Yerushalmi to Selected Mishnah-Chapters in the Division of Moed. Erubin Chapter One, and Moed Qatan Chapter Three.* Atlanta, 1993: Scholars Press for South Florida Studies in the History of Judaism.

The Bavli's Unique Voice. A Systematic Comparison of the Talmud of Babylonia and the Talmud of the Land of Israel. Volume Four. *Bavli and Yerushalmi to Selected Mishnah-Chapters in the Division of Nashim. Gittin Chapter Five and Nedarim Chapter One. And Niddah Chapter One.* Atlanta, 1993: Scholars Press for South Florida Studies in the History of

Judaism.

The Bavli's Unique Voice. A Systematic Comparison of the Talmud of Babylonia and the Talmud of the Land of Israel. Volume Five. *Bavli and Yerushalmi to Selected Mishnah-Chapters in the Division of Neziqin. Baba Mesia Chapter One and Makkot Chapters One and Two.* Atlanta, 1993: Scholars Press for South Florida Studies in the History of Judaism.

The Bavli's Unique Voice. A Systematic Comparison of the Talmud of Babylonia and the Talmud of the Land of Israel. Volume Six. *Bavli and Yerushalmi to a Miscellany of Mishnah-Chapters. Gittin Chapter One, Qiddushin Chapter Two, and Hagigah Chapter Three.* Atlanta, 1993: Scholars Press for South Florida Studies in the History of Judaism.

The Bavli's Unique Voice. Volume Seven. *What Is Unique about the Bavli in Context? An Answer Based on Inductive Description, Analysis, and Comparison.* Atlanta, 1993: Scholars Press for South Florida Studies in the History of Judaism.

Introduction to Rabbinic Literature. N.Y., 1994: Doubleday. The Doubleday Anchor Reference Library. Religious Book Club Selection, 1994. Paperback edition: 1999.

Talmudic Dialectics: Types and Forms. Atlanta, 1995: Scholars Press for South Florida Studies in the History of Judaism. I. *Introduction. Tractate Berakhot and the Divisions of Appointed Times and Women.*

Talmudic Dialectics: Types and Forms. Atlanta, 1995: Scholars Press for South Florida Studies in the History of Judaism. II. *The Divisions of Damages and Holy Things and Tractate Niddah.*

Rationality and Structure: The Bavli's Anomalous Juxtapositions. Atlanta, 1997: Scholars Press for South Florida Studies in the History of Judaism.

Judaism. The Evidence of the Mishnah. Chicago, 1981: University of Chicago Press. *Choice*, "Outstanding academic book list" 1982-3. Paperback edition: 1984. Second printing, 1985. Third printing, 1986. Second edition, augmented: Atlanta, 1987: Scholars Press for Brown Judaic Studies.

Hayyahadut le'edut hammishnah. Hebrew translation of *Judaism. The Evidence of the Mishnah.* Tel Aviv, 1987: Sifriat Poalim.

Il Giudaismo nella testimonianza della Mishnah. Italian translation by Giogio Volpe. Bologna, 1995: Centro editoriale Dehoniane.

Judaism in Society: The Evidence of the Yerushalmi. Toward the Natural History of a Religion. Chicago, 1983: The University of Chicago Press. *Choice,* "Outstanding Academic Book List, 1984-1985." Second printing, with a new preface: Atlanta, 1991: Scholars Press for South Florida Studies in the History of Judaism.

Judaism and Scripture: The Evidence of Leviticus Rabbah. Chicago, 1986: The University of Chicago Press. [Fresh translation of Margulies' text and systematic analysis of problems of composition and redaction.] Jewish Book Club Selection, 1986.

Judaism: The Classical Statement. The Evidence of the Bavli. Chicago, 1986: University of Chicago Press. *Choice,* "Outstanding Academic Book List, 1987."

Judaism and Story: The Evidence of The Fathers According to Rabbi Nathan. Chicago, 1992: University of Chicago Press.

The Making of the Mind of Judaism. Atlanta, 1987: Scholars Press for Brown Judaic Studies.

The Formation of the Jewish Intellect. Making Connections and Drawing Conclusions in the Traditional System of Judaism. Atlanta, 1988: Scholars Press for Brown Judaic Studies.

The Four Stages of Rabbinic Judaism. London, 2000: Routledge.

What, Exactly, Did the Rabbinic Sages Mean by "the Oral Torah"? An Inductive Answer to the Question of Rabbinic Judaism. Atlanta, 1999: Scholars Press for South Florida Studies in the History of Judaism.

A Theological Commentary to the Midrash: I. *Pesiqta deRab Kahana.* Lanham, 2001: University Press of America. STUDIES IN ANCIENT JUDAISM SERIES.

A Theological Commentary to the Midrash: II. *Genesis Rabbah*. Lanham, 2001: University Press of America. STUDIES IN ANCIENT JUDAISM SERIES.

A Theological Commentary to the Midrash: III. *Song of Songs Rabbah*. Lanham, 2001: University Press of America. STUDIES IN ANCIENT JUDAISM SERIES.

A Theological Commentary to the Midrash. IV. *Leviticus Rabbah*

A Theological Commentary to the Midrash: V. *Lamentations Rabbati*

A Theological Commentary to the Midrash VI. *Esther Rabbah I and Ruth Rabbah*

A Theological Commentary to the Midrash VII. *Sifra*

A Theological Commentary to the Midrash VIII. *Sifré to Numbers*

A Theological Commentary to the Midrash IX. *Sifré to Deuteronomy*

A Theological Commentary to the Midrash X. *The Theological Foundations of Rabbinic Midrash*

The Talmud of Babylonia. A Complete Outline. Atlanta, 1995-6: Scholars Press for *USF Academic Commentary Series*.

I.A   *Tractate Berakhot and the Division of Appointed Times. Berakhot, Shabbat, and Erubin.*
I.B   *Tractate Berakhot and the Division of Appointed Times. Pesahim through Hagigah.*
II.A.   *The Division of Women. Yebamot through Ketubot*
II.B.   *The Division of Women. Nedarim through Qiddushin*
III.A   *The Division of Damages. Baba Qamma through Baba Batra*
III.B   *The Division of Damages. Sanhedrin through Horayot*
IV.A   *The Division of Holy Things and Tractate Niddah. Zebahim through Hullin*
IV.B   *The Division of Holy Things and Tractate Niddah. Bekhorot through Niddah*

The Talmud of The Land of Israel. An Outline of the Second, Third, and Fourth Divisions. Atlanta, 1995-6: Scholars Press for for USF Academic Commentary Series.

I.A   *Tractate Berakhot and the Division of Appointed Times. Berakhot and Shabbat*

I.B   *Tractate Berakhot and the Division of Appointed Times. Erubin, Yoma, and Besah*

I.C   *Tractate Berakhot and the Division of Appointed Times. Pesahim and Sukkah*

I.D   *Tractate Berakhot and the Division of Appointed Times. Taanit, Megillah, Rosh Hashanah, Hagigah, and Moed Qatan*

II.A.   *The Division of Women. Yebamot to Nedarim*

II.B.   *The Division of Women. Nazir to Sotah*

III.A   *The Division of Damages and Tractate Niddah. Baba Qamma, Baba Mesia, Baba Batra, Horayot, and Niddah*

III.B   *The Division of Damages and Tractate Niddah. Sanhedrin, Makkot, Shebuot, and Abodah Zarah*

The Two Talmuds Compared. Atlanta, 1995-6: Scholars Press for USF Academic Commentary Series.

I.A   *Tractate Berakhot and the Division of Appointed Times in the Talmud of the Land of Israel and the Talmud of Babylonia. Yerushalmi Tractate Berakhot*

I.B   *Tractate Berakhot and the Division of Appointed Times in the Talmud of the Land of Israel and the Talmud of Babylonia. Tractate Shabbat.*

I.C   *Tractate Berakhot and the Division of Appointed Times in the Talmud of the Land of Israel and the Talmud of Babylonia. Tractate Erubin*

I.D   *Tractate Berakhot and the Division of Appointed Times in the Talmud of the Land of Israel and the Talmud of Babylonia. Tractates Yoma and Sukkah*

I.E   *Tractate Berakhot and the Division of Appointed Times in the Talmud of the Land of Israel and the Talmud of Babylonia. Tractate Pesahim*

I.F   *Tractate Berakhot and the Division of Appointed Times in the Talmud of the Land of Israel and the Talmud of Babylonia. Tractates Besah, Taanit, and Megillah*

I.G   *Tractate Berakhot and the Division of Appointed Times in the*

*Talmud of the Land of Israel and the Talmud of Babylonia. Tractates Rosh
Hashanah, Hagigah, and Moed Qatan*
II.A   *The Division of Women in the Talmud of the Land of Israel and
the Talmud of Babylonia. Tractates Yebamot and Ketubot.*
II.B   *The Division of Women in the Talmud of the Land of Israel and
the Talmud of Babylonia. Tractates Nedarim, Nazir, and Sotah.*
II.C   *The Division of Women in the Talmud of the Land of Israel and
the Talmud of Babylonia. Tractates Qiddushin and Gittin.*
III.A   *The Division of Damages and Tractate Niddah in the Talmud
of the Land of Israel and the Talmud of Babylonia. Tractates Baba
Qamma and Baba Mesia*
III.B   *The Division of Damages and Tractate Niddah in the Talmud
of the Land of Israel and the Talmud of Babylonia. Baba Batra and Nid-
dah.*
III.C   *The Division of Damages and Tractate Niddah. Sanhedrin and
Makkot.*
III.D   *The Division of Damages and Tractate Niddah. Shebuot, Abo-
dah Zarah, and Horayot.*

The Components of the Rabbinic Documents: From the Whole to the Parts. Volume
   I. *Sifra.* Atlanta, 1997: Scholars Press for USF Academic Commentary Series.

   Part i.   *Introduction. And Parts One through Three, Chapters One
   through Ninety-Eight*
   Part ii. *Parts Four through Nine. Chapters Ninety-Nine through One
   Hundred Ninety-Four*
   Part iii. *Parts Ten through Thirteen. Chapters One Hundred Ninety-
   Five through Two Hundred Seventy-Seven*
   Part iv. *A Topical and Methodical Outline of Sifra*

The Components of the Rabbinic Documents: From the Whole to the Parts. Volume
   II. *Esther Rabbah I.* Atlanta, 1997: Scholars Press for USF Academic Commentary Series.

The Components of the Rabbinic Documents: From the Whole to the Parts. Volume
   III. *Ruth Rabbah.* Atlanta, 1997: Scholars Press for USF Academic Commentary Series.

The Components of the Rabbinic Documents: From the Whole to the Parts. Volume
   IV. *Lamentations Rabbati.* Atlanta, 1997: Scholars Press for USF

Academic Commentary Series.

The Components of the Rabbinic Documents: From the Whole to the Parts. Volume
V. *Song of Songs Rabbah.* Atlanta, 1997: Scholars Press for USF
Academic Commentary Series.

> Part i.   *Introduction. And Parashiyyot One through Four*
> Part ii.   *Parashiyyot Five through Eight. And a Topical and Methodical*
> *Outline of Song of Songs Rabbah*

The Components of the Rabbinic Documents: From the Whole to the Parts. VI. *The*
Fathers Attributed to Rabbi Nathan. Atlanta, 1997: Scholars Press
for USF Academic Commentary Series.

The Components of the Rabbinic Documents: From the Whole to the Parts. VII. *Sifré*
to Deuteronomy. Atlanta, 1997: Scholars Press for USF Academic
Commentary Series.

> Part i.   *Introduction. And Parts One through Four*
> Part ii.   *Parts Five through Ten*
> Part iii.   *A Topical and Methodical Outline of Sifré to Deuteronomy*

The Components of the Rabbinic Documents: From the Whole to the Parts. VIII.
Mekhilta Attributed to R. Ishmael. Atlanta, 1997: Scholars Press for
USF Academic Commentary Series.

> Part i.   *Introduction. Pisha, Beshallah and Shirata*
> Part ii   *Vayassa, Amalek, Bahodesh, Neziqin, Kaspa and Shabbata*
> Part iii.   *A Topical and Methodical Outline of Mekhilta Attributed to R.*
> *Ishmael.*

The Components of the Rabbinic Documents: From the Whole to the Parts. IX. *Gene-*
sis Rabbah. Atlanta, 1998: Scholars Press for USF Academic
Commentary Series.

> Part i.   *Introduction. Genesis Rabbah Chapters One through Twenty-*
> *One*
> Part ii.   *Genesis Rabbah Chapters Twenty-Two through Forty-Eight*
> Part iii.   *Genesis Rabbah Chapters Forty-Nine through Seventy-Three*
> Part iv.   *Genesis Rabbah Chapters Seventy-Four through One Hundred*
> Part v.   *A Topical and Methodical Outline of Genesis Rabbah. Bereshit*

through Vaere, Chapters One through Fifty-Seven
Part vi. *A Topical and Methodical Outline of Genesis Rabbah. Hayye Sarah through Miqqes. Chapters Fifty-Eight through One Hundred*

The Components of the Rabbinic Documents: From the Whole to the Parts. X. *Leviticus Rabbah.* Atlanta, 1998: Scholars Press for USF Academic Commentary Series.

Part i. *Introduction. Leviticus Rabbah Parashiyyot One through Seventeen*
Part ii. *Leviticus Rabbah Parashiyyot Eighteen through Thirty-Seven*
Part iii. *Leviticus Rabbah. A Topical and Methodical Outline*

The Components of the Rabbinic Documents: From the Whole to the Parts. XI. *Pesiqta deRab Kahana.* Atlanta, 1998: Scholars Press for for USF Academic Commentary Series.

Part i. *Introduction. Pesiqta deRab Kahana Pisqaot One through Eleven*
Part ii. *Pesiqta deRab Kahana Pisqaot Twelve through Twenty-Eight*
Part iii. *Pesiqta deRab Kahana. A Topical and Methodical Outline*

The Components of the Rabbinic Documents: From the Whole to the Parts. XII. *Sifré to Numbers.* Atlanta, 1998: Scholars Press for USF Academic Commentary Series.

Part i. *Introduction. Pisqaot One through Eighty-Four*
Part ii *Pisqaot Eighty-Five through One Hundred Twenty-Two*
Part iii *Pisqaot One Hundred Twenty-Three through One Hundred Sixty-One*
Part iv *Sifré to Numbers. A Topical and Methodical Outline*

The Documentary Form-History of Rabbinic Literature. I. *The Documentary Forms of the Mishnah.* Atlanta, 1998: Scholars Press for USF Academic Commentary Series.

The Documentary Form-History of Rabbinic Literature II. *The Aggadic Sector: Tractate Abot, Abot deRabbi Natan, Sifra, Sifré to Numbers, and Sifré to Deuteronomy.* Atlanta, 1998: Scholars Press for USF Academic Commentary Series.

The Documentary Form-History of Rabbinic Literature III. *The Aggadic Sector:.Mekhilta Attributed to R. Ishmael and Genesis Rabbah.* Atlanta, 1998: Scholars Press for USF Academic Commentary Series.

The Documentary Form-History of Rabbinic Literature IV. *The Aggadic Sector:.Leviticus Rabbah, and Pesiqta deRab Kahana.* Atlanta, 1998: Scholars Press for USF Academic Commentary Series.

The Documentary Form-History of Rabbinic Literature V. *The Aggadic Sector: Song of Songs Rabbah, Ruth Rabbah, Lamentations Rabbati, and Esther Rabbah I.* Atlanta, 1998: Scholars Press for USF Academic Commentary Series.

The Documentary Form-History of Rabbinic Literature. VI. *The Halakhic Sector. The Talmud of the Land of Israel. A. Berakhot and Shabbat through Taanit.* Atlanta, 1998: Scholars Press for USF Academic Commentary Series.

The Documentary Form-History of Rabbinic Literature. VI. *The Halakhic Sector. The Talmud of the Land of Israel. B. Megillah through Qiddushin.* Atlanta, 1998: Scholars Press for USF Academic Commentary Series.

The Documentary Form-History of Rabbinic Literature. VI. *The Halakhic Sector. The Talmud of the Land of Israel. C. Sotah through Horayot and Niddah.* Atlanta, 1998: Scholars Press for USF Academic Commentary Series.

The Documentary Form-History of Rabbinic Literature. VII. *The Halakhic Sector. The Talmud of Babylonia. A. Tractates Berakhot and Shabbat through Pesahim.* Atlanta, 1998: Scholars Press for USF Academic Commentary Series.

The Documentary Form-History of Rabbinic Literature. VII. *The Halakhic Sector. The Talmud of Babylonia.* B. *Tractates Yoma through Ketubot.* Atlanta, 1998: Scholars Press for USF Academic Commentary Series.

The Documentary Form-History of Rabbinic Literature. VII. *The Halakhic Sector. The Talmud of Babylonia. C. Tractates Nedarim through Baba Mesia.* Atlanta, 1998: Scholars Press for USF Academic Commentary

Series.

The Documentary Form-History of Rabbinic Literature. VII. *The Halakhic Sector. The Talmud of Babylonia.* D. *Tractates Baba Batra through Horayot.* Atlanta, 1998: Scholars Press for USF Academic Commentary Series.

The Documentary Form-History of Rabbinic Literature. VII. *The Halakhic Sector. The Talmud of Babylonia.* E. *Tractates Zebahim through Bekhorot.* Atlanta, 1998: Scholars Press for USF Academic Commentary Series.

The Documentary Form-History of Rabbinic Literature. VII. *The Halakhic Sector. The Talmud of Babylonia.* F. *Tractates Arakhin through Niddah. And Conclusions.* Atlanta, 1998: Scholars Press for USF Academic Commentary Series.